In a culture where the obvious is o[...] takes a refreshing look at age-old [...]ship. Thoroughly rooted in Scripture and sensibly colored by tradition, this work will prove to be a vital tool in equipping and preparing church and corporate leaders for years to come. Bishop Blue argues with sensitivity and purpose, creating a safe context for discourse on some of the most difficult dimensions of church relationships as it pertains to leadership. This is necessary reading for all who desire to be more effective followers and leaders for the kingdom of God.

—BISHOP-ELECT ERIC J. FREEMAN (M.A. THEOLOGICAL ETHICS)
SENIOR PASTOR, THE MEETING PLACE CHURCH INTERNATIONAL,
COLUMBIA, SOUTH CAROLINA

Secondary leaders are much like thoroughbred stallions, full of strength and power, but able to run aimlessly without guidance or direction. Through this book, Bishop Michael Blue meets that challenge for leadership by constructing the tool equivalent to the pedigree's bit, which is attached to the bridle, to harness that power and give direction, supervision, and instruction. The application of this concept allows senior leadership consistent forward motion without opposition from those in the ancillary position.

—PASTOR STEVEN FORD
GREAT GATHERING CHURCH, NEWARK, DELAWARE
(WORLD RENOWNED MUSICIAN, COMPOSER, AND PRODUCER)

Building Credibility In Leadership is one of the greatest works on this subject of our time. Bishop Michael Blue not only defines, clarifies, and gives structure to the responsibilities of primary leadership; he also articulates carefully and clearly the importance, value, and responsibility of secondary leadership. This book should be required reading as it will instruct, affirm, and strengthen those who desire to take their knowledge, understanding, and execution of leadership responsibilities to another dimension.

—BISHOP BOBBY HILTON, PhD
WORD OF DELIVERANCE MINISTRIES FOR THE WORLD,
FOREST PARK (GREATER CINCINNATI), OHIO

A must read for all the flock of God.

—BISHOP ANDREW J.D. MERRITT
STRAIGHT GATE INTERNATIONAL CHURCH

MICHAEL A. BLUE

BUILDING CREDIBLITY *in*

LEADERSHIP

PRINCIPLES
for
SECONDARY
LEADERS

CREATION
HOUSE

BUILDING CREDIBILITY IN LEADERSHIP by Michael Blue
Published by Creation House Books
A Charisma Media Company
600 Rinehart Road
Lake Mary, Florida 32746
www.charismamedia.com

Scripture quotations are from the King James Version of the Bible.

Design Director: Bill Johnson
Cover design by Rachel Lopez

Visit the author's websites: www.dohcc.com and
www.buildingcredibilityinleadership.com

Library of Congress Cataloging-in-Publication Data: 2011925314
International Standard Book Number: 978-1-61638-586-6
E-book ISBN: 978-1-61638-587-3

First edition

11 12 13 14 15 — 9 8 7 6 5 4 3 2 1
Printed in the United States of America

DEDICATION

THIS WRITING IS dedicated to unsung leaders, senior and secondary, those who paid the price of devotion to God's little ones, without recognition, sometimes without compensation, and sometimes with their very graves left unmarked. There are people who touched me and didn't know the profound impact that they made. Isaiah states that the servant of the Lord is blind. (See Isaiah 42:19.) These servants of God served "blindly." They were not focused on their abilities, but upon Him.

They could not have seen, could not have known, the full implication of their work—they did not see all those whom they were inspiring, whom they were parenting, whom they were lifting from degradation. For they walked by faith, not by sight. I am the grateful beneficiary of blind servants of God...

ACKNOWLEDGMENTS

I MUST ACKNOWLEDGE MY wife, Malinda, the MVP on my life team. More than any other person, you validate whatever credibility my voice carries. I owe you more than I can repay for your love, loyalty, and sacrifice.

I am grateful for my children, Michala and Michael II, who are my greatest legacy and my delight.

I appreciate my sisters: Laura, Gearl, and Vanessa—each of you, uniquely, has been a blessing to me.

To the Door of Hope Christian Church, a committed body of believers among whom many of these principles have been crystallized and demonstrated: you are a great people of great power. Thank you for the privilege of having served you for these years. We continue to grow together.

To the Christian Covenant Fellowship of Ministries—your unfailing support has provided strength for this journey. It is an honor to be vitally associated with, and accountable to, such a God-ordained kingdom movement.

To Marion School District 1 (and particularly Marion High School), Marion, South Carolina, where I have spent most of my life as a learner and as a teacher—I hope that I have made a legitimate contribution to the great educational heritage of our community, for I am definitely its beneficiary.

To the great cloud of witnesses that has grown and become more precious as the years have gone by: many loved ones who have blessed us have gone before us: Apostle Robert Evans, Bishop Raymond Johnson, departed members of DHCC, and others.

To those who read the manuscript and generously shared their feedback—I pray that this reflects the fact that I heard you and genuinely value your input.

To Dr. Myles Munroe for your inspiration as an iconic kingdom oracle in our generations: through your ministry the Word of God continues to be "made flesh."

To Bishop Michael E. Goings, a great prophetic voice and mentor from my earliest years in Christ—your labors continue to yield fruit in my life.

To my premier spiritual father—the late Bishop John W. Barber—"If I be not an apostle to others, yet doubtless I am to you" (1 Cor. 9:2), you taught me that Jesus is the same, yesterday, today, and forever.

To my spiritual mother and natural "Momma," my Fan #1, the late Mother Alberta Franklin—sometimes I wish you were still here, but I have no doubt that you're there, with the Lord.

To my deceased brother, Deacon Christopher Blue...we shared a dream.

To all of those who have contributed a piece to my "coat of many colors": thank you for being the Father's vessels in my life.

Above all...

to the great God and our Savior, the Lord Jesus Christ—through Your precious Holy Spirit, You are my Teacher, my Life, my Strength, and my Hope. Thank You, again... and again...

TABLE OF CONTENTS

FOREWORD

THIS ERUDITE, ELOQUENT, and immensely thought-provoking work gets to the heart of one of the most important aspects of true leadership. It is indispensable reading for all progressive leaders and professionals who want to live life above the norm. This is a profound authoritative work, spanning the wisdom of the ages yet breaking new ground in its approach.

This exceptional work by Bishop Michael Blue is one of the most profound, practical, principle-centered approaches to this subject I have read in a long time. The author's approach captivates the heart, engages the mind, and inspires the spirit. His ability to leap over complicated theological and metaphysical jargon and reduce complex theories to simple practical principles is amazing. This book challenges the intellectual while embracing the laymen, dismantles the mysteries of the soul search of mankind and delivers the profound with clear simplicity.

Bishop Blue's approach awakens in the reader the untapped inhibiters that retard our personal development as leaders and his antidotes empower us to rise above these self-defeating, self-limiting factors to a life of exploits in spiritual and mental advancement in leadership. The author also integrates into each chapter time-tested precepts that give each principle a practical application to life making the entire process people-friendly.

Every sentence of this book is pregnant with wisdom and I enjoyed the mind-expanding experience of this exciting book. I admonish you to plunge into this ocean of knowledge and watch your life change for the better.

—DR. MYLES MUNROE
BAHAMAS FAITH MINISTRIES INTERNATIONAL
INTERNATIONAL THIRD WORLD LEADERS ASSOCIATION
NASSAU, BAHAMAS

Preface

SECONDARY STATUS IS FOR EVERYONE

Look Out for Number One

Y OU'VE GOT TO look out for Number One!" is an old expression that means, "Put yourself, your needs, and your desires first!" It is an old adage, but there is Someone far older who said, "Greater love hath no man than this, that a man would lay down his life for his friends" (John 15:13). The same ancient One said also, "If any man desire to be first, the same shall be last of all, and servant of all" (Mark 9:35). Another way to express "last of all, and servant of all" is simply this: an individual chooses to prioritize the benefit of another before his or her own—the other person is *first*, and he or she embraces *second* place.

The scope of this secondary concept is broader than one might think! It applies to all members of the body of Christ because all of us are secondary to Jesus, the head of the church. Furthermore, everyone—in some aspect of life—is called to be second: the wife in submission to her husband, who is the head of the marriage; the husband in submission to his wife, who is the heart of the marriage; the children, secondary to their parents' position of first authority; the parents, placing their own needs as secondary to the needs of their children.

To successfully live, everyone must posture himself or herself as secondary to someone else at some time for the good of all. In particular, every believer is challenged to serve, provide for, support, and sacrifice for another *before himself*. This is exactly what Jesus did. He took his position as "the Second Man." He placed His own comfort second to the needs of all of mankind by placing His own will "second" to the will of the Father. And He is our example:

> But it shall not be so among you: but whosoever will be great among you, shall be your minister: and whosoever of you will be the chiefest,

shall be servant of all. For even the Son of Man came not to be ministered unto, but to minister, and to give his life a ransom for many.

—MARK 10:43–45

Let this mind be in you, which was also in Christ Jesus: who, being in the form of God, thought it not robbery to be equal with God: but made himself of no reputation, and took upon him the form of a servant, and was made in the likeness of men: and being found in fashion as a man, he humbled himself, and became obedient unto death, even the death of the cross. Wherefore God also hath highly exalted him, and given him a name which is above every name.

—PHILIPPIANS 2:5–9

The first man is of the earth, earthy; the second man is the Lord from heaven.

—1 CORINTHIANS 15:47

If Christians are ever truly to be like Jesus, they must be willing to place themselves second. That is the "this mind" to which Paul refers in Philippians 2:5. Consider the prescription of "this mind," the attitude that Christ Himself had, found in verses 1–4 of the same chapter:

If there be therefore any consolation in Christ, if any comfort of love, if any fellowship of the Spirit, if any bowels and mercies, fulfil ye my joy, that ye be likeminded, having the same love, being of one accord, of one mind. Let nothing be done through strife or vainglory; but in lowliness of mind let each esteem other better than themselves. Look not every man on his own things, but every man also on the things of others.

—PHILIPPIANS 2:1-4

The same truth is taught in Romans:

Be kindly affectioned one to another with brotherly love; in honour preferring one another.

—ROMANS 12:10

Love—The Basis of Secondary Posture

Love is the hallmark of Christianity, and it is the "why" of Christian service. Notice the prominence of the word *love* in the verses quoted above. "Preferring one another" means putting another first, which makes me second. Love is the only reason that justifies second place to the human heart, a heart so naturally prone to self-centeredness. Jesus said:

> By this shall all men know that ye are my disciples if ye have love one
> to another.
>
> —JOHN 13:35

The Old and New Testament mandate of God for His people is that they would love Him and love one another. Without love, one's service in the kingdom is not authentic in God's sight.

But what is love?

True Love is a Choice

Biblical love is the propensity to care for another and to benefit another by the giving of oneself:

> For God so loved the world, that he gave his only begotten Son, that
> whosoever believeth in him should not perish, but have everlasting
> life.
>
> —JOHN 3:16

> Be ye therefore followers of God, as dear children; and walk in love, as
> Christ also hath loved us, and hath given himself for us an offering and
> a sacrifice to God for a sweetsmelling savour.
>
> —EPHESIANS 5:1–2

Love includes two fundamental components: the *emotional* and the *volitional*. Affection is the emotional side, and commitment is the volitional side.

Commitment is a decision, and it is the most important aspect of true love. In pop culture, love has been reduced to a mere feeling, personified in the mythical, mischievous archer, Cupid. Cupid flits around and shoots whomever he wills, and his wounded victims "fall" in (and often out of) love, having little to no ability to control the experience. Love "just happens."

Strangely, God's idea of love seems less coincidental and more deliberate. God says, "Thou *shalt* love the Lord...and thy neighbor ..." (Mark 12:30–31). They are commands—the most important of the Ten Commandments. Wouldn't it be unjust of God to demand of people that which they cannot produce "on demand" as an act of their will? It would be, and God is not unjust. Therefore, the natural inference is that true love involves a choice, a decision. It is one's choice to give oneself on behalf of another for his or her benefit. Love may have warm, fuzzy feelings associated with it sometimes, but above all love is a choice, a long-term decision, a commitment.

Commitment in the Culture

Our culture, at least in America, tends to be very strong on feelings but very weak on quality decision-making and the commitment that should accompany it. Commitment in our culture is at an all-time low. These days, it is politically incorrect to be committed to anything except, paradoxically, that which defies (and *defiles*) commitment. For generations now, commitment has been gradually eroding. It has been lampooned and reviled for decades, and, predictably, society on all levels has gotten the message. Multitudes of fathers and mothers brazenly abandon their dependent children. Patriotism is mocked in many public forums. Long-term bonds between employers and employees are a thing of the past, threatened by spontaneous downsizing and overnight mergers, not to mention economic collapse.

In the church there is little difference. Christians migrate from ministry to ministry upon the slightest displeasure with the previous church or preacher. Mand Christians today do not even support (commit to) the ministries that they do supposedly love. And not only do ministries feel the heat—commitment to God Himself, the only One who is flawless, is also lacking, for some Christians only appreciate God when they can feel His presence or see His blessings. When they cease to feel Him, some become offended at Him.

Perhaps the most glaring, tragic example of the commitment crisis is marriage, the fundamental institution of civilization. Many husbands and wives are increasingly uncommitted. "As long as ye both shall live" from the traditional wedding vows has been replaced with "as long as we both shall *love*," meaning *feel*, which is a perverse distortion. What is left of the vows themselves is often preceded by a prenuptial agreement. In effect, the couple says, "I'll marry him or her. I just don't trust him or her, so I won't commit." Is this not at least slightly ludicrous? One trusts another to sleep in his or her presence unguarded but cannot trust him or her with one's material possessions?

Cold Love

Where there is not real commitment, there can be no real love. Perhaps our times were the times that Jesus had in mind when He said, "And because iniquity shall abound, the love of many shall wax cold" (Matt. 24:12). A *cold* love—that is what many are left with. It is a love that may build a house but cannot make a home. It is a love that can furnish sex but cannot produce intimacy. It is a love that will save a whale but murder a human fetus. It is a love that gives a child an existence but no identity. It is a love that is faithful "for better" but not "for worse," "in health" but not "in sickness," not "till death us do part" but "till I've had enough." It is a love that eats its nation's benefits yet despises patriotism. It is a love that will murder its own mother.

Yes, cold love has even made its way to church. It manifests there as a love that will speak in tongues but not in kind greeting to another. It is a love that will raise hands to God but not shake hands with a brother or sister.

Cold love threatens to rend the entire fabric of the culture, leaving us with a postmodern tolerance of all but commitment to none. Society descends as this coated-over selfishness becomes the underlying motive for all political decisions, economic policy, ethical codes, and moral edicts. Cold love does away with the servant's heart and leaves every man for himself in a "me-first" mindset.

Kingdom leadership cannot flourish where fervent love is not found, for true leadership is first for the benefit of the ones being led, then for those who are leading, if leadership benefits at all. There is an urgent need in the body of Jesus Christ for a return to commitment. The contemporary believer must regain a healthy view of the power of submissive commitment to God and to other believers—the power of second place.

Second Is a Place, Not a Person

For God so loved the world, that he gave his only begotten Son, that whosoever believeth in him should not perish, but have everlasting life.

—JOHN 3:16

There is neither Jew nor Greek, there is neither bond nor free, there is neither male nor female: for ye are all one in Christ Jesus.

—GALATIANS 3:28

God loves and values all of His children equally, regardless of any attributes or traits. None of these—color, gender, social class, talent, education, or beauty—endears God to one person above another.

Primary or Secondary?

A primary leader is one who executes a function or office that bears the greatest weight of responsibility and authority in a given system. A secondary leader is one whose function or office is designed to complement the function or office of a primary leader in a given system.

For example, suppose that the pilot and a flight attendant on a given plane have the same illness. One of the symptoms of that illness is that without proper daily nutrition, a person with this malady may pass out without warning.

Now, suppose the pilot and the flight attendant are former classmates: same age, same gender, same ethnicity, same marital status, same political views, and so on. The pilot makes more money, but the flight attendant belongs to a more affluent family, so they have the same financial status. In this example, considering most aspects of existence, they are equal in *worth*.

Now, suppose they are on duty at the same time on the same flight. If the flight attendant passes out, the passengers may not get their nuts and drinks. They may not have blankets or pillows handed out if it is a long flight. That's tough, but they can do without some of the ambience expected on a luxurious flight. However, if the pilot passes out, the passengers and the plane may experience great damage and destruction. The two professionals are not equal in *function*. The weight of their worth is the same; the weight of their work is different.

The work of the attendant—keeping passengers secure and comfortable on their trip—is complementary to the work of the pilot—transporting passengers alive and whole as they travel to their destinations.

Though the pilot's work is more vital, most passengers never interact with the pilot or even think of him or her unless something goes wrong, such as when the plane hits turbulence. But the passengers almost always interact with the attendant: Their opinion of the airline is shaped by their encounters with the secondary leader—the flight attendant—far more than with the primary one—the pilot. And if they gain an unfavorable view of the airline, they may refuse to ride, which will affect the attendant, the pilot, and the entire airline. So although the secondary person's work may not be vital for keeping customers alive, it is very vital for keeping the airline itself alive!

Even the Senior Leader's Place Is Second

In regard to my role as a bishop, I've been asked more than once, "How many churches are you over?" I have examined the phrasing and the ideology behind the question. The word *episcopos*, translated "bishop" in the English Bible, can literally be translated "overseer." Therefore, the question is legitimate as asked, and the concept of "covering" is legitimately associated with the bishopric.

Nevertheless, I have thought that the question could be better asked this way: "How many churches are you under?" Jesus, and those whom He used to help establish the church (and churches), is referred to in Scripture using the symbolism of a foundation, not a roof; of stones, not shingles; of a cornerstone, not a capstone. Jesus placed Himself *under* mankind, bearing the burden of its sin and elevating those who receive Him to His own seat in the heavenly places. He committed Himself to mankind forever, putting us first and Himself second.

Lead From Beneath

Christ's purpose is that we likewise undergird and lift people toward the fulfillment of God's destiny for them, individually and collectively. The believer who wishes to flow in harmony with Christ's purpose must ask himself or herself, "How many people have I committed to place

myself underneath, to raise them upward—heavenward—toward God?"
An effective leader, regardless of the office title—secular or sacred—is the
individual who recognizes both the necessity and the power of placing
others first. Embracing this principle, he or she is ready to discover the
dynamic possibilities of the place called *second*.

I Second That!

In parliamentary procedure, no motion can be carried into the questioning
or voting phase unless there is a "second," where another official member of the
organization comes into agreement with the member who has initially offered
the motion. Regardless how great the idea or how important a development
the motion may connote, unless there is a seconding of the motion, it dies.
Even so, no heavenly "motion" of God will be "carried" on the earth without
a "second."

> For all the promises of God in him are yea, and in him Amen, unto the
> glory of God by us.
>
> —2 CORINTHIANS 1:20

> Verily I say unto you, Whatsoever ye shall bind on earth shall be bound
> in heaven: and whatsoever ye shall loose on earth shall be loosed in
> heaven.
>
> —MATTHEW 18:18

God seeks someone earthly to agree with His message, or His motion,
with a second. In turn, God will raise up another person to agree with the
one who has agreed with Him. And:

> In the mouth of two or three witnesses every word may be established.
>
> —MATTHEW 18:16

The motion has been given... is there a second?

Introduction

SCRIPTURAL FOUNDATIONS

And Moses' father in law said unto him, The thing that thou doest is not good. Thou wilt surely wear away, both thou, and this people that is with thee: for this thing is too heavy for thee; thou art not able to perform it thyself alone. Hearken now unto my voice, I will give thee counsel, and God shall be with thee: be thou for the people to Godward, that thou mayest bring the causes unto God: And thou shalt teach them ordinances and laws, and shalt shew them the way wherein they must walk, and the work that they must do. Moreover thou shalt provide out of all the people able men, such as fear God, men of truth, hating covetousness; and place such over them, to be rulers of thousands, and rulers of hundreds, rulers of fifties, and rulers of tens: And let them judge the people at all seasons: and it shall be, that every great matter they shall bring unto thee, but every small matter they shall judge: so shall it be easier for thyself, and they shall bear the burden with thee. If thou shalt do this thing, and God command thee so, then thou shalt be able to endure, and all this people shall also go to their place in peace.

—Exodus 18:17–23

And there came of the children of Benjamin and Judah to the hold unto David. And David went out to meet them, and answered and said unto them, If ye be come peaceably unto me to help me, mine heart shall be knit unto you: but if ye be come to betray me to mine enemies, seeing there is no wrong in mine hands, the God of our fathers look thereon, and rebuke it. Then the spirit came upon Amasai, who was chief of the captains, and he said, Thine are we, David, and on thy side, thou son of Jesse: peace, peace be unto thee, and peace be to thine helpers; for thy God helpeth thee. Then David received them, and made them captains of the band.

—1 Chronicles 12:16–18

Most men will proclaim every one his own goodness: but a faithful man who can find?

—Proverbs 20:6

And he goeth up into a mountain, and calleth unto him whom he would: and they came unto him. And he ordained twelve, that they should be with him, and that he might send them forth.

—Mark 3:13–14

But I trust in the Lord Jesus to send Timotheus shortly unto you, that I also may be of good comfort, when I know your state. For I have no man likeminded, who will naturally care for your state. For all seek their own, not the things which are Jesus Christ's. But ye know the proof of him, that, as a son with the father, he hath served with me in the gospel.

—Philippians 2:19–22

Thou therefore, my son, be strong in the grace that is in Christ Jesus. And the things that thou hast heard of me among many witnesses, the same commit thou to faithful men, who shall be able to teach others also.

—2 Timothy 2:1–2

Defining Leadership

Leadership is defined many different ways. John Maxwell defines it as "influence." But what is the biblical definition of leadership? It is probably embodied in one word: service. Leadership connotes service—first to the glory of God, then for the benefit of others, and finally resulting in the fulfillment of oneself. The word *minister* means "servant"—how many ministers know this?—and almost everyone agrees that ministers lead the church. So, the kingdom leader is an *influential servant*.

Unfortunately, when the average person thinks of a leader, the image that emerges is that of the man or woman in charge and on top—bossing, not serving. That is a very narrow view of leadership, and a harmful view, particularly in the body of Christ.

In the secular world, the organizations that achieve success most often do so through their acceptance of the team concept. Although in any leadership structure there must always be someone with final authority because he or she has ultimate responsibility, the best leadership models optimize the power of teams. These systems (e.g., corporations, educational institutions, and businesses) affirm that within the team, every member—not just the captain—has a key role. This principle is derived from none other than the Creator Himself. Actually, all human organizational systems that succeed do so to the degree that they employ universal principles of leadership, and these universal principles derive from the God of the universe. God is the original Leader, and when we look at God and His leadership style, we see the quintessential example of teaming.

God is self-existent. He has need of nothing and no one. Yet He is love, and love is creative and relational. Because of His love nature, God chooses to create someone to whom to reveal Himself, with whom to share Himself, and through whom to express Himself. He willingly shares, allocates, and delegates His power and authority among His creatures. His angels have certain powers and duties. And yes, man has been uniquely called to share God's power and duties as well. Walking in submission to Him, humans become "laborers together with God," members of the God Team. (See 1 Corinthians 3:9.)

The outcome of the God Team's work is that greater good is wrought and greater glory is brought—for everyone involved—than individual members could ever hope to attain on their own. God is shown to be even more glorious, and His kingdom is revealed as ever more excellent when people witness the wonders He does through the team of persons who walk with Him.

So it is in human institutions and organizations. When leadership is based on the team model, whatever is undertaken and accomplished is far richer than what one individual, no matter how chosen, gifted, and talented, could do alone.

> Two are better than one; because they have a good reward for their labour. For if they fall, the one will lift up his fellow: but woe to him that alone when he falleth; for he hath not another to help him up. Again, if two lie together, then they have heat: but how can one be warm alone? And if one prevails against him, two shall withstand him; and a threefold cord is not quickly broken.
>
> —ECCLESIASTES 4:9–12

So, in the leadership systems of given organizations, there are those who are primarily responsible and have primary authority. There is usually one per organization or level of organization. In the case of the heavenly kingdom, there is one Leader, God. In the case of earthly organizations, there is typically a president, a prime minister, a chairman, a senior pastor, a governor, or some other primary leader. But while there is one primary leader in each system, there must be an ever-increasing number of other leaders who support the primary leader's efforts if those systems are to grow and remain healthy—extending, refining, enhancing, implementing, and replicating. God, as the model Leader, establishes this precedent, and man, as a leader, must embrace this precept. Those people who are called to the side of God, or to the side of other human leaders, help to make what happens, happen. We refer to this precious group and their essential position or function as *secondary leadership*.

Necessary in Every Realm

The role of secondary leadership is necessary in every realm. The most important example of this is illustrated in the relationship between God and humanity, since the fall of man. God, though omnipresent, is personally present in heaven, and man is on earth. Since the fall of Adam from his original relationship with God, God earnestly desires to reach man, and mankind desperately, instinctively, searches for a higher power, God, even if they do not recognize that power as God. So who is responsible for—or even capable of—reinstating the connection between God and man? Mankind itself is powerless to lay hold upon God by its own strength.

Enter Jesus—the Secondary Leader

But then enters Jesus—the God-Man. He is God, in all His glory and splendor, but He humbles Himself and becomes obedient to the will of the Father. He positions Himself as the *secondary leader*. Consequently, He is the One who is able to bring heaven and earth into tandem. He is "Jacob's Ladder," reconciling the will of God and the will of man. He is "Job's Daysman" who can lay one hand on divinity and the other on humanity and cause them to clasp in a covenantal grip. It is His secondary place that makes this possible.

> For there is one God, and one mediator between God and men, the
> man Christ Jesus.
>
> —1 TIMOTHY 2:5

He is even referred to as the second Person of the Godhead. He has purchased salvation for all humanity by His sinless life, vicarious death, and glorious resurrection. This glorious purchase transaction is called redemption, done by the ministry of Someone willing to place Himself second.

The Secondary Leaders of Jesus

Let's take the illustration a step further. Christ has accomplished redemption and has ascended. He is seated at the right hand of the Majesty on high, operating in the heavenly aspect of His ministry as Lord and High Priest. However, on earth, countless men and women still live without the benefits that redemption provides. There are still multitudes who do not even know that Jesus came, and there are even more who do not know why He came. Thus, they remain in bondage to sin and Satan. They are in situations similar to those of the people that Jesus encountered during His earthly walk. He brought spiritual, emotional, physical, and material deliverance to thousands when He was personally here on earth. Now that He has ascended, did the earthly aspect of His ministry end? Was it supposed to? Is it exclusively a heavenly ministry from the Ascension forward? How are earthbound humans supposed to appropriate redemption's effects?

Finish It

Luke wrote, "The former treatise have I made, O Theophilus, of all that Jesus began both to do and teach until the day in which he was taken up" (Acts 1:1–2). When Jesus died on the cross, He cried, *"It is finished."* What was finished was the reign of Satan, sin, and death. What was finished was the necessity to observe the ceremonial laws that could not cleanse humanity's hearts or consciences from the Adamic taint. What was finished was the payment of the ransom that satisfied the claims of divine justice against Adam and his progeny.

Jesus said, *"It* is finished." What He did not say was, *"Everything* is finished." That must be understood in order to appreciate Luke's assertion, quoted above, that all Jesus did in His earthly ministry—the entire narrative called the gospel of Luke—was not a finishing of all but a *beginning*.

Jesus' life, death, burial, and resurrection constituted the beginning of mankind's restoration to God's original plan for mankind from eternity, which was disrupted with the fall of Adam. Redemption was finished in Christ's passion, but restoration? That had just begun—it was not finished. It remains unfinished.

It was not finished because the preaching of the gospel of the kingdom was not finished. Up to the time of Christ's death, it had been shared in incomplete measure with "the lost sheep of the house of Israel" (Matt. 15:24) and an occasional Gentile audience. It may have been taken into all of Palestine but definitely not all of the Middle East, much less "all the world":

> And this gospel of the kingdom shall be preached in all the world for a witness unto all nations; and then shall the end come.
> —MATTHEW 24:14

The implications of redemption were for every person on the face of the earth—past, present, and future. Because of this, Jesus issued a mandate for His followers—those alive then, plus all their successors—to go into all the world and preach the gospel, announcing that redemption had been wrought and that all who are willing can experience restoration. In other words, He deputized all His followers as His secondary leaders.

> Go ye therefore, and teach all nations, baptizing them in the name of the Father, and of the Son, and of the Holy Ghost: Teaching them to observe all things whatsoever I have commanded you: and, lo, I am with you always, even unto the end of the world. Amen.
> —MATTHEW 28:19–20

Jesus implied the following:

- Reality #1: the salvation (by God) of mankind is *finished* in heaven—He is ever reaching down.

- Reality #2: the search (by mankind) for God *continues* on earth—man forever reaches up.

- Reality # 3: the first two realities *can never be reconciled* unless somebody (Somebody) gets in the middle, connecting Reality #1 with Reality #2—bringing searching mankind into contact with the saving God.

The Man in the Middle

The Somebody who stands in the middle is the Lord Jesus Christ. Paul wrote, "For there is one God, and one mediator between God and men, the man Christ Jesus" (1 Tim. 2:5). But we knew that. We knew Christ had a *mediatorial* role. What we did not acknowledge is that Christ has a body, the church. The Head took responsibility as God redeemed man; the body is responsible as God endeavors to restore man, through the knowledge of what Jesus has done. The Head, the corporeal Christ, has done His part; now His body, the corporate Christ, must *finish* what the Head began. His body is His secondary leadership on the earth.

Because as he [Christ] is, so are we in this world.

—1 JOHN 4:17

There exists a view held widely among Christians and non-Christians alike. It is the idea that God's sovereignty means that He can and will do pretty much whatever He wills, indiscriminately. For instance, if God wants people saved, if He wants their lives changed and their environments illuminated by His presence, He just shows up like the dawn, and *boom!* Change just happens! Or if God wants to communicate with people, He will do it—using whatever means He wills, whenever He is ready for me to be saved, He will "bring me in."

I believe this hinders the church from fully accepting the Great Commission mandate. The church must realize that when it comes to the restorative work of Christ in the lives of people, "Without Him, we cannot—but without us, He will not." God needed the physical body of Jesus Christ to bridge the gap in redemption. He needs the corporate, mystical body of Jesus Christ to bridge the gap in restoration. Now that the price has been paid, the good news about that price must be published, for the gospel itself is God's power to deliver. (See Romans 1:16.) God wills that all be saved, but all are not; only when people hear and believe the gospel message will they appropriate the grace that has been provided in the cross. It is only then that they experience the benefit of Jesus' purchase.

> How then shall they call on him in whom they have not believed? And how shall they believe on him of whom they have not heard? And how shall they hear without a preacher?
>
> —ROMANS 10:14

The New Testament preacher is not exclusively the five-fold minister of Ephesians 4:11 or the professional clergy who specialize in ministering the Word. The preacher here is "ye" of Matthew 28:19, Mark 16:15, Luke 24:48, and Acts 1:8, and "you" of John 20:21. In other words, every believer is a preacher in the general sense. It is the responsibility of every believer to make known what God has done so that their fellow human beings may believe and be born again, becoming sons of God. As they are reborn, humanity enters the path of restoration to the original course that God laid for mankind in eternity past.

> And all things are of God, who hath reconciled us to himself by Jesus Christ, and hath given to us the ministry of reconciliation; to wit, that God was in Christ, reconciling the world unto himself, not imputing their trespasses unto them; and hath committed unto us the word of reconciliation.
>
> —2 CORINTHIANS 5:18–19

You see, God had a plan for man that did not include sin, death (separation), and the need for a Savior. That's right. It was man who chose to forsake that original plan—we will call it Plan A—and God, having foreknown (but not preordained) that man would fall, had already formulated the all-glorious backup plan—"the Lamb slain before the foundation of the world" (Rev. 13:8). But that was not His original design.

Some suggest that God ordained Lucifer, the rebellious angels, Adam, Eve, and all their descendants to sin against Him and be estranged from Him. If this were true, then it would follow logically that God planned the atrocities of slavery, the horrors of the Holocaust, the ravages of war, and the decimation of tsunamis and hurricanes. This further implies that God was dependent upon Satan's and man's fall for Him to have something to do in order to show Himself mighty. This is ludicrous, for it implicates God as having initiated sin, evil, and rebellion against His own holiness. God is not a kingdom divided against Himself.

Satan's Sin

Ye are of your father the devil, and the lusts of your father ye will do. He was a murderer from the beginning, and abode not in the truth, because there is no truth in him. When he speaketh a lie, he speaketh of his own: for he is a liar, and the father of it.

—JOHN 8:44

Man's Sin

Let no man say when he is tempted, I am tempted of God: for God cannot be tempted with evil, neither tempteth he any man; But every man is tempted, when he is drawn away of his own lust and enticed. Then when lust hath conceived, it bringeth forth sin: and sin, when it is finished, bringeth forth death.

—JAMES 1:13–15

It was not the intention of God to have a plan of redemption, or Plan B. No, God had a plan A ordained for man. He still has it. It is a course of glory and beauty that "eyes have not seen, nor ears heard" (1 Cor. 2:9).

Plan A, in a Sentence

And God said, Let us make man in our image, after our likeness: and let them have dominion over the fish of the sea, and over the fowl of the air, and over the cattle, and over all the earth, and over every creeping thing that creepeth upon the earth.

—GENESIS 1:26

God declares the end from the beginning. In the above verse, God provides a glimpse of what He originally intended for all of mankind. He declares that man will be in His image, after His likeness, and that he will exercise dominion on the earth. The New Testament reveals that Christ is the image of God, so for man to be in God's image is for Him to be in Christ. Man fell from his original "in Christ" status (the capacity to represent God), but he retained the likeness of God in a measure (bearing resemblance to God). And man allowed a disproportionate measure of his authority to be subverted by Satan, though Satan's exercise of the authority is still dependent upon the cooperation of men and women. So you see, Plan B was the decision of man, and God's foreknowledge thereof.

Grand Parentheses

All of this leads us to the conclusion that all of human history—beginning in Genesis 3 and continuing until Revelation 20—is merely a pause in the sentence of God's original design, bracketed in an elaborate set of parentheses: Genesis 1–2 and Revelation 21–22.

Human history since the fall is a miniscule parenthetical moment between eternity past and eternity future. God is working now between the parentheses. And He will use what is accomplished here—redemption and restoration (or, in other words, Plan B)—to get men and women ready to proceed with God's sentence: "And let them have dominion" (Gen. 1:26), which is God's Plan A.

The message of the gospel is about getting mankind positioned to go back to the essence of Genesis 1–2, back to the alpha moment to experience what God really had in mind when He said, "Let us make man in Our image." Those who are born again, then, have re-entered Plan A.

God desires that we receive revelation concerning the scope of our calling in Christ, what being His secondary leaders really means:

> That ye may know what is the hope of his calling, and what the riches of the glory of his inheritance in the saints, And what is the exceeding greatness of his power to us-ward who believe, according to the working of his mighty power, Which he wrought in Christ, when he raised him from the dead, and set him at his own right hand in the heavenly places, Far above all principality, and power, and might, and dominion, and every name that is named, not only in this world, but also in that which is to come: And hath put all things under his feet, and gave him to be the head over all things to the church, Which is his body, the fullness of him that filleth all in all.
>
> —Ephesians 1:18–23

Fullness = Completion

The Scriptures teach that the church is "the fullness of Him that filleth all in all." The world *fullness* is the Greek *pleroma*, and it means "completion." The church is the completion of Christ (Him) Who fills (completes) all things. He is the Alpha and Omega. He is the Author and Finisher of our faith.

When He finished/completed the work of creation of heaven and earth with all their hosts, He rested.

When He finished/completed the purchase of redemption through the cross, He sat down.

Yet today, He is still at work, bringing all things to fullness, making them complete!

Jesus Christ makes individual lives complete. He makes broken hearts completely whole. He makes broken bodies completely healed. He makes marriages completely strong and healthy. He completes all things. But on a larger scale, He invigorates communities, He revitalizes cities, and He even resurrects nations. Christ desires to make all things complete!

That Jesus Christ completes all things is a powerful truth. The other side of that truth, however, is shocking! The church completes Him, as He completes all things. Or, in other words, all the things catalogued above, which are completed by Him in His role as Redeemer, are completed by means of His body, the church! Ephesians 1:23 teaches that it is by means of the church that Jesus makes mankind complete. It is by means of the church that He makes broken hearts completely whole. It is by means of the church that He makes broken bodies completely healed. It is by means of the church that He makes marriages completely strong and healthy. Communities, cities, and nations are completed by Christ through the church, for the church is the fullness—the completion—of Him who completes all things.

When Will This Completion Be Completed?

This completion will not come to pass in our generation if God's secondary leaders, the entire body of Christ on earth, do not decide to buy totally into His program of the restoration of mankind, taking ownership of God's vision: restoration through redemption. If this generation of the church does not rise up and fully assume its place as the body of Jesus

Christ, just as with Israel and its Exodus, God must tragically allow us, too, to pass off the scene. He will raise up our children to take our place.

What if Believers Believed?

But what if believers believed? What would happen if believers knew that we complete, or complement, Jesus and His continued earthly work? What would happen if we believed that if we do nothing then nothing will be done to impact people for God? As incredible as it may seem, God has ordained that the work He "began both to do and teach" (Acts 1:1) in the physical body of Jesus Christ be brought to complete fruition and maturity through the aggregate, composite body of Jesus Christ—the church! Is this why Jesus said, "Verily, verily, I say unto you, He that believeth on me, the works that I do shall he do also; and greater works than these shall he do because I go unto my Father" (John 14:12)? Is this why He said, "Ye have not chosen me, but I have chosen you, and ordained you, that ye should go and bring forth fruit, and that your fruit should remain: that whatsoever ye shall ask of the Father in my name, He may give it to you" (John 15:16)? Is this why He said, "As the Father hath sent me, so send I you" (John 20:21)?

If the responsibility for completing Christ's work is ours, if this *is* why He said these things, He lets us know that He is depending on His secondary leaders—on *us*—to get the biggest, most important job in history done: the realization of mankind being restored to God.

Most Shocking of All

What may really be hardest thing of all to believe is that it's really going to happen! The church is actually going to finish the job that Jesus prescribed. God does not indicate in Scripture that He has, or that He needs, a Plan C. No, Jesus said, "Upon this rock I will build my church; and the gates of hell shall not prevail against it" (Matt. 16:18).

Hell can't win! Sin cannot win! Regardless of the narrow, hyper-dispensationalist view that the church will be a limp, totally Laodicean mess when Jesus comes for us, Paul disagrees, and so must we. (The seven churches existed concurrently; therefore, characteristics of all seven of the "seven churches" in Revelation are symptomatic of various segments of the body of Christ concurrently.)

And hath raised us up together, and made us sit together in heavenly places in Christ Jesus: That in the ages to come he might shew the exceeding riches of his grace in his kindness toward us through Christ Jesus.

—EPHESIANS 2:6–7

To the intent that now unto the principalities and powers in heavenly places might be known by the church the manifold wisdom of God, According to the eternal purpose which he purposed in Christ Jesus our Lord.

—EPHESIANS 3:10–11

Husbands, love your wives, even as Christ also loved the church, and gave himself for it; That he might sanctity and cleanse it with the washing of the water by the word, That he might present it to himself a glorious church, not having spot, or wrinkle, or any such thing; but that it should be holy and without blemish.

—EPHESIANS 5:25–27

Regardless of how far-fetched it might seem, the writers of Scripture indicate that the church will prevail because Christ must prevail—and has prevailed! Granted, by the time these things are fully consummated, the church manifest then may be vastly unlike that which we see today. But inevitably, Christ will have a glorious church!

Chapter 1

THE FOUNDATIONAL ROLE
OF THE LOCAL CHURCH

AN ELDERLY MINISTER, internationally noted and widely respected, was asked on a Christian talk show what he thought God was doing in this hour. He replied in tacit form that God was doing what He has always done, transforming lives through the blood of Jesus by the power of His Word and of His Spirit. However, he went on to state that one significant development was the growing impact of local churches. He asserted that he believed the move of God in these last days would be seen in the increasing power of the local church.

The Hub of Ministry

This gentleman's ideas are biblical: the local church is the hub of Christian ministry. The local church is a visible witness of the invisible God and His kingdom. It is a haven where the lost are saved and safe. Also, at its best, it is an empowerment center, a "filling station" for individual Christians. When believers come together, acknowledging their common identity in the Spirit of God, there is an irresistibly invigorating dynamic that hurls them back into their ordinary lives refilled with extraordinary power and perspective.

An Empowerment Center

The Bible tells of Isaiah the prophet, who had a vision of God in the temple. Whether Isaiah was literally inside the Jerusalem temple having the vision, or he was elsewhere and had a vision both of the temple and of God in it—in either case, the temple is quite significant. Because the temple system, the system of worship in those days, constituted Isaiah's "local church," we could say that Isaiah saw God in his own local church and was ministered to by one of His flaming ones, the seraphim. Once Isaiah had

had this encounter, he was ready to go back to the street, among his people, and fulfill God's vision and God's mission in response to God's request. After the God encounter, Isaiah said, "Here am I, send me" (Isa. 6:8).

A Fresh Awe

It is a wonderful thing when believers can find God in their local church. The local church now, as Isaiah's did, must have "burning ones," ministers who, as keepers of the flame, are ready to ignite anew those who come to commune with God. Even so, when individual Christians get a true view of God in His temple, the assembled body flowing in the corporate anointing, they are awe-stricken afresh at His power to save and to transform.

> For ye are the temple of the living God; as God hath said, "I will dwell in them, and walk in them; and I will be their God, and they shall be my people."
> —2 CORINTHIANS 6:16

And when they are served a burning coal, a living Word from God, by one of His flaming ministers, they are made ready to go back home to their spouses and their children. They are ready to go back to work, back to school, back to business, and back to their communities—but differently this time. They are not going casually, but *causally*. This time, they are saying, "Here am I, Lord; send me. I'm here in Your presence, and I am willing to obey You. I am willing to leave the assembly to go back into the everyday environment. But this time, I'm not just going. You're sending me to my spouse. You're sending me to my children. You're sending me into the world, across the street or across the planet. I go empowered because of what I experienced in the Temple—not merely at the church, but *as* the church."

Some Principles Upon Which the Local Church Is Built

The Bible is the Word of God, the ultimate guide and test of doctrine, conduct, and experience for all. Consequently, it is the basis for the structure and order of the church on every level.

This is important because, more importantly than creeds, discipline books, and manuals, the Book is to be the guiding Light for the local church.

The church's identity and viability depend upon the guidelines that Jesus and His sent ones articulated in the Bible. The life and ministry of the Lord Jesus (recorded in the Gospels), the book of Acts, and the epistles provide the first and final model of what ministry ought to be. The rest of the Bible provides guidance and undergirding, as well, for life and godliness. Therefore, no local church can be successful without the highest regard for the Word. *Sola scriptura* should be our rallying cry, even as it was of the Reformers. Of course, it is necessary to make rules and policies in the church that address the particulars of our times and our culture. However, denominational, organizational, and operational rules must all be subjected to the scrutiny of the written Word of God.

All Leaders Are Fallible, but the Word Is Infallible

Furthermore: because this lesson is primarily about relationships between human beings as they strive to fulfill the will of God for their lives and ministries as leaders, it is important to strongly iterate this truth: no human being is above the Bible. All of us are obligated to live according to the plain sense of Scripture. No man or woman has the right to demand, expect, give to, or accept from another man or woman that which is not wholly consistent with Scripture. God gave mankind dominion over the earth and everything in nature; however, He did not give mankind dominion over one another. Furthermore, there is nothing in the Scripture that gives one human the right to dominate or exploit another. The standard for leadership is not human leaders: it is the Word of God, with God in Christ as the Prototype.

What Makes Human Leadership Legitimate, Then?

All humans are equal in the sight of God, though their roles in society differ. And all Christians are equal in worth, though their functions in the body of Christ may vary. Therefore, kingdom leadership is based upon two fundamentals.

First, because all human beings are equal, the only way that one person may effectively lead another is for the one being led to give the leader permission to lead by submitting to his or her leadership. One cannot biblically lead by coercing another; the follower must choose to follow.

Secondly, every office of leadership exists because a need exists. The office is responsible to fulfill a need in some aspect of the kingdom. In order to fulfill that responsibility, the office is assigned a corresponding measure of authority.

The office is to be respected, even when the officeholder is not particularly respectable. This is a supremely sensitive area because the best and the worst of what has happened in the church and in civilization has been because of its leadership dynamics. Because of the basic self-centeredness of the Adamic human nature, all leaders and leadership styles must be continually reassessed. For though God's principles of leadership are absolutely perfect, our understanding and application of them are naturally imperfect. Everything that leaders in the house of God attempt should ultimately be to the glory of God. No principle should be misconstrued for the fleshy motive of a man or woman.

The Lord Jesus Christ Is
the Head and Chief Shepherd

Deists believed that God created the universe. However, they viewed the universe under the metaphor of a clock, which its Maker created, wound up, and then left to run on its own according to certain principles. A similar paradigm seems to exist pertaining to the church in these times. We sometimes forget that the church is not ours but Christ's. How dare a church formulate doctrines and accept practices that violate the very teachings and values of Jesus Christ Himself, some which even question His own Being? Jesus purchased the universal and local church with His own blood. Consequently, in all that is done, Jesus Christ is to be acknowledged. Pastors, officers, and all members must understand that they will give a strict account to the Lord Jesus Christ for how they "transact business" in His name.

> For we must all appear before the judgment seat of Christ; that every one may receive the things done in his body, according to that he hath done, whether it be good or bad.
>
> —2 CORINTHIANS 5:10

The Church on Two Levels

An ecclesiastical hierarchy, if a given church exists within such a framework, may properly have a chain of command and accountability. However, it must be remembered that God and the Scriptures primarily recognize the church on two primary levels: the universal and the local. Ultimately, the universal church is the voice and presence of the Lord Jesus Christ to the global community, and the local church is the voice and presence of the Lord Jesus Christ to its local community.

Intermediate strata within the universal church, such as fellowships, conferences, communions, organizations, denominations, and parachurch ministries, are biblically valid. They find their validity within the framework of the apostle's ministry—networking—and the timeless concepts of covenant and fellowship. However, their validity exists only to the degree that they enhance the universal and local church. If these groupings of churches or ministries do not make the greater body of Christ greater still, and if they do not ultimately edify and support local ministry, they are outside the will of God. They have no biblical legitimacy.

The church is the body of Jesus Christ and is responsible to make the kind of impact on its environment now that the physical body of Jesus did two thousand years ago.

Church Redefined

One other thing. The term *church* must be redefined for our day, recapturing the definition that Jesus and the apostles gave it in His and their day. We have too often reduced *church* to mean a building where ceremonial religious activities are carried out, or to refer to the activities themselves. "Having church" has thus come to mean "engaging in religious activities in a building set apart for such purposes." These activities are typically self-fulfilling and self-contained.

At first glance, this may not seem significant, but when a term is defined a certain way, the term becomes a concept. The processing of concepts constitutes thinking, and "as he thinketh in his heart, so is he" (Prov. 23:7). The impotence that characterizes the lives of too many Christians—if they are truly born again and not merely nominal Christians—is the result of flawed thinking.

Oversimplification?

This may seem an oversimplification for such a complex issue as Christian ineffectiveness and defeat. However, the Scriptures bear it out. "My people are destroyed," God said, "for lack of knowledge" (Hos. 4:6). The apostle Paul states that a major aspect of the believer's warfare is "casting down imaginations and every high thing that exalteth itself against the knowledge of God, and bringing into captivity every thought to the obedience of Christ" (2 Cor. 10:5).

The way we think about the church necessarily involves the way we view God and ourselves because the church is the nexus between God and humanity. When we are joined to God through Jesus Christ, we become His body, the church. We are in Him, and He is in us. That thought alone has explosive potency. It is so powerful that, according to Paul, it is the mystery that was hidden from ages and generations: "Christ in you, the hope of glory" (Col. 1:27). And Paul declares further that it is through the church that God will demonstrate to the principalities and powers in the heavenly places—which I believe also includes the celestial ones and the Satanic ones—His own manifold wisdom throughout all eternity.

The Church's Impact in the Past

The worldwide, transcendent impact of the church upon history and civilization could not have occurred if these definitions, "religious activities" and "literal buildings," had been in use from the beginning. The martyrs who laid down their lives over the centuries were so deeply convicted as to face murder, and no one would knowingly lay down his life for fairly well-crafted religious activities or a building where such activities were held. They laid down their lives in honor of the message of a bodily risen Christ and His abiding presence in a people—the church, which is His body.

Church meant the "called-out" people who are the composite Christ, His body, bringing the living God to dying humanity in every sector where these called-out ones exist: the marketplace, the educational community, the political arena, and everywhere else believers exist. The assembly of the believers, the church, was and is of far more significance than the physical location, for Jesus said, "Where two or three of you are gathered together in my name, there am I in the midst of them" (Matt. 18:20).

Impotent and Irrelevant

The church is rendered impotent when it allows the spirit of this age to define it. The so-called "separation of church and state" ideology has further misdefined the church, causing it to be marginalized in the minds of many believers and unbelievers. These people deal with two realities: the reality that exists when they are safe behind the walls of the church and the reality of the nitty-gritty, everyday details of life. Such ideas make the church largely irrelevant; thus, it should not surprise us that people who really want to "live" don't see the church as an avenue toward fulfillment in their lives. Respect for the church is at an all-time low, at least in Western culture. People tend to be irreverent to what they perceive as irrelevant.

The Importance of Definitions

Definitions are important. They affect the whole of an individual or a corporate entity such as the church. "No human being can define you. Don't allow anyone to try. Remember, whatever or whoever can define you can confine you. In relation to your place in Christ, human beings or society, at best, can only describe you—only God in His Word should be allowed to define you."

The Damage of Poor Definitions

The Christian has often been confined to a life of mediocrity and dullness because *church* or *Christian* has been defined for him or her as repeated religious activity or a religious person. The outcome of this mind-set is that neither the church nor the Christian deliberately affects anyone for God. There is a shyness there, an "I don't want to offend anybody" attitude.

And not only is there confinement in this life—many Christians even embrace a bleak misdefinition of eternity. They envision it to be one in which the saints will spend the everlasting ages sitting at huge tables, wearing long white robes, wings, halos, golden crowns, and golden slippers, while drinking milk and eating honey. (What about the honey? How will we eat the honey? Will there be spoons to eat the raw honey from bowls? Nobody said anything about biscuits—could we at least have some biscuits to "sop" the honey and wash it all down with milk?) This is not the clear picture of what believers have to look forward to in the world to come. As you can see, fact has been intertwined with fiction, and the misdefinition damages one's perspective.

The Equippers of the Saints

The Lord Jesus Christ gave apostles, prophets, evangelists, pastors, and teachers to the church for the purpose of equipping the saints for the work of serving God and others, resulting in the building up of the church in quality and quantity.

There exists much fervent debate as to whether all the members of this four- or five-fold set of servants still exists in the church today. The perspective of this text is that they have always existed, continue to exist, and are needed in this day more than ever. Furthermore, it is the nomenclature that has changed. Many people, because of abuses or (again) wrong definitions, are uncomfortable with being called an apostle or prophet, though they have occupied those roles. They've opted for more generic labels.

Even if one disagrees with this position, allowing only for the latter two or three ministries, he or she should agree that the stated purpose for these ministries has not changed. Ministers are placed in the church not to be the professional practitioners of religion at the religious activity buildings where the bravely devout visit at least once weekly (or weakly!). Rather, they are placed in the Christian community and the world to model Christlikeness and to empower fellow believers. They are to love, inspire, mentor, train, challenge, discipline, and develop Christians and send them back into the everyday world. They are positioned there to make trouble for the devil, to make a positive difference in the lives of others, and to bring glory to God. These ministers are called to be servants of God's children, "tutors and governors" (Galatians 4:2) to prepare His offspring for the appointed time, in this life and the next, to rule and reign with Christ.

The local church is the hub of Christian ministry. It is the place where the rubber meets the road.

The Local God

God has always wanted to be local. This is obvious in many places in the Scriptures. Beginning with the first man, God came down and visited man time and again. He instructed Moses to build Him a tabernacle so that He could dwell among His people. Finally, the Word was made flesh and dwelt among us—God became local, with a birth certificate and a street address. And when the Word-Made-Flesh departed from this earth, He promised that God would soon become more local yet: this time He would not only dwell with His people, He would dwell *in* them. And by means of indwelling them, they would become a composite local expression of the Deity to those who do not know Him. Jesus instructed His followers to make Him local: "Go and teach all nations"; "Go into all the world"; "among all nations"; "Jerusalem, Judea, Samaria, and the uttermost parts of the earth." (See Matthew 28:16–20.)

The Early Local Church

The "early church," that pristine model to which most of us reverently look and desire to emulate, was first and foremost a local church. First, it was the church at Jerusalem, and then it became "the church at…(Rome, Corinth, Ephesus)," whatever the geographical setting. Most of the epistles are letters sent to local churches, either individual churches or groups of local bodies, making the letter "encyclical" (to be taken and read from one local congregation to another).

A Place Where People Meet God

And so it is that the local church becomes the place where people meet God. It is in the local church context that people are born again, lives are changed, people receive counsel and assistance in crises, marriages are made and restored, children are dedicated to the Lord and instructed, disciples receive the call to special ministry, the sick are ministered to, and the dead are buried. Justly or not, most people's view of the Lord Jesus Christ is largely determined by what they have seen in whatever local church is in their lives or communities. Even with the advent of tremendous media ministries, many of which do great good in the lives of people, nothing has or can replace the power of the personal touch. And this is found, primarily, in the local church.

All believers, including all ministers, should have a wholesome, personal relationship and commitment to some local church:

> And let us consider one another to provoke unto love and to good
> works: Not forsaking the assembling of ourselves together, as the

manner of some is; but exhorting one another: and so much the more, as ye see the day approaching.

—HEBREWS 10:24–25

The Value of Local Church
Relationships in the Early Church

When reading about the lives of early Christians in the Scriptures, one thing is abundantly clear: there was a high premium placed upon relationships with other Christians. There was nothing acceptable about being a "god unto oneself" in that historical context. To the contrary, it is explicit from the beginning that fellowship was the proper attitude for believers:

> And when they were come in, they went up into an upper room, where abode both Peter, and James, and John, and Andrew, Philip, and Thomas, Bartholomew, and Matthew, James the son of Alphaeus, and Simon Zelotes, and Judas the brother of James. These all continued with one accord in prayer and supplication, with the women, and Mary the mother of Jesus, and with his brethren. And in those days Peter stood up in the midst of the disciples.
>
> —ACTS 1:13–15

> And when the day of Pentecost was fully come, they were all with one accord in one place.
>
> —ACTS 2:1

> Then they that gladly received his word were baptized: and the same day there were added unto them about three thousand souls. And they continued steadfastly in the apostles' doctrine and fellowship, and in breaking of bread, and in prayers. And fear came upon every soul: and many wonders and signs were done by the apostles. And all that believed were together, and had all things common; And sold their possessions and goods, and parted them to all men, as every man had need. And they, continuing daily with one accord in the temple, and breaking bread from house to house, did eat their meat with gladness and singleness of heart, Praising God, and having favour with all the people. And the Lord added to the church daily such as should be saved.
>
> —ACTS 2:41–47

And the multitude of them that believed were of one heart and of one soul: neither said any of them that ought of the things which he possessed was his own; but they had all things common. And with great power gave the apostles witness of the resurrection of the Lord Jesus: and great grace was upon them all. Neither was there any among them that lacked: for as many as were possessors of lands or houses sold them, and brought the prices of the things that were sold, And laid them down at the apostles' feet: and distribution was made unto every man according as he had need.

—Acts 4:32–25

Not Only for Laity but for Leadership

The line of demarcation between laity and clergy may not have been as clear in the early church as it is in the present. It was not that the ministry gifts were not honored; rather, it was because the definition of *church* was dynamically inclusive of all believers, not exclusive to the professionals. All who professed Christ were expected to possess the power and character of God in their daily lives. Therefore, not only was the laity known to embrace principles of relationship, but the apostles, prophets, evangelist, pastors, teachers, elders, bishops, and deacons were known to embrace the need to belong to a community of believers, too.

See, for example, Saul's relationship with the disciples after his conversion:

And when Saul was come to Jerusalem, he assayed to join himself to the disciples: but they were all afraid of him, and believed not that he was a disciple. But Barnabas took him, and brought him to the apostles, and declared unto them how he had seen the Lord in the way, and that he had spoken to him, and how he had preached boldly at Damascus in the name of Jesus. And he was with them coming in and going out at Jerusalem.

—Acts 9:26–28

Notice also, the example of the church at Jerusalem and among the Gentiles:

And the hand of the Lord was with them: and a great number believed, and turned unto the Lord. Then tidings of these things came unto the ears of the church which was in Jerusalem: and they sent forth Barnabas, that he should go as far as Antioch. Who, when he came, and had seen the grace of God, was glad, and exhorted them all, that with purpose of heart they would cleave unto the Lord. For he was a good man, and full of the Holy Ghost and of faith: and much people was added unto the Lord.

—ACTS 11:21–24

The following describes Barnabas and Saul's relationship with the church at Antioch:

Now there were in the church that was at Antioch certain prophets and teachers; as Barnabas, and Simeon that was called Niger, and Lucius of Cyrene, and Manaen, which had been brought up with Herod the tetrarch, and Saul. As they ministered to the Lord, and fasted, the Holy Ghost said, Separate me Barnabas and Saul for the work whereunto I have called them. And when they had fasted and prayed, and laid their hands on them, they sent them away.

—ACTS 13:1–3

Later, Paul and Barnabas returned to their "home church" at Antioch and remained in relationship with those who fellowshipped there:

And there came thither certain Jews from Antioch and Iconium, who persuaded the people, and, having stoned Paul, drew him out of the city, supposing he had been dead. Howbeit, as the disciples stood round about him, he rose up, and came into the city: and the next day he departed with Barnabas to Derbe. And when they had preached the gospel to that city, and had taught many, they returned again to Lystra, and to Iconium, and Antioch, Confirming the souls of the disciples, and exhorting them to continue in the faith, and that we must through much tribulation enter into the kingdom of God. And when they had ordained them elders in every church, and had prayed with fasting, they commended them to the Lord, on whom they believed. And after they had passed throughout Pisidia, they came to Pamphylia. And when they had preached the word in Perga, they went down into Attalia: And thence sailed to Antioch, from whence they had been recommended to the grace of God for the work which they fulfilled. And when they were come, and had gathered the church together, they rehearsed all that God had done with them, and how he had opened the door of faith unto the Gentiles. And there they abode long time with the disciples.

—ACTS 14:19–28

Additionally, Paul, Barnabas, and Peter share their ministry experiences at the Jerusalem Council:

> And being brought on their way by the church, they passed through Phenice and Samaria, declaring the conversion of the Gentiles: and they caused great joy unto all the brethren. And when they were come to Jerusalem, they were received of the church, and of the apostles and elders, and they declared all things that God had done with them.... And the apostles and elders came together for to consider of this matter.... Then pleased it the apostles and elders, with the whole church, to send chosen men of their own company to Antioch with Paul and Barnabas; namely, Judas surnamed Barsabas, and Silas, chief men among the brethren.... So when they were dismissed, they came to Antioch: and when they had gathered the multitude together, they delivered the epistle: Which when they had read, they rejoiced for the consolation. And Judas and Silas, being prophets also themselves, exhorted the brethren with many words, and confirmed them.... And after they had tarried there a space, they were let go in peace from the brethren unto the apostles.... And he went through Syria and Cilicia, confirming the churches.
>
> —ACTS 15:3–4, 6, 22, 30–31, 33, 41

Paul also consulted with Peter:

> Then after three years I went up to Jerusalem to see Peter, and abode with him fifteen days. But other of the apostles saw I none, save James the Lord's brother.
>
> —GALATIANS 1:18–19

Furthermore, Paul conferred with leaders of the Jerusalem church concerning his ministry for doctrinal accountability:

> And I went up by revelation, and communicated unto them that gospel which I preach among the Gentiles, but privately to them which were of reputation, lest by any means I should run, or had run, in vain.... And when James, Cephas, and John, who seemed to be pillars, perceived the grace that was given unto me, they gave to me and Barnabas the right hands of fellowship.
>
> —GALATIANS 2:2, 9

All Christians—professionals and laypersons, the mature and the novice—all of them need the kind of relationship that being a part of the local church community provides.

Chapter 2

THE MOST VITAL LEADERSHIP ROLE IN THE LOCAL CHURCH: THE SENIOR LEADER (PASTOR)

T HE BIBLE TEACHES that "God hath set some in the church, first apostles, secondarily prophets, thirdly teachers, after that miracles, then gifts of healings, helps, governments, diversities of tongues" (1 Cor. 12:28). Scripture also states, "He gave some apostles, and some prophets, and some evangelists, and some pastors and teachers" (Eph. 4:11).

Local Church Leader

In the local church relationship network, as in all things, there is a primary, or senior, leader. This leader is someone who serves as an initiator, an "articulator of vision," while others in the church—all of whom are yet leaders—serve as facilitators. In the local church, that initiator, who is also the guardian and "feeder," is generally called a pastor. Some groups may use different terminology (pastor-teacher, ruling elder), and it is taught in some settings that the primary leader of a local house does not necessarily have to be the ministry gift of pastor. Nevertheless, it is almost universally believed that, under Christ, the head (at least, the spiritual head) of a local church should be some person(s) specially called, gifted, and qualified for the position.

Angel of the Church

Classically, Bible scholars believe that the seven angels of the seven churches of Asia Minor, referred to in the Book of Revelation, are actually the pastors of those churches: the Greek term *angelos* means "messenger," whether heavenly or earthly. Furthermore, the Revelation calls these angels "seven stars" in the hand of the Lord Jesus Christ. If the stars are the angels, and the angels are the pastors, then the pastors are in the direct charge of the Lord Himself. Peter refers to them as elders taking oversight, under-shepherds who will one day stand before the Chief Shepherd, the Lord Jesus Christ, to give account of their service as pastors (1 Peter 5: 1–4). Therefore, the most vital leadership role of the local church is that of the "set gift," variously labeled as the pastor, senior elder, or senior pastor. This individual is the administrative and spiritual head of a local church, under Christ.

The Pastor's Authority

The pastor is the one in whom God invests the highest authority in the local church in order to fulfill his or her mandate to feed, lead, and guard the flock of God. In all settings, there should be a plurality of voices lending varied insights for the wholesomeness, security, and grounding of the ministry. Whether this plurality is of a high official nature, as in the Presbyterian or Congregationalist church government model, or in a more "independent church" leadership setting, or in an Episcopal governmental context, "in the multitude of counselors there is safety" (Prov. 24:6).

The Bible is clear about the fact that dictatorship is not God's plan for His kingdom. Though all are kings in the church—believers are a royal priesthood—there is only one King of the church, the Lord Jesus Christ. God has placed His wisdom within more than any one of us, more than those who are ministers in the official sense. Our ability to listen, to defer, to take one another seriously, and to respect Christ's presence in His whole body—this strengthens the entire church.

God Selects One

Nevertheless, the Bible pattern is that God always has an individual, a chief spokesperson, who leads His enterprises. This individual is given primacy in authority because he or she is held primarily responsible for the well-being and outcomes of all involved, not because of any inherent superiority to others, though he or she should have proven Christian maturity, integrity, and a corresponding gifting and calling. He or she may be called by different titles in different settings, but this person is the under-shepherd of the local church.

Though there are distinctly gifted persons inside and outside the local church who will be used to bless and support it, the place of the pastor is a unique one. No other leader—no apostle, no prophet, no bishop—has authority that supersedes the authority of the local pastor inside the local church, so long as he or she is operating within scriptural guidelines.

Other Ecclesiastical Leaders in Relation to the Pastor

To state it positively, all leaders, from outside or within the local church, are subject to the pastor with respect to that church. Even if a leader from the outside is the spiritual father of the pastor, a prelate, or a superintendent, his first obligation is to minister to the pastor, not to dominate that pastor's church.

Of course, these are basic principles. Their application would vary widely, based upon denominational, organizational, or other policies to which a church or fellowship subscribes. For example, there may be a newly planted church in which a newly appointed pastor is on probation of sorts, proving that he or she is capable of leading a congregation. Naturally, those who are his or her leaders would deal with him or her and that local church based upon the provisions of their covenant, fellowship, communion, and denomination. Nevertheless, there should eventually come a point of maturity in the ministry when that newly inducted pastor is able to securely lead the flock to which he or she has been assigned, according to a God-inspired, Bible-based vision.

An Example of "Out-of-Order"

It is out of order for me, having been invited to minister in a given local church or other ministry setting, to attempt to take over aspects of that church outside the parameters of my assignment. If I have been asked to teach on a certain aspect of ministry and to assist in its structure, then I am at liberty—and even then with great caution and discretion—to address and perhaps modify something in that regard. If I have been called to minister concerning praise and worship, I have no right to change the ushers' uniforms. If I have been asked to conduct prayer, I should not start a business meeting. If I have been asked to come as a revivalist, I have no right to conduct private consultations with members of that congregation.

I may greet members of the congregation the same as I would greet anyone anywhere, but beyond this, we have no official interactions. As a guest minister, I relate to the members of that congregation primarily through the pastor. If the host pastor refers a member to me because there is a particular topic in which the member and I share interest or experience, only then will I confer with that parishioner as a parishioner. And when that exchange is over, I am open and willing to brief that pastor on what transpired. I need to assist in holding that brother or sister accountable to his or her local fellowship, because if triumph or trouble arises in his life, he should be able to look to God and to his local church and leadership—not to me.

Assigned to Serve

When I am called to a local ministry and I accept the invitation, I am there as the servant of the Lord first, of course. But I am also there as the servant of the pastor and that local house. Instead of being there to take over, I am there to be told how I can best help to promote what the Lord is doing in that ministry.

There will be times when I am told to take my liberty and flow in whatever is on my heart in a given season. But there also may be times when I am asked to teach on, preach on, or lecture on a given theme or area where the ministry needs emphasis. I am to do what I have been asked to do because I expect the pastor to have insight as to what the congregation needs most.

I may feel like leading a praise service, but if the pastor perceives that the church needs a lesson on prayer, I should teach prayer. If I genuinely sense the compulsion of the Spirit to go another way, I should at least determine whether I have the latitude to go with that prompting. Most pastors who believe in the leading of the Spirit will welcome this unction, but respect still requires that I acknowledge that senior leader because I am not only accountable to God, but to him or her. If it turns out that I am inhibited or prohibited from giving all that I have from God for that local house, God will hold that leader responsible, but I will not be unruly.

Another Example

Furthermore, if I am the spiritual father or big brother of the pastor, my relationship with that pastor does not automatically entitle me to special prerogatives where the congregation and its affairs are concerned. Again, this could vary if the spiritual father figure is also the planter or builder of that local church. In that case, he may have a special "founder's rapport" with that congregation: he would be not merely the pastor's father but also the whole congregation's spiritual father. Even then, however, if the spiritual father does not graciously assist the congregation in shifting its primary leadership focus from himself to the "new" pastor, he may effectively handicap that congregation and that pastor, preventing them from ever becoming stable from within.

Crippling a Congregation

If the people are never able to make the transition into seeing the present pastor as a senior leader, they will never be a complete spiritual family. For the longer-term members, who may have "grown up" spiritually with, or even before, the new leader, they must at least see the pastor as elder brother #1 in the church. If not, there will never be the level of cohesiveness that a church should have. The church's development will have to wait until the members who have been peers with the new pastor do one of the following:

- conform and accept the new leadership,

- depart and find a spiritual father, or

- go home to be with the Lord.

The other alternative is the worst one: remain unchanged and cause all kinds of havoc and division within the congregation.

In summary, only as the pastor grants me, the "outside leader," the privilege of speaking into the life of that church may I do so. Otherwise, my assignment is to the pastor as a father, pastor, or mentor. The church is his or her assignment, not mine.

Respect for Human Authority

Let every soul be subject unto the higher powers. For there is no power but of God: the powers that be are ordained of God. Whosoever therefore resisteth the power, resisteth the ordinance of God: and they that resist shall receive to themselves damnation.

—ROMANS 13:1–2

Most widely, this passage is taught regarding civil authorities and magistrates, showing that their authority is actually delegated by God and that therefore their offices should be respected. But would not this principle of respect for delegated authority be even more relevant as applied to leadership within the body of Christ, those to whom He has delegated spiritual authority?

God Himself Respects Human Authority

This is a truth that seems little known or regarded. People, in their folk wisdom, seem to think of the God of the Bible, or whatever god they regard, as a renegade. They say things about God that He never says of Himself, and they do so without qualification and stipulation. These are statements such as, "God can do anything He wants to do, whenever He wants to, however He wants to!" This is supposedly a definition of divine sovereignty. Another one is, "God don't need nobody!" or "I don't believe in all this prophesying! If God's got something to tell me, He can tell me Himself!" or "You ain't got to have no preacher and go to no church to know God! You can have all the church you want at home by watching Christian TV or listening to the radio."

All these statements are and without stipulation, and some are outright false. When God created man, He put the care of the earth into his hands. When man failed, God did not revoke man's status as custodial steward over this planet. Man relinquished full exercise of his authority on the earth, and a Man would have to regain it. So God did what He had to do in order to protect His own Word: He became a Man to legally redeem man from sin. To intervene in these affairs as God, He would have violated His own Word.

Pharaoh

When it was time to bring Israel out of Egypt, God possessed the raw power to bring His people out at any time, without any negotiation. Yet God respects human authority—the authority that He had delegated and allocated to man. He was so respectful that He used a man, Moses, to tell another man, Pharaoh, to let His people go. Pharaoh was told to permit the people to leave Egypt.

If God just does anything, anyway, at any time, why didn't He just snatch Israel out of Egypt?

Yes, God did get glory and demonstrate His power on Pharaoh through hardening Pharaoh's heart—but the hardening of heart was Pharaoh's choice (Romans 9:17). God uses those who reject Him as vessels of wrath, but only because of His infinite knowledge of their rejection of Himself. To suggest otherwise is to imply that God creates some humans to destine them for destruction, with no hope of salvation available to them. What about statements such as "who will have all men be saved and come to the knowledge of the truth" (1 Tim. 2:4)? What about "not willing that any should perish but that all should come to repentance" (2 Pet. 3:9)? God respects the authority that He gave each human to accept Him or to refuse Him, with the corresponding consequences in either case.

This is because God honors authority—He honors protocol. Even if the officeholder is unrighteous, God respects the office. If the officeholder respects God, he does not have to incur the wrath of God. Pharaoh didn't respect God, and he and his nation paid a dreadful price. Notice, too, that before each of the plagues, God would solicit Pharaoh to let the people go. In the end, it was still only after Pharaoh told them to depart that Moses and the Israelites left Egypt.

Other Examples of God Respecting Human Authority

Throughout the Scriptures, examples are shown of God honoring human authority and those who do likewise.

- When Adam and Eve sinned, God, knowing all things, did not challenge the serpent or the female without first addressing the man. Even though the serpent and the woman had sinned first, God dealt with Adam because he was the one who was directly given the charge by God not to eat of the forbidden tree—he was not deceived when he sinned. Secondly, Adam was the leader of his marriage; he was primarily responsible for his wife to have been informed of God's mandate. (See Genesis 3 and 1 Timothy 2:14.)

- God consulted with Abraham before destroying Sodom and Gomorrah, and the consultation ended only when Abraham ceased to intercede. (See Genesis 18:17–19.)

- The angels said they "could not" destroy Sodom and Gomorrah until Lot was brought out. (See Genesis 19:21–22.) David did not rise up against Saul, even after Saul had lost the anointing. (1 Samuel 24:24, 26.)

- When the king of Nineveh called a fast, God turned the destruction that Jonah had predicted. (See Jonah 3.)

- God instructed the captive Jews to pray for the peace of Babylon while they were in bondage.

- Jesus said, "Render unto Caesar" (Matt. 22:21). Jesus said, "Honor the Pharisees for sitting in Moses' seat, but do not emulate them" (Matt. 23:1–3).

- Even though Jesus came to the earth to die, the Father did not allow Him to be betrayed, even at the very last moment, until He as a Man said, "Thy will be done" (Matt. 26:42).

- Paul taught, "Let every soul be subject to the higher power, for there is no power but of God" (Romans 13:1).

- Paul also taught, "first of all prayers, supplications, intercessions, giving of thanks, be made for kings and all that are in authority" (1 Tim. 2:1).

- Jude taught that the angels do not presume to speak evil of dignities, that the Archangel Michael did not bring a railing accusation against Satan but said, "The Lord rebuke thee" (Jude 1:8–9).

- Jesus Himself said, "Behold, I stand at the door and knock if any man hear my voice and open unto me I will come in unto him" (Rev. 3:20). He does not kick the door in; He waits to be invited.

If our God respects authority—personal and official, natural and spiritual—then certainly we who seek to follow Him should do likewise.

By all means, we should respect His representatives, particularly those who walk upright, living and teaching the Word of God.

The Pastor's Responsibility

Consequent to this high level of authority, the pastor is held to a higher level of responsibility. First, the pastor is not independent. Yes, there are "independent churches"—churches that have legal, fiscal, and visionary autonomy and are not affiliated with any denomination or organization. And yes, each ministry gift has a uniqueness of anointing and calling upon a person's life. However, in the truest sense, no member of the body of Christ is independent any more than the parts of a physical body are independent of each other. Rather, we are interdependent: we each depend upon the other, and we all depend upon God. This interdependence includes accountability; though men and women of God may opt not to be legally tied to one another, the bond of covenant must be maintained to ensure that no one becomes a god unto himself.

Pastors Need Relationship

Pastors, and all leaders, need other pastors and other ministry gifts for networking that provides covenant relationships. With covenant relationships, all of the following elements, and more, are found: camaraderie, accountability, confirmation, encouragement, credibility, correction, counsel, covering, and corporate strength. Leading ministry gifts need relationship, of which doctrinal, professional, and personal accountability are critical ingredients. There is a strong cry for genuine covenant relationship—"real-ationship"— where leaders are not merely joined at the hip (carrying credentials from the same organization) but joined at the heart. These "real-ationships" for leaders are found in fathers, friends, and followers.

Real-ationship #1: Fathers

For though ye have ten thousand instructors in Christ, yet have ye not many fathers: for in Christ Jesus I have begotten you through the gospel.

—1 Corinthians 4:15

The Cry and the Need for Fathers

One of the greatest yearnings in the hearts of leaders, even many who are accomplished ministers in their own right, is the desire for a father. This absence and silence of fathers is mirrored in the natural. As a matter of fact, I believe that the Bible shows the Last Day scenario to be parallel between natural and spiritual.

Several passages suggest that the cultural climate of the end times will be clouded by a breakdown of the family, necessitating a restoration of the "office of father." Children and parents are foretold to become estranged from each other. "Behold, I will send you Elijah the prophet before the coming of the great and dreadful day of the LORD: And he shall turn the heart of the fathers to the children, and the heart of the children to their fathers, lest I come and smite the earth with a curse." (Mal. 4:5–6). (See also Isaiah 3:12; Mark 13:12; II Timothy 3:1–2.)

The sociological backdrop of our day is largely affected by the absence and silence of fathers and the breakdown of families—poverty, illiteracy, gangs—all these things are traceable to the father void. And often, what is true in the natural is a portrayal of what is happening in the spirit realm; there is a dearth of spiritual fathers and a decay of wholesome spiritual family relationships. Paul said there were not many spiritual fathers in his day (See 1 Corinthians 4:15)—how much less in ours?

Premature Parents

For example, so many contemporary households consist of women who have children and no husband, forcing women to attempt to master motherhood and fatherhood at once. Often these women became mothers while still children themselves, having the God-given physical "equipment" to be a mother but not the other corresponding qualifications. (Their male counterparts are usually in a similar situation; it is just that most often the female is left holding the proverbial bag of parental responsibility.) Reproduction is God's will for their lives, but they have become parents prematurely. They are able to procreate but unprepared to parent. Furthermore, some faithful grandmothers, grandfathers, uncles, aunts, principals, pastors, and coaches are playing multiple roles trying to be surrogate mothers and fathers to the fatherless.

Even so, there are many young men and women who are called of God and have the God-given spiritual "equipment" to preach, prophesy, start a church, and conduct evangelistic outreach. However, they are in need of someone who will give them a sense of grounding, support, and discipline—a sense of identity and validation that can only come from a father in the gospel. Often these senior leaders have come into spiritual "parenting" themselves prematurely. Though fulfilled in part in Christ's First Advent, this prediction has great significance in connection with the time of His Second Coming as well.

Preemies: Trauma and Risk

Premature babies experience much trauma and risk—far more than those who stay in the womb until full term. The landscape is littered with ministries and ministers that are on the scene before their time. They did not stay in the womb of the local church—the womb of discipline, the womb of correction, and the womb of encouragement for the set time.

Zion, which is the church above us, is the "mother of us all," according to Paul. (See Galatians 4:26; Hebrews 12:22–23.) But not everyone has waited in the invisible womb of obscurity until the time for temporal manifestation. The Bible says that we should humble ourselves under the mighty hand of God and that He will exalt us in due time. The five-fold ministry has been likened to the hand ministry of God. As a man or woman humbles himself under the leadership of God's appointed equippers, God will exalt that man or woman to the fulfillment of destiny.

Abortion Attempts

Abortion is legal in our day, in the natural realm. But that doesn't make it right. Even so, in the Spirit, taking the child out of the womb before it is time because of the inconvenience of spiritual parenting may be popular, but is isn't proper. This is another cause of premature birth. Somebody tried to kill a spiritual baby, tried to cancel God's assignment on a man or woman's ministry, but the baby survived. He or she may have the cut marks and the bruises that accompany the surgery of death, but he or she survived.

Miscarriage

Miscarriages are also common in our day. May God help us to have strong prenatal, intrauterine ministries in our local churches to which the babies may be engrafted to Christ and His cause. The lining of sound doctrine, prayer, worship, love, and holiness will be suitable to hold and feed the little ones. May the mothers (the local church ministries) understand that what they ingest, they are feeding to the babies! May we remember that if we have been divisive in order to begin ministries, that the spirit of division can infect our offspring as well. How many babies are born already addicted to chemicals, such as with fetal alcohol syndrome or crack babies, not because of what they have done, but because of what their parents had in their system when the babies were conceived? May we be quick to repent for rebellion, before we have to reap what we have sown.

Hope for the Premature

However, thank God, premature babies—those ministers, ministries, and leaders that came forth before the right time—don't have to die. The ministry of the spiritual father includes supporting the preemies. The incubator is the next best thing to the womb. It is the special grace for nurturing and mentoring with which God anoints true spiritual fathers to minister.

Isaiah refers to "nursing fathers" (Isa. 49:23) and God, our Father, calls Himself El-Shaddai, which means "the many-breasted One." Fathers can be nurturers in the Spirit—and must be for the premature minister or ministry to have a valid opportunity to succeed. It is incumbent upon the one who realizes that he or she is a preemie in some regard, whether by rebellion, by rejection (addressed later), or by any other circumstance, to acknowledge this plight, repent, and make restitution for any part that his or her actions caused and to seek God's guidance as to whether a spiritual father may not be a need in his or her life for wholeness. (Note: "Father" is not a physical gender term here; it is an "in-Christ" concept.) In the meanwhile, the spiritual parent types must be sensitive to look beyond behaviors to the heart and destiny of the premature minister. If the leader has a nurturing, rescuing heart, God will even cause those in need to gravitate toward him or her.

What Is a Spiritual Father?

When the Bible refers to God as our Father, it means He is infinitely more than a male parent. It means he is our origin, source, generator, and pattern. He is our Father, but He is not a human. Whoever God uses as His primary resource, His means of encoding and revealing Himself to us and in us—that individual is a spiritual father. Not only may a father lead us to the initial knowledge of Christ in the born-again experience, but a father will lead us to deeper levels of the knowledge of God. A father will help us to come to greater awareness of the body of Christ and the kingdom of God in general, while also bringing us to an increasing realization of our own distinctive callings and gifts, which otherwise may lie dormant.

Affirmation and Confirmation

A father affirms and confirms his children. A father articulates to his child a sense of identity. He tells his children who God says they are, and he confirms the voice of the Lord when He begins to speak to them. He is aware of his child's purpose. And as Eli did to Samuel, he perceives that the Lord is calling the child and teaches the child how to respond to the call. Every leader must be grateful to God for someone who taught him or her how to respond to the voice of God.

Groomed for the Throne

A father is provided to discipline and groom his son or daughter for "the throne," that person's place of divine destiny. He is to spare no expense to train him or her to reign:

1) He accepts the expense of risking the child's displeasure for rebuking and reproving the child when he or she goes astray.

2) He accepts the expense of acknowledging it when the girl becomes a woman or when the boy becomes a man. It is costly to some fathers' egos when those who were once totally dependent on him in some regard no longer need him in that area. Everyone needs to be needed, and fathers can be stuck at the point of being needed. A wise parent understands that he never ceases to be needed—it is just that the nature of the need changes.

3) He accepts the expense of being identified with the children, even when they mess up.If there is truly a father/child relationship, that tie is not severed when the child takes a fall. Anyone who only identifies with his covenant child when he

or she has done all things perfectly does not have the true
spirit of fatherhood, and he may be an opportunist, hoping
to somehow benefit from the child's accomplishments.

A child should "requite" parents when he or she is able. (See 1 Timothy 5:4.)
However, the true father does not demand anything from the child except
his or her love and respect.

> Behold, the third time I am ready to come to you; and I will not be
> burdensome to you: for I seek not your's , but you: for the children
> ought not to lay up for the parents, but the parents for the children.
> —2 Corinthians 12:14

The role of the parent evolves, as does the role of the child. In order to
avoid the possibility of estrangement and strain on the relationship, the
parents and the children have to understand that the relationship will
change. It will grow. One with the true spirit of fatherhood understands
that as he gives his life for his children, God uses him to transmit His life
to His children.

Transgenerational Increase

> A good man leaveth an inheritance to his children's children.
> —Proverbs 13:22

A father wants more for the child than he has accomplished himself.
Abraham died leaving Isaac rich. Isaac imparted blessing to Jacob who
became Israel, the prince. Joseph was richer than all of the above, becoming
prime minister of Egypt. Moses left Joshua with a nation organized for
conquest, though he had found them a cantankerous collection of clans.
Saul, though not a particularly good father, organized the monarchy in
Israel, which was ultimately passed on to David; God obviously had used
David's tenure in Saul's house for him to learn kingly protocol. And finally,
Jesus leaves His children with more.

> Verily, verily, I say unto you, He that believeth on me, the works that I
> do shall he do also: and greater works than these shall he do; because
> I go to the Father.
> —John 14:12

The father/child relationship is one that is anything but casual. For a true father, everything that he has ultimately belongs to the child. The father provides for his offspring a sense of belonging—a security that having possessions or accolades cannot provide.

Abandonment and Rejection

Another scenario of fatherlessness is abandonment and rejection by fathers. It is the Saul/David syndrome. David is the biological son of Jesse, a father who evidently either (1) underestimates his son, or (2) recognizes his son's worth but wants to exploit it for his own purposes. Neither case is wholesome.

David's brother Eliab attempts to belittle him. Later, David becomes an adopted "spiritual son" (and son-in-law) of King Saul and accomplishes great things in God for Saul and his kingdom's benefit. Apparently, God ordains the association between David and Saul as a means of equipping David with kingly protocol for his destiny as king. (Note: God rejected Saul as king, not as a person. If Saul had repented, God still could have used him. There is nothing to suggest he could not have been a vital advisor for David.)

As soon as David gets a little more press than Saul, however, Saul becomes his nemesis for life. It is a sad but true commentary that there are fathers who are able to discern greatness in their children—often the greatness that God has imparted through those very fathers—but they see that greatness as a threat to themselves!

Why a Threat?

What should those fathers expect? After the sons or daughters have assimilated what their senior leaders have taught and exemplified, internalizing their very principles, why is it amazing when the same grace of God that worked in the leaders now works in the followers? Why is it amazing when "the works that I do shall he do also" principle begins to manifest? Why would any spiritual father or mother want to kill the sons or daughters who have become what the father or mother prophesied?

> When my father and my mother forsake me, then the Lord will take me up.
>
> —Psalm 27:10

The Flip Side

> A son honoureth his father, and a servant his master: if then I be a father, where is mine honour? and if I be a master, where is my fear? saith the Lord of hosts unto you, O priests, that despise my name.
>
> —Malachi 1:6

Some children are ungrateful; in fact, ingratitude is at an all-time high. The quoted Scripture directly refers to God being dishonored, but the principle includes natural parents, mentors, and parents-in-Christ. Paul predicted thanklessness as a sign of the End Times and listed it as precipitating a reprobate mind.

> This know also, that in the last days perilous times shall come. For men shall be lovers of their own selves, covetous, boasters, proud, blasphemers, disobedient to parents, unthankful.
>
> —2 Timothy 3:1–2

> For the invisible things of him from the creation of the world are clearly seen, being understood by the things that are made, even his eternal power and Godhead; so that they are without excuse: Because that, when they knew God, they glorified him not as God, neither were thankful; but became vain in their imaginations, and their foolish heart was darkened.... Wherefore God also gave them up to uncleanness.
>
> —Romans 1:20–21, 24

This is true of spiritual children as well as of natural children. There are those spiritual children who will hang around leadership just long enough to assimilate the giftings, skills, or talents of the spiritual father or mother with no intention of "requiting" them, as Paul instructed Timothy.

Absalom

There are those who have actually committed the sin of Absalom, turning the hearts of the people against the father or mother and dividing the congregation, leading their contingent in open rebellion. They have even gone so far as to commit a spiritual form of the "rooftop orgy" that Absalom committed, becoming intimately involved with the sheep when another man or woman is the actual under-shepherd of the flock, and using that intimacy to embarrass the David figure.

May all Absalom spirits beware. Absalom was known for his beauty, and the crowning aspect of his beauty was his hair. In other words, he was known for his obvious traits, those that had appeal in the carnal realm. His masculine beauty was his area of giftedness. However, he did not regularly cut his hair. He did not consistently harness the gift of hair with the shears of discipline and character. And finally, while fleeing for his life, his hair became entangled in the trees, and it cost him his life.

Let the rebellious sons and daughters beware. The gift that you will not temper with character and discipline may become the snare that costs you your life, your ministry, your marriage, your health, your walk with God, your credibility—*everything*.

Weep With David

> And the king was much moved, and went up to the chamber over the gate, and wept: and as he went, thus he said, O my son Absalom, my son, my son Absalom! would God I had died for thee, O Absalom, my son, my son!
>
> —2 SAMUEL 18:33

Let us weep with the David figure, for Absalom. We weep for what should have been and what could have been. What should have been is a much closer relationship between father and son, closeness made difficult by the responsibilities of an emerging kingship that included wars, stabilizing the fledgling kingdom, and leading the people into true worship of Jehovah. These external difficulties were complicated by the internal discomfort of David's multiple wives and their offspring, a complexity forever exemplified in Amnon's rape of Tamar and David's tragic affair with Bathsheba. Was there a rage in Absalom that manifested in his killing of Amnon but was not resolved because it flowed much deeper, including frustration with his overall family's plight?

Notice that after David exiled Absalom and then rescinded the exile, David refused to see Absalom. Absalom took it upon himself to get his father's attention one way or the other, resorting to arson, at Joab's expense. Finally, he was willing to subvert his father's entire kingdom and make him a fugitive again in his latter years.

There was no excuse for Absalom's behavior—no justification. But we know, from God's own mouth, that Absalom's rebellion was the fruit of David's sin: "The sword was not to depart from his house." Was it not only David's sins of commission with Bathsheba (adultery, conspiracy, and murder), but also the grave sin of omission—parental negligence? David wept. He wept because he loved his son. He may also have wept because "the sword" that God had spoken of had become guilt's arrow, pointing as directly at him as Nathan had, saying, "Thou art the man."

As God turns the hearts of the children to the fathers, He also has declared that He will turn the hearts of the fathers to the children. Let fathers beware, lest they provoke their children to wrath and they become discouraged, never fulfilling their destiny, and causing pain to the ones they love and are beloved of the most, their own parents.

For that man or woman of God who is without a spiritual parent, or who has come through parental dysfunction: remember these things.

Honor your spiritual parents. "Honour thy father and mother; which is the first commandment with promise" (Eph. 6:2). This has natural and spiritual significance. We do not choose our parents, in the natural or in the spiritual. If we could, many of us would have chosen the wealthiest, most famous, most powerful people to be our mother and father. Instead, that choice was made for us by God, even if the context of our conception, birth, or upbringing was contrary to His will. God chose who would bring us into the earth, and He chose who would bring us into the kingdom. There was something in them that was an essential ingredient in the composition that became you. Even if, like David, the Saul who adopted you has made you a fugitive, you must still honor him for what God has used him to accomplish in you. Though God anointed David, it was in the house of Saul that David was first exposed to the protocols of royalty. God made David a king, but Saul apparently taught him the order of kingdom.

We must honor our fathers, even those who may disown us, because willingly or not, they have been used by God to make an indispensable, undeniable deposit in us. Ideologically, you may not agree, but the example of David is that you should not speak disparagingly of them, you should not seek to retaliate against them for wrongs, and you should honor your parents for who they are to you and to God, even if you cannot respect them for what they do. If you have risen against your spiritual parents in the spirit of dishonor, if you have attempted to subvert them, if you have attacked their character because they attacked yours, you are going to miss out on your true place in the kingdom—your promise. Repent to God and to them. They can't stop your blessing, but you can—by dishonor.

Do not deny your spiritual heritage. As stated earlier, we do not choose our parents, natural or spiritual. There were times when a country boy who made it big in life would be asked where he was from. Well, knowing he was from "the backside of the woods," he was afraid that if he admitted being from Mayberry, someone might look down on him. So, he would think of the nearest metropolis and name that as his home.

The same kind of thing happens in the spiritual. Some leaders, as God shows them favor, are ashamed to admit their spiritual background. If they are not from a major religious organization or well-known ministry, they will tend to whisper about where they originated. Or they will claim someone more prestigious as their father in the Lord. Well, God knew where the back of the woods was, and if He had been ashamed of your originating there, he would have planted you elsewhere. It is not your problem if someone has a problem with where you come from.

I have not made it big at all, but my heritage is enough of a patchwork quilt that I will use it as an example. I was baptized in the apostolic church, reared for part of my pre-teen years in the African Methodist Episcopal (A.M.E.) Church, fellowshipped with the Missionary Baptist church, ended up back in the apostolic church, and now pastor a nondenominational church. And, by the way, I have a deep Church of God In Christ (COGIC) background on my maternal family's side. What does that make me? It gives me a respect for the oneness of God, His saving Name, and the Pentecostal experience; an appreciation for Wesleyan-style hymns, the Apostles' Creed, liturgy, and the Triune nature of God; a knowledge of the black gospel preaching and singing tradition; and a knowledge of the gifts of the Spirit, the power of praise, and a consecrated life. It gives me a connection with the greater body of Christ. It renders me better, richer, and fuller than I could ever be with even one of these elements missing. Don't be ashamed of who or what God used to make you who you are.

Do not claim to be a self-made wonder. All of us had somebody who helped us to become what God called us to be. Many of us had to learn some things without the luxury of a systematic, classroom-style instruction.

Many of us have felt so lonely at various points in ministry (and leadership is, by definition, a lonely place). Yet God didn't speak directly to us from heaven every time, though He did so at times.

Instead, there were occasions when He used our own spiritual parents, even when we thought they were missing it, to sow into our lives things that proved invaluable later. Even if they taught us by their example what not to do, if we learned it they were still effectively teaching. He also used someone's book, someone's radio or television broadcast, someone's reel-to-reel tape, LP, "45," eight-track, audiocassette, video cassette, CD, DVD, or MP3 (any of these you don't recognize tells your age!).

God used someone to impact us and impart to us. It may not have been as we would have had it, but even if God chose to send ravens, you still ate, Brother or Sister "Elijah." Let us not act as if we got there by ourselves. To do so is to manifest the spirit of ingratitude. Let us be willing to tell someone thank-you besides Jesus. We ourselves desire to be appreciated. Let us appreciate our forefathers and matriarchs in Christ.

All My Heroes Are Dead? Really?

And they're not all dead, either. Often, when a leader wants to avert being seen honoring another human being, because of his or her own insecurities, he or she will claim that all the people who inspired him or her are dead. This is sometimes a shabby excuse for not showing high regard to one's contemporaries. It may be a fear of being associated with the living person's failures, as heroes in one aspect of life can blow it in other areas. No, many of the greats are indeed gone on, but more often than not there is still somebody "on this side" to whom we owe a debt of tribute and honor. Let us be real, honest, and thankful.

God Compensates for Lack: He Will Make It Up To You

> When my father and my mother forsake me, then the Lord will take me up.
>
> —Psalm 27:10

> Then Peter began to say unto him, Lo, we have left all, and have followed thee. And Jesus answered and said, Verily I say unto you, There is no man that hath left house, or brethren, or sisters, or father, or mother, or wife, or children, or lands, for my sake, and the gospel's, But he shall

receive an hundredfold now in this time, houses, and brethren, and sisters, and mothers, and children, and lands, with persecutions; and in the world to come eternal life. But many that are first shall be last; and the last first.

—MARK 10:28-31

All along, God put father figures in David's life: Samuel, whom God sent to anoint David and who had to be instructed not to miss David by looking at "looks"; Nathan, who so admired David's great heart toward God that he affirmed his heart before God corrected his actions, and yet was bold to call David to account for his sins; and Gad, who is called the king's seer and watched David's back although David was a prophet himself, yet proclaimed the judgment of God to David when he had numbered Israel. These men were there for David when others should have been. They were also there to correct him when he sinned against God.

God will make it up to you. Just know that God will compensate for every pain and every loss. He will place people in your life, in His time, who will fill those void places in your life.

And until such time, rather than mourning over what you do not have, purpose to obey God's will for yourself and accept the challenge to be to someone else what no one else would be, or could be, to you.

Real-ationship #2: Fraternal Friends

Leadership: A Lonely Place

Leadership is a lonely place. By definition, being a leader means seeing further than others see, going further than others go, and getting there, at least in spirit, before others do. By definition, being a visionary means to be able to see what most others do not see. It is a lonely place. The loneliness is intensified by the fact that the leader will often be surrounded by people and yet find no one who relates to where he or she is within.

In the natural, a shepherd may be surrounded by a multitude of sheep, yet at best the sheep can only communicate to the shepherd their basic needy situations: hunger, fear, fatigue, or maybe contentment. The shepherd and the sheep may enjoy one another's company. They may play together and have positive emotional bonds. However, their relationship is limited to these rudimentary levels. There is no communion possible at all because communion only exists where communication can occur.

This is also true in ministry.

The Shepherd's Communication

To whom does the shepherd communicate his hunger, fear, fatigue, or contentment? Only to a peer—and most poignantly, to another shepherd— is this possible. Likewise, often a senior leader only receives gripes or grins from those who follow him or her. Beyond this, there tends to be very little opportunity for true unburdening of the heart of the leader with others. Too often, all the parishioner seems to care about is, "How will my needs be met? Who is going to console me, feed me, and give me rest?" The pastor has to keep all his "deep stuff" to himself.

A Friend: Everybody Needs One

Enter—a friend. The senior leader needs someone who sees eye to eye with him or her and can relate to him or her in the highs and the lows. The senior leader needs someone who does not primarily need him or her as feeder, protector, and cuddler. A friend can celebrate and appreciate the leader's victories without envy. The friend can support the leader when he or she weeps privately while ministering powerfully to the multitudes. A friend can reprimand the leader privately for human weakness while respecting his or her divine anointing. A friend has more confidence in the leader than the leader has in himself or herself.

A friend—everybody needs one, and everybody should be one.

Real-ationship #3: Followers

Believe it or not, it is God-ordained that each of us would have followers. Granted, all of us may not be pastors of churches or heads of ministries. And this is definitely not an encouragement toward personality cults, celebrity fan clubs, and such. Rather, as God blesses an individual, He holds him or her responsible to give to a succeeding generation. God desires to take the life of one who knows Him and make him a seed to be planted in others, invested in their becoming what God has planned for their lives.

No gift, no talent, and no aptitude that God has given an individual is primarily for that person alone. Even in the parables of the monetary talents and pounds, Jesus commends the servants who invest what they have been given to gain more for the master. Spiritual leaders must understand that "burying their talent in the earth"—keeping the principles, wisdom, and resources God has entrusted them to themselves—will cause God to frown upon them. He wants His treasure invested—not hoarded, and not wasted. And the greatest investment is the next generation.

Better Than I

> Whatever God has given me is for someone else. I must pour out the sum total of my experiences, my knowledge, my strengths, such as they are, to benefit someone else. And as a spiritual father or mother, this is the most essential reason why parents exist anyway: to make others better—better than themselves.

> My responsibility is not only to enhance others generally. It is specifically to make them better than I am. If I do not exert every effort to allow those who "follow me as I follow Christ" to so profit from my life that they exceed me, then, as a spiritual (or even a natural) father, I have failed. Making them better, and making things better for them, does not preclude their learning discipline, sacrifice, and structure. Indeed, the discipline and sacrifice are vital components of their becoming better and not merely "fatter." We want them to live better, have more, minister under greater circumstances, and achieve more that we ever did, for in their accomplishments we accomplish. In their success, we succeed. This is an element of a true father or mother's spirit: I want my child to go further than I have ever gone.

Picking Cotton and Cropping Tobacco

We want our children to have "the better," but we also must be careful to help them to become "the better" through character building. Sometimes in our efforts to protect our children from hardships we went through, we deprive them of the character-building that some of us gained through those hardships.

For example, some of my generation and I had the experience of wood stoves, outhouses, cropping tobacco, picking cotton, and digging potatoes. These were austere circumstances compared to the typical lifestyles of today. However, coming through that era helped us develop stamina and an appreciation for life that those who have not experienced them may lack.

Even so, in the spiritual, some of us came through pioneering situations, difficult parental situations, and extreme demands with little if any notice or recognition. Compensation—what was that?

We will be kinder to our children than some of our spiritual parents were to us. However, we must not be "sugar daddies" to those whom God places in our charge. We must hold them accountable, and God holds us accountable, to provide for the development of their character and their behavior.

Dogs and Hogs in the House

It was stated earlier that it is God's intent that the treasure He puts in a leader be invested, not squandered or wasted. Jesus said:

> Give not that which is holy unto the dogs, neither cast ye your pearls before swine, lest they trample them under their feet, and turn again and rend you.
>
> —MATTHEW 7:6

Jesus was not referring to literal hogs and dogs in this text. Rather, He is referring to the attitudes of people who receive ministry or who do not receive ministry. There are dog and swine spirits in the house of God. Few things can be more grievous to the servant of a local church than to perceive that his or her efforts to bring people to a greater knowledge and demonstration of God are unappreciated. More specifically, it is a burden on the heart of a spiritual parent when spiritual children will not allow themselves to be parented.

Mother Ministry, Father Ministry

Perhaps it has always been so, but definitely in this generation, people are selective about what they receive and what they refuse to receive from the servant of the Lord. As long as what is being said is what they define as "encouraging" (i.e., something that has a syrupy-sweet connotation), they will shout and celebrate—and contribute financially—to no end.

Those who receive personal prophecy anticipate those prophecies that state, "I see you having a worldwide ministry," "I see God causing everyone who did you wrong to have to apologize," "I see you being the next so-and-so or having the spirit of fill-in-the-blank leader." Granted, there are some blatantly false prophecies along these lines to be categorically dismissed.

But some such prophecies may be essentially accurate. God does take the anointing upon one life and seed it into another, because in every generation there must be witnesses unto Jesus' power. God will give us a sense of our destiny, though He does not intend for prophetic insight to puff us up.

These kinds of experiences are what we will call "mother ministry." That is, it is a nurturing, cuddling, "you're so special" kind of ministry, which is vital to the well-being of the spiritual child. This may be done by a male or female spiritual parent; physical gender is not an issue here. The illustration is that even in the natural, in a two-parent situation, often the mother is the softer touch, and children generally like that.

Spiritual parenting may not involve two parents, but it is two-sided. Enter now: "father ministry."

Father Me?

Many secondary leaders find aspects of "father ministry" revolting, so ultimately they revolt. Why is it that in virtually every prophesying service, all the prophecies are good? Why do they promise everyone involved the same kinds of things, whether they are faithful or not, whether they are committed or not, whether they are humble or not? Someone would say, "It is because of the goodness of God." But what we must remember is that "the goodness of God leadeth thee to repentance" (Rom. 2:4).

These people are forever reveling in the goodness of God, but often they are not repenting for their immaturity, lack of commitment, and divisiveness in the body of Christ. If someone is a spiritual parent, why does he or she never give a prophecy such as, "Brother _____, the Lord said that you can be more disciplined in your lifestyle, but you refuse. If you don't change, it will hinder you from the greater blessings"? Why are there no prophecies such as, "I see you on the telephone spreading gossip about your brethren. Repent or God will judge you." Or what about, "You are hateful to your spouse and children. God says, 'Don't preach again until you go home and get it right!'"

I believe that the potential for that kind of prophetic ministry exists as well. I believe that God does talk to people about more than the size of their new house, car, or new church building. What happens is that the spiritual parents know that if they were to come down on some of these present secondary leaders with such a word, those secondary leaders might leave the church, or worse: they might attack the church or its leadership. Spiritual parents may be intimidated, but scripturally, anyone who will not receive "father ministry" is not a son.

Truly Illegitimate Children

Everybody in the midst is not necessarily in the mix: "They went out from us, but they were not of us; for if they had been of us, they would no doubt have continued with us: but they went out, that they might be made manifest that they were not all of us" (1 John 2:19).

God says in Proverbs and later in Hebrews that one true mark of sonship is the ability to accept discipline:

> And ye have forgotten the exhortation which speaketh unto you as unto children, My son, despise not thou the chastening of the Lord, nor faint when thou art rebuked of him: For whom the Lord loveth he chasteneth, and scourgeth every son whom he receiveth. If ye endure chastening, God dealeth with you as with sons; for what son is he whom the father chasteneth not? But if ye be without chastisement, whereof all are partakers, then are ye bastards, and not sons. Furthermore we have had fathers of our flesh which corrected us, and we gave them reverence: shall we not much rather be in subjection unto the Father of spirits, and live? For they verily for a few days chastened us after their own pleasure; but he for our profit, that we might be partakers of his holiness. Now no chastening for the present seemeth to be joyous, but grievous: nevertheless afterward it yieldeth the peaceable fruit of righteousness unto them which are exercised thereby.
>
> —HEBREWS 12:5–11

Any secondary leader or so-called spiritual offspring who is not willing to take rebuke and correction in the right spirit, knowing that it doesn't feel good but that it will do him or her good is, according to the Scriptures, illegitimate. The King James Version calls that person a "bastard." (See Hebrews 12:6–8.) There are, unfortunately, many bastardized leaders and ministries the sole reason for whose existence and function is that they could not, or would not, receive instruction. So they left the church or other ministry—or in some cases attempted a *coup d'etat*. Like Lucifer, these orchestrated the split of a ministry, appealing to other disgruntled pseudo-sons and -daughters.

If one is in a ministry where the senior leader is a man or woman of God who strives to please the Lord with life and doctrine, even though that senior leader is not perfect, God demands submission. And should circumstances ultimately make it necessary for the dissolution of a ministerial relationship, it should be done with much grace and care not to cause casualties in the kingdom and in the world, where people cannot understand why those who claim to love God cannot get along. The proof of sonship is that one can flow with his or her leader even when their opinions are contradictory and the secondary leader does not see why it is necessary to do what the senior leader asks. Anybody can claim to be obedient when nothing is being asked of him or her. There are those members who pledge with tears to do all they can to support ministry, but the moment their comfort level is challenged, they draw back.

If parents truly love a child, they will discipline that child. And if your pastor or other senior leader loves you, secondary leader, it will be necessary for him or her to correct you, speaking the truth in love, but speaking the truth.

> As an earring of gold, and an ornament of fine gold, so is a wise reprover upon an obedient ear.
> —PROVERBS 25:12

> Against an elder receive not an accusation, but before two or three witnesses. Them that sin rebuke before all, that others also may fear.
> —1 TIMOTHY 5:19–20

> All scripture is given by inspiration of God, and is profitable for doctrine, for reproof, for correction, for instruction in righteousness: That the man of God may be perfect, thoroughly furnished unto all good works.
> —2 TIMOTHY 3:16–17

> Preach the word; be instant in season, out of season; reprove, rebuke, exhort with all longsuffering and doctrine. For the time will come when they will not endure sound doctrine; but after their own lusts shall they heap to themselves teachers, having itching ears.
> —2 TIMOTHY 4:2–3

If a person cuts the ties with his spiritual parents, not because they are living unholy lives or teaching or practicing false doctrine, but just because he or she refuses to obey or submit to their godly principles, God said that he or she is a bastard. This is sad, but true.

Yes, the senior leader, along with all leaders, needs these three tiers of relationship to hold him both secure and accountable because he is responsible. Just as God upholds righteous leadership, He deals very strictly with a leader who mishandles His charge. One needs only to look at the Old Testament leaders (who were pastors, in a sense) who were greatly blessed as they conducted themselves with honor and humility fulfilling their call. However, one cannot help but note those who came under the severe judgment of God for the misappropriation of divinely granted privilege.

Examples of the Judgment of Leaders

Lucifer and the fallen angels
Because of their rebellion in heaven, Lucifer and the fallen angels were cast out of their glorious estate. Lucifer lost his anointing, and they were all sentenced to burn forever in the lake of fire with no hope of reprieve.

Adam
Because of his disobedience to God's mandate concerning the tree of the knowledge of good and evil, Adam was put out of the garden and subjected (he and his billions of descendants) to misery, sickness, poverty, war, and death.

Abraham
Because of his taking Hagar in order to generate seed by his own means, Abraham precipitated the strife between his descendants that has the world in turmoil until this day.

Moses
Because he did not honor God at the waters of Meribah, striking the rock instead of speaking to it, Moses was not permitted to see the Promised Land.

Saul
Because of two incidents illustrative of his rebellion toward God, Saul forfeited the throne, and ultimately his life.

David

Because of his sin with Bathsheba, David saw his family and his kingdom plunged into civil war, and he saw some of his children die. Because of his numbering Israel, seventy thousand of his citizens were killed in a plague.

Ahab

Because of his idolatry, Ahab was fatally wounded in battle, though in disguise, died in disgrace, yet lives in infamy as the embodiment of weak manhood.

Manasseh

His idolatry led to his being taken to Babylon in chains.

Nebuchadnezzar

His pride caused him to be bereft of his senses for seven years, living like an animal.

Herod Agrippa I

He died while giving an oration during which he was proclaimed to be a god. An angel smote him, and worms ate him.

In our day also, we have seen those who were appointed to leadership judged because they refused to judge themselves. God is merciful, and His mercy endureth forever. But sometimes the most merciful thing He can do is to allow the consequences of the believer's actions to befall him or her.

> It is reported commonly that there is fornication among you, and such fornication as is not so much as named among the Gentiles, that one should have his father's wife....In the name of our Lord Jesus Christ, when ye are gathered together, and my spirit, with the power of our Lord Jesus Christ, to deliver such an one unto Satan for the destruction of the flesh, that the spirit may be saved in the day of the Lord Jesus.
>
> —1 CORINTHIANS 5:1, 4–5

> Of whom is Hymenaeus and Alexander; whom I have delivered unto Satan, that they may learn not to blaspheme.
>
> —1 TIMOTHY 1:20

My brethren, be not many masters, knowing that we shall receive the
greater condemnation.

—JAMES 3:1

Like People, Like Priest

There is a phrase in Hosea: "like people, like priest" (Hos. 4:9). Zechariah
also says, "smite the shepherd, and the sheep shall be scattered" (Zech. 13:7).
The writer of Proverbs says, "When the righteous are in authority, the people
rejoice: but when the wicked beareth rule, the people mourn" (Prov. 29:2).

God demands that His leaders be credible, that they be those who can say
with the apostle Paul, "Be ye therefore followers of me as I am also of Christ"
(1 Cor. 11:1). Peter says that senior leaders should serve as "ensamples" to
the flock. The Pastor's character, behavior, and reputation are the first and
bottom line of credibility in the leadership of the local church, and they set
the stage and the standard for all other leaders.

A Foregone Conclusion

That the high character of leadership is to reside in the senior leader first,
that he or she is to exemplify what is expected of a subordinate leader is a
foregone conclusion. No senior leader has the right to expect a follower to
exhibit qualities that he himself has not integrated into his own life—how
else may the secondary leader be assured that the principles he or she is
taught are legitimate, holding the promise of God's pleasure and success in
his or her calling? All of the traits we urge upon the secondary leader should
already be highly obvious in the life of the primary leader. Remember,
one of the most important facets of the senior leader's calling is to "be
secondary to his or her secondaries," placing to place their development and
achievement first. And the most effective teacher or leader is an example of
what is taught.

If the biblical principles contained in this study are not present in one's
senior leadership, the validity of such leadership is questionable.

The Stabilizing Effect of the Senior Leader's Credibility

This cannot be overstated: if the senior leader has credibility, it serves as a stabilizing force within his ministry and actually is projected onto the church and ministry overall, in the eyes of the world. It is a launching pad for ministerial effectiveness and impact in the community. However, if the senior leader has no credibility or has damaged credibility, the ministry is in the most critical trouble; the sharp blade of the gospel sword is blunted, the effectiveness of ministry is stunted, and most importantly of all, God is displeased, for the name of Jesus is reproached.

Chapter 3

THE CRITICAL ROLE OF THE SECONDARY LEADER

Section I – Critical to the Success of the Vision

To a large degree, the success of an organization will depend upon secondary leadership. It is a mistake to assume that a senior leader, regardless of how charismatic, how gifted, or how administratively sound, can singlehandedly bring a ministry to its full fruition. God's purposes are fulfilled in pluralistic oneness—unity is the first principle, but diversity empowers and enhances unity. God is One; yet He has diversity within His unity. And in all of God's great enterprises, we are shown the facets of His diversity working in harmony to bring glory to His unity. An example of this is the creation of man. God says, "Let us make man" (Gen. 1:26).

A Diversified Unity

Granted, we are not God. Yet the principle of a diversified unity, as opposed to unilateralism, is proven to be most effective for success. God's imprint is on mankind, and man is at his best when he acts like God.

Human beings were designed to accomplish the great causes by means of diversified unity. When God created man, He created one man, yet within that one man was all mankind. More specifically, when God formed Adam, Eve was already there, potentially, within the form of the male man.

This may sound a little controversial, but let us look at the text. The Scripture says that when God formed the male man, He derived his form, his body, from the dust. However, when He formed the female man (the womb-man), He did not return to the dust for her form. He went to the body of the man and took out a rib (in the Hebrew, a side or chamber).

This underscored two facts: first, that the male man, the female man, and mankind, were one in origin: God made them, and God made them one.

To remain in God's will, they would have to remain one. Second, they were given distinctives: different traits, different anatomies, different functions, and different perspectives—and these differences were God-ordained for the enhancement of their oneness. The contrasts were not designed to be contradictory, but complementary.

Man's Purpose Was to Glorify God

Having used Adam and his creation as an illustration, one more point is necessary. When God created Adam, He created him the same way that He created anything then or creates anything now: He spoke. The creation of Adam is recorded in Genesis 1, whereas the formation of Adam is chronicled in Genesis 2. And the Scripture states that God not only spoke of man, He spoke of man's purpose, his calling. The Lord stated that man would have dominion over the various aspects of creation. This dominion would be a co-regency under God, on the earth. And since man would bear God's image and likeness, God would be glorified.

The Creation of Man

When God created, He did not see it is as the finite creation of one human person. He literally created at least two, a male and a female. Yet, in the truest sense, He acknowledged the entire human race in that creative act, with the first individual as the "federal head" of the race. And the "great commission" that he gave to Adam was not for Adam only: it was for the entire race of mankind. The command to be fruitful and multiply, to replenish the earth, to subdue, and to have dominion was give to all men, to all women, when God spoke to the original man. When God called Adam, he called those who would walk and work with him to fulfill his "great commission." When God called him, He called them, the billions of Adamite descendants yet unborn.

As in Adam, So in Christ

When God called Christ, the Last Adam, He chose "them" (the church) who would be with Him. They were "chosen...in Him before the foundation of the world" (Eph. 1:4).

And So in Christ's Leaders

Even so, when God calls an earthly leader to fulfill the Last Man, Adam's, great commission, He calls the people who will walk and serve with him or her. They may reside in different cities, states, or nations, but the sovereign God can and will bring them together. From the ends of the earth, He will gather those who are needed to fulfill His will.

An Individual Can't Do It Alone

This discussion is intended to point out that no individual has ever been intended to accomplish the calling of God alone. There is protocol; there can be sequence and priority in roles, but having one who does all of them—long term—is not God's will. Leadership is a vital key to successful accomplishment of goals. What is not as commonly understood is that the first leader—the senior leader—is not the only leader requisite to their achievement. The breadth of success in any undertaking is measured by a flow of influential impact.

A Flow of Influential Impact

That is, there is first a vision that is established in the heart of the senior leader. The fulfillment of that vision becomes the central principle governing the senior leader and the philosophy of the organization. That central principle captivates and drives the senior leader. In turn, the senior leader articulates the central principle to those around him or her, training and empowering them to believe in the vision and implement it. Ultimately, they are to become leaders as he or she is: passionate, disciplined, and progressively effective. These secondary leaders reciprocally touch the masses, who are their target audience, replicating their own development's process in many others, and thereby taking their message, methods, and means to the endless reaches of the world. Let us illustrate the flow of influential impact.

**From Central Principle
To Senior Leader
To Secondary Leader
To Target Audience**

Central Principle: Christ and His Great Commission

Senior Leader:
The Pastor With a God-Given Vision
for Fulfillment of the Great Commission

Secondary Leader:
Officers and Members With a God-Inspired Commitment
to the Protection and Realization of the Vision
for the Fulfillment of the Great Commission

Target Audience:
The Congregation, the Community, and the World
Becoming Believers, Then Disciples, Then Leaders
Who Bring the Vision to Realization and Perpetuate
the Fulfillment of the Great Commission

The Parable of Wal-Mart

Consider Wal-Mart. Whether one is a fan or a foe of Wal-Mart, the illustration is valid.

Central principle

The central principle is the vision and legacy of Sam Walton. Apparently his great commission was to provide goods/services to neighborhoods, establishing and expanding stores and other venues throughout the US and beyond.

Senior leader

The senior leader is the CEO, and his vision is the plan for fulfilling the Walton mandate.

Secondary leaders

The secondary leaders are the district managers, the distribution centers, the truckers, the store managers, and their staff persons. They are the ones who actually touch the public.

Target audience

That's easy. The target audience is the public: in Benton, in Arkansas, in America, and the entire world.

Central Principle: Sam Walton and His Vision and Legacy

Primary Leader: Chairman of the Board/CEO of Wal-Mart

Secondary Leaders: District Managers, Distribution Centers, Truckers, Store Managers, Staff

Target Audience: The Public, Which Is Bentonville, all of Arkansas, America, and the World

When the world is impacted by Wal-Mart, when Wal-Mart finally becomes the World's Mart, Sam's dream will be realized. Yet, the Wal-Mart that the average citizen thinks of most is not the huge corporate conglomerate; it is the local Wal-Mart with local workers and neighbors who smile, frown, help, or ignore customers. It is the local level upon which the success of the rest of this commercial gargantuan depends.

So Also Is the Kingdom of God

The kingdom of God is not like Wal-Mart, but Wal-Mart (and every other truly successful corporation) is successful because it utilizes kingdom principles, whether consciously or not. Furthermore, it is sad that sometimes the secular world uses God's precepts much more effectively than believers. Just as the average consumer judges the Wal-Mart conglomerate by the Supercenter in his own town, so the average unbeliever judges the whole body of Christ (and often Jesus Himself) by the church in his or her neighborhood. We should wonder what the unbelievers on our block think about Jesus and His church, after having been exposed to us.

Secondary Leadership: Makes It or Breaks It

Indeed, the secondary leadership of an organization will propel it to great heights or plummet it to disastrous depths. The Bible is full of examples of this principle.

God and Adam

God's purpose for Adam included Adam's role as secondary to God on the earth.

> And God said, Let us make man in our image, after our likeness: and let them have dominion over the fish of the sea, and over the fowl of the air, and over the cattle, and over all the earth, and over every creeping thing that creepeth upon the earth.
> —GENESIS 1:26

> The heaven, even the heavens, are the Lord's: but the earth hath he given to the children of men.
> —PSALM 115:16

God is referred to as King of kings and Lord of lords. Mankind was destined to be the secondary kings and lords. When God placed Adam in the garden, He gave him full sway of the garden, to dress it and to keep it. Only one prohibition was placed upon man, with many privileges suitable to one of such dignity and authority.

Moses and the builders of the tabernacle

When God instructed Moses to build the tabernacle and showed him the pattern on the mountain, God told Moses that He had specially qualified some men to build what Moses had seen.

> And let them make me a sanctuary; that I may dwell among them. According to all that I shew thee, after the pattern of the tabernacle, and the pattern of all the instruments thereof, even so shall ye make it.
> —EXODUS 25: 8–9

> And the Lord spake unto Moses, saying, See, I have called by name Bezaleel the son of Uri, the son of Hur, of the tribe of Judah: And I have filled him with the spirit of God, in wisdom, and in understanding, and in knowledge, and in all manner of workmanship, To devise cunning works, to work in gold, and in silver, and in brass, And in cutting of stones, to set them, and in carving of timber, to work in all manner of workmanship. And I, behold, I have given with him Aholiab, the son of Ahisamach, of the tribe of Dan: and in the hearts of all that are wise hearted I have put wisdom, that they may make all that I have commanded thee.
> —EXODUS 31:1–6

It is interesting to note that the same Holy Spirit who had anointed Moses to see the tabernacle had anointed them to build the tabernacle. The same Spirit was upon both Moses and his workers. They were developing the same building project. Yet there was a different anointing for their differing roles in the project. Moses was anointed to prophesy, to say what he saw. His team was anointed to conceive and apply, to see what he said. He was anointed for articulation. They were anointed for interpretation and application. He was anointed to instruct, and they were anointed to construct.

Moses and the seventy

> I am not able to bear all this people alone, because it is too heavy for me. And if thou deal thus with me, kill me, I pray thee, out of hand, if I have found favour in thy sight; and let me not see my wretchedness. And the Lord said unto Moses, Gather unto me seventy men of the

elders of Israel, whom thou knowest to be the elders of the people, and officers over them; and bring them unto the tabernacle of the congregation, that they may stand there with thee. And I will come down and talk with thee there: and I will take of the spirit which is upon thee, and will put it upon them; and they shall bear the burden of the people with thee, that thou bear it not thyself alone.... And Moses went out, and told the people the words of the Lord, and gathered the seventy men of the elders of the people, and set them round about the tabernacle. And the Lord came down in a cloud, and spake unto him, and took of the spirit that was upon him, and gave it unto the seventy elders: and it came to pass, that, when the spirit rested upon them, they prophesied, and did not cease.

—NUMBERS 11:14–17, 24–25

Did God Call Me to Kill Me?

When Moses petitioned God concerning the burden of responsibility for the people, God said that He would empower others to bear the burden with Moses, so that Moses would not be consumed. This is somewhat reminiscent of the counsel that Jethro had given Moses earlier concerning the delegation of authority. (Had Moses not learned that lesson? Or had he been so burned by some of the prior appointees that now he was suffering from insecurity, fear of a repeated insubordination?) God stated that He would take of the Spirit that was upon Moses and put it upon the seventy. It is interesting that God takes the anointing not directly from heaven but from Moses and puts it upon the new leaders.

Three key lessons are found here.

God Has to Anoint

First, God has to anoint: no man has an anointing of his own to give anyone. The senior leader's divine enablement comes from God, and only He has the right to imbue and endow.

Anointing Is Transgenerational

Second, God's anointing is not merely for one era. Once He has bestowed this anointing, it can be (and should be) transmitted generationally. A generation is not intended to imply biological kinship only, but from life to life, from epoch to era, God can take the anointing upon one and use it to equip another for service.

You Need Your Leader's Spirit

Third, in order to flow with the senior leader, the secondary needs that leader's spirit. That first system of leaders that Moses would have set up following Jethro's counsel is not noted to have had Moses' spirit, even though they would have been honorable persons, and they shared Moses' authority. Is it ever wise for people to share a leader's authority if they do not first share his heart, his passion, or his spirit?

Although all children of God are unique in Him, when it comes to leadership, there can only be one senior leader and one central vision for a ministry. Therefore, all secondary leaders need a spiritual connection to the senior leader (as he or she must have with Christ). This necessitates an attitude of meekness—being teachable. With this attitude, and by sharing their primary leader's unction, the secondary leaders may serve as extensions and extenders of the divine calling of the senior leader and of the ministry.

It Was Theocracy, Not Democracy

Please note that God took the spirit that was upon Moses and put it upon the seventy, in order for them to assist in leading the people. He did not take the spirit of the people and put it upon the seventy in order for them to lead Moses. The first responsibility of the seventy was to represent Moses to the people, not to represent the people to Moses.

Could there have been, in this context, an element of representation of the people, with the seventy serving as "senators" of sorts? In all likelihood, yes. However, this was not the inauguration of a representative form of government in the modern sense of a democratic republic. God's government, in ancient Israel then and in the church now, is a theocracy, not a democracy. God rules His kingdom.

Knowing Who "Theo" Is Not

Again, "Theo" means God—not Moses. So every "Moses" must submit to an accountability system because he is human and, therefore, subject to error. However, this accountability system for Moses' humanity must never degenerate into a controlling system of his or her divine mandate.

Furthermore, to assert that the seventy, or secondary leaders, need the spirit (divine enablement for service) of their senior leader is not to proclaim them to be innately inferior to him or her or anyone else, for all believers are sons of God. Secondary leaders need the spirit that is upon their Moses: the Holy Spirit's distinctive dispensation (pouring forth) of His grace through His chosen senior leader. They do not need that leader's human spirit, and not necessarily his or her personality, interests, political leanings, food preferences, or anything else in the natural realm. They are not called to be clones or pawns—lobotomized, robotized non-entities. When we compare and contrast Moses with Joshua or Elijah with Elisha, it becomes apparent that they were not facsimiles of each other. Yet these secondary leaders most definitely had their primary leader's spirit.

The Man, the Master, the Mantle, and the Mandate

The example of Elijah and Elisha is the classic example of how God uses one generation of leadership to prepare the next. Is is seen through Elisha's relationship with Elijah the man, Elijah the master (mentor, teacher), Elijah's mantle (gift-set, anointing), and Elijah's mandate (his assignment to bring reformation to the nation of Israel).

The Man: Humanity
Elijah confronts Elisha.
Lesson: God somehow acquaints us with the man (or woman) that He has chosen to mentor us.
It is possible that we know (or know of) the mentor before the pivotal encounter, but there is a God-ordained moment of connection.

The Master: Authority
Elisha follows Elijah with a pure heart and expectation of God.
Lesson: He or she becomes our instructor (rabbi, or master, is synonymous for "teacher").
It has been said that "when the student is ready, the teacher will appear." We begin to realize there is something that God has placed in this teacher that will bring us to our own destiny's fulfillment.

The Mantle: Ability

Elisha desired a double portion of Elijah's spirit and received the mantle. Even before Elijah's departure, Elisha began to experience supernatural revelation—he knew of Elijah's departure in advance.

Lesson: We become captivated by God's Word, anointing, and grace flowing through the mentor as God reveals more of Himself to us through that leader's life and ministry, and we "covet" what we see. (The mantle is the gift set and divine enablement; see 1 Cor. 12:31.)

The Mandate: Responsibility

Elisha understands that Elijah is not merely his teacher but his father, positioning him to assume prophetic protective oversight for the nation. The true "chariot of Israel" is not in the arsenal of Ahab but in the word of the Lord through Elijah. He assumes the leadership of the prophetic community and ministers to Israel and its leaders.

Lesson: Finally, we gain perspective and take ownership of the mentor's mandate. This component takes more maturity than any of the others. We come to share our mentor's burden; we come to realize the divine why and how of his or her ministry, not merely the who and what.

All four components are necessary to secure continuity and succession in leadership.

If the focus is on adulating the man, not on emulating the master, desiring the mantle, or understanding the mandate, admirers may be cultivated, but not disciples. (The disciple should be as his master.) On the other hand, if the leader is "just another man" in the secondary's eyes and not a master at all, then there can be affection without respect. The sin of familiarity can prevent one from receiving the destiny impartation from his or her leader. If one goes after the mantle without the man, one may become envious and strive to replace the leader instead of preparing to support and succeed the leader. If one embraces the mantle and mandate without the man, he or she can be unappreciative of the human cost of seeking divine revelation and carrying divine anointing.

If one embraces the mantle without understanding the mandate, he will exalt gifts as an end, rather than as a means of accomplishing God's plan. He may actually use spiritual weaponry for entertainment and exploitation. (Often the mandate of the mentor involved him or her carving out a place in business, ministry, or life in general where there was none before. This person actually has set a precedent that generations afterward follow, many of whom are not even aware that their reaping was precipitated by someone else's sowing.) "I sent you to reap that whereon ye bestowed no labour: other men laboured, and ye are entered into their labours" (John 4:38).

Jesus and the Apostles

Jesus, God in flesh, having accomplished eternal redemption for mankind, left the propagation of the gospel in the hands of His secondary leaders: the apostles, the other disciples, and ultimately all of the church. The Great Commission was given most directly to Jesus' handpicked secondary leadership.

> Then the eleven disciples went away into Galilee, into a mountain where Jesus had appointed them. And when they saw him, they worshiped him: but some doubted. And Jesus came and spake unto them saying, All power is given unto me in heaven and in earth. Go ye therefore, and teach all nations, baptizing them in the name of the Father, and of the Son, and of the Holy Ghost: Teaching them to observe all things whatsoever I have commanded you: and, lo, I am with you always, even unto the end of the world. Amen.
>
> —MATTHEW 28:16–20

> Afterward, he appeared unto the eleven as they sat at meat, and upbraided them with their unbelief and hardness of heart, because they believed not them which had seen him after he was risen. And he said unto them, Go ye into all the world, and preach the gospel to every creature. He that believeth and is baptized shall be saved: but he that believeth not shall be damned. And these signs shall follow them that believe: In my name shall they cast out devils; they shall speak with new tongues; They shall take up serpents; and if they drink any deadly thing, it shall not hurt them; they shall lay hands on the sick, and they shall recover. So then after the Lord had spoken unto them, he was received up into heaven, and sat on the right hand of God. And they went forth, and preached every where, the Lord working with them, and confirming the word with signs following. Amen.
>
> —MARK 16:14–20

> Then opened he their understanding, that they might understand the scriptures, And said unto them, Thus it is written, and thus it behooved Christ to suffer, and to rise from the dead the third day: And that repentance and remission of sins should be preached in his name among all nations, beginning at Jerusalem. And ye are witnesses of

these things. And, behold, I send the promise of my Father upon you: but tarry ye in the city of Jerusalem, until ye be endued with power from on high.

—LUKE 24:45–49

But ye shall receive power, after that the Holy Ghost is come upon you: and ye shall be witnesses unto me both in Jerusalem, and in all Judea, and in Samaria, and unto the uttermost part of the earth.

—ACTS 1:8

It is by the power of the Holy Ghost that these miracles were wrought, but the Holy Ghost used people to bring the gospel to the ends of the earth.

First Disciples, Then Apostles

Jesus gathered disciples very early in His ministry. He evidently understood that one of the most significant elements of His work was leadership development for those who would perpetuate His message. From among His disciples He chose Twelve and trained them intensely before He sent them on preliminary missions as apostles. Many of their failures and human flaws are graphically depicted in the gospels, yet in spite of their mortal weaknesses, God chose to use them as foundational (second only to Christ Himself) to the church.

Isn't it amazing that although none of the people God calls to leadership, primary or secondary, are perfect (with the exception of One), He has decreed that the gates of Hades shall not prevail against the church? It is!

Jesus' Secondary Leaders Were Effective

After His resurrection, Jesus gave the apostles an irrevocable assignment—to them and to the rest of the church, those who would believe on Him through the apostles' teachings. And in one generation, the civilized world had been indelibly impacted with the gospel—impacted with no television, no radio, no telephone, no automobile, and no Internet. It had been so impacted, in fact, that the comment was made that the world had been turned upside down by the ministry of Christ's followers. (See Acts 17:6.) This "motley crew" of believers forever changed the world, its history, its culture, and its future. What was viewed initially as a mere personality cult or an aberrant sect of Judaism when Christ died had shaken the Roman Empire fifty or so years later by the works of His secondary leadership. We have the Bible and the best of Western civilization as the result of the effectiveness of Jesus' secondary leadership team.

The High Priestly Prayer

The longest recorded prayer of Jesus is His high priestly prayer the night He was betrayed. One of the key concerns in that prayer was the disciples that God had given Him. He expressed His great love and protectiveness over them. He was concerned that they would become all that they were destined to be. He prayed that they would be preserved from evil while they remained His representatives in this world. He expressed that His desire for them was that they would be a living part of the mystical relationship between Him and the Father.

He Prayed for Secondary Leaders

In Jesus' high priestly prayer, He prayed not only for His apostles (His own secondaries), but also for their secondaries:

> Neither pray I for these alone, but for them also which shall believe on me through their word; That they all may be one; as thou Father, art in me, and I in thee, that they may be one in us: that the world may believe that thou hast sent me.
>
> —JOHN 17:20–21

Jesus knew that not only must His generation of followers, disciples, and apostles be strong, but that their successors must be sustained as well. He looked beyond the present leadership and asked the Father's guidance, development, and protection for all those who would believe through His first followers' teachings. We, all disciples of Jesus Christ who are extant today, are secondary—spiritual sons and daughters—of that first-century band of Christ-ones. The existence of the church and much of what is good on this planet are largely attributable to the apostles (Christ's secondaries) and their secondaries.

Secondary Leaders: Essential to the Detriment of the Vision

To a large degree, the success or failure of an organization will depend upon secondary leadership. On the other hand, the worst things that have ever happened in the plan of God have happened because of problems with leadership, and, yes, with secondary leadership in particular.

God and Lucifer

Many traditional Bible scholars affirm that Ezekiel 28, Isaiah 14, along with Luke 10:18, and Revelation 12 give a retrospective view into the origin of Satan, the devil. As it turns out, he was not intended to be diabolical at all; he was in a class all by himself, an "anointed" (empowered by God Himself) cherub (created angelic being associated with the throne and presence of God) "that covereth" (apparently served as an honor guard for God Himself). (See Ezekiel 28:11–15.) The Scriptures state that He was multifaceted with various gifts and abilities. Many believe that he was the highest of the angelic beings, second only to the Godhead. And yet his lofty position did not satisfy him. He was not satisfied with being second. He wanted the first place. (See Isaiah 14:12–15.) In his tragic story there are some sad lessons to which we should take heed.

God is God

Lucifer obviously did not understand that God is God, not because of what seat He holds, but because of who He is. He *is* the only One who is God by nature, having no creator, no beginning, no end, and no one to whom He looks for delegation of power. He did not understand that God does not merely hold a position as God: He *is* God, and is the *only* God. No one elected or appointed Him, and no one can fire Him. Even if people decide not to serve Him, to deny His existence, or to mock His name, it makes Him no less God. God is not what He does or an office He has acquired: *God is who He is.*

The ministry gift is a gift

Even so, secondary leaders in the church must understand that if their senior leaders are God-anointed and God-appointed, their man-made positions (as CEO, legal head of the ministry, etc.) do not make them who they are in the kingdom. As important as those positions are, they are of less significance than the offices that Christ has prescribed for His body. God "set some" (1 Cor. 12:28), and Christ "gave some" (Eph. 4:11) in His five-fold ministry. And the "some" are the individuals whom He has chosen. The secondary leader, in relation to his primary leader, may be a gifted person, perhaps even more gifted than his leader. However, the essential difference, the eternal difference, is that though the secondary leader may have a gift from God for the body, the senior leader is a gift from God to the body.

Secondary: a gift as well

This is not to suggest that a secondary leader may not be a ministry gift as well. To the contrary, the will of God is that diversities of giftings flow within and out from the local church. Nevertheless, it means that the primary gift to the local body will be the "set man" or woman of that house; therefore, the first obligation of any other ministry gifts within the church is to complement the vision and work of the primary ministry gift.

You can't keep what's not yours

Finally, it is pointless for a secondary leader to attempt to supplant a senior leader. Even if he is successful (for a season) in taking away what the senior leader has, he can never take away who the senior leader is, if this senior leader is God's man or woman. Presuming to put on God's crown (like Lucifer did) or attempting to steal the senior leader's mantle makes no angel become God—makes no follower become the leader—any more than putting on a cowboy hat makes the wearer John Wayne.

God and Adam

It was the will of God that Mr. and Mrs. Adam and their descendants would walk in fellowship with Him forever, in peace, in life, and health. There was no sin, no death, and none of death's offspring on the earth until God's secondary leader refused to take responsibility and utilize his delegated authority. Instead, he disobeyed God and subjected himself to Satan's will. Consequently, Adam and all his descendants were infected with the nature of Satan, the sin nature. And everything evil that could have happened began to happen, with all humans and all of nature being made victims.

Who was more responsible?

Specifically, the one more responsible for order in the garden was Mr. Adam. The scripture states that he was with Mrs. Adam when the serpent was dialoguing with her and she yielded to its deception. He refused to act; he refused to intervene when he saw something in the garden challenging the mandate of the Senior Leader, God Himself. Adam remained inactive and silent. He was not deceived, and God confronted him before He confronted his wife. (See 1 Timothy 2:14; James 4:17; and Genesis 3:9.)

Secondary leaders need to speak up!

When a secondary leader sees a challenge to God's word, the senior leader's scriptural directives, or the enemy attacking one of God's children to whom that secondary leader is assigned, he is to speak up! He does not need a prophecy or some special dream to know that there is a challenge to the authority of his leader or that one of God's children is about to be deceived.

All of the wars, plagues, floods, and pestilences that ever occurred have taken place through Adam's silence. The death of the Lord Jesus Christ was caused by Adam's silence. The secondary leader, Mr. Adam, who refused to speak up cost God and His kingdom dearly.

Secondary leaders who did speak up

Joshua and Caleb

When the children of Israel had been discouraged by the evil report of the ten other spies, it was Joshua and Caleb who stood up to "still the people before Moses" (Num. 13:30). They took the initiative, after having seen Moses go through time after time of reassuring the people of God's faithfulness. They were not intimidated because they were not in the majority opinion among the spies. The congregation at large did not take heed to their admonitions, but Joshua and Caleb received places of honor in the conquest of the Promised Land.

Phineas, the Son of Aaron

And, behold, one of the children of Israel came and brought unto his brethren a Midianitish woman in the sight of Moses, and in the sight of all the congregation of the children of Israel, who were weeping before the door of the tabernacle of the congregation. And when Phinehas, the son of Eleazar, the son of Aaron the priest, saw it, he rose up from among the congregation, and took a javelin in his hand; And he went after the man of Israel into the tent, and thrust both of them through, the man of Israel, and the woman through her belly. So the plague was stayed from the children of Israel. And those that died in the plague were twenty and four thousand. And the LORD spake unto Moses, saying, Phinehas, the son of Eleazar, the son of Aaron the priest, hath turned my wrath away from the children of Israel, while he was zealous for my sake among them, that I consumed not the children of Israel in my jealousy. Wherefore say, Behold, I give unto him my covenant of peace: And he shall have it, and his seed after him, even the covenant of an everlasting priesthood; because he was zealous for his God, and made an atonement for the children of Israel.

—NUMBERS 25:6–13

We do not recommend literal spears or weapons of any kind among God's people! The principle is vivid, however. Moses did not have to deal with this blatant act of iniquity—Phineas' zeal provoked him to action. Zeal, or passion, for God and the vision of God is a priceless asset. Many times the masses of people go astray because those in position to help Moses rebuke ungodliness cannot: as Moses, they must first live pure, passionate, loving lives in the midst of the flock. This will qualify them to repudiate unrighteousness in order to save the wandering sheep.

Jesus and Judas

Perhaps the most infamous example of a secondary leader undermining a senior leader is the story of Judas's betrayal of the Lord Jesus Christ. This story is well known, but sometimes it is not closely examined. *Judas* is the Greek for *Judah*, a Hebrew name meaning "praise." Isn't it tragic that the disciple, the apostle, who betrayed Jesus was named "praise"? Furthermore, one of the key Greek words for *worship* may be translated "kiss." Judas kissed Jesus in order to betray Him: "Praise" "worshipped" Jesus in order to betray Him.

Judas was probably not a "bad fellow"

Another aspect is that Judas had to have been very highly respected among the apostles:

- Nobody would have selected Judas as a treasurer if he were considered anything less than totally trustworthy.

- Judas was among the apostles preaching the gospel, healing the sick, and raising the dead.

- According to Jesus, Judas, as a part of the twelve, had a destiny in the millennial kingdom of the Lord Jesus. (See Matthew 19:27–30.)

- When Jesus said that one of the apostles would betray Him, none of the other apostles suspected Judas any more than himself. Even when Judas left the room, none of them were suspicious, nor would any have known, apparently, had Jesus not revealed it to Peter and John.

- Judas was not the monster that some people have made him out to be, until he was possessed by Satan:

  - It has already been noted that Jesus said he was destined for the Millennium.

  - Satan entered him in John 13. If Satan entered him, Satan did not previously indwell him.

  - Jesus called him a devil indirectly. However, he was speaking figuratively, obviously. He called Herod a fox, yet Herod was a human, not an animal. Jesus knew what was in Judas, and He knew what Judas would eventually do.

  - Peter states that by transgression Judas fell from his place. Judas could not have fallen if he had never been in a God-ordained high place from the beginning.

  - Judas, shortly after the betrayal of Jesus, expressed remorse and an awareness that he had done wrong and betrayed innocent blood—he even confessed as much.

  - Judas had so much regret for what he did that he threw away the money (clearly against his usual nature) and hanged himself. If he had been so filled with the nature

of Satan at that time, as some claim, why did he not gloat
and grin at the prospect of Jesus' hideous torture and
gruesome death?

Don't die like a fool

Simply put, the enemy took advantage of Judas' flesh and used him to
betray his Senior Leader and to make a fool, an eternal fool, of himself.
Anyone who will follow Judas's example and work to undermine his or
her own leader will end up in the posture of a fool. God ultimately caused
Judas's crime to work for good: Jesus' death redeemed us all. However, Judas
is in hell now, and his name lives on in infamy as an example of the vilest
of men. As my pastor stated it, he is "the only man who kissed the door of
heaven and (still) turned around and went to hell."

The secondary leader

Virtually every organization, secular and sacred, is crying out for leaders
who can be developed to secure the organization's legacy and carry it to
the next level for the next generation. Where are the true sons, in spirit, of
Moses, of David, of Elijah?

Three Positions of the Secondary Leader

Forerunning—Before the Senior Leader: John the Baptist

It is notable that God often gives a secondary leader a role which precedes
and facilitates that of his senior leader. John the Baptist understood his role
as the forerunner of Jesus Christ. He understood that Jesus' role was more
important than his, but that he (John) had been sent to prepare the way for
the entrance of Jesus' ministry. Furthermore, John ministered to the people,
directing them not to look to him but to believe on the One would come
after John and who would baptize with the Holy Ghost. John never directed
attention toward himself or away from Christ.

He knew his role

Even when the misguided could have believed that John the Baptist was
the Messiah, he freely acknowledged that he was not; he claimed to be only a
voice. (Jesus later said that he was the greatest prophet born of woman and that

he was Elijah who had been foretold to come again, in spirit.) Furthermore, John stated that Jesus, who came after him, was preferred before him.

He knew his mission: using the metaphor of the traditional Jewish wedding, he stated that he was the friend of the Bridegroom. He said to his disciples, "Behold, the Lamb of God." He, in essence, told them not to look to him but to Jesus. Even when Jesus' following outgrew his own, John said that this gave him joy, not a sense of envy. Even when Jesus began His ministry preaching "John's sermon," John did not demand royalties for his word being spoken. He knew his role.

Others in the "John the Baptist" function

Though no one is Jesus or John the Baptist personally on the earth today, the parallels are priceless. Consider the role of Sunday school teachers, of ushers, of praise and worship leaders, and of the choir. They usually come into contact with the congregation before the senior leader. And a major part of their role is to prepare the congregation to receive the ministry of the Word shared by the pastor. The pastor may be ever so anointed, but if the atmosphere has not been prepared, if the soil of the hearts has not been cultivated, the seed may fall by the wayside rather than on good ground.

And what of administrative assistants, custodians, and aides to the pastors or other fivefold ministers? Do they not often carry out vital preliminary functions before ministry ever takes place and without which the minister's effectiveness would be greatly hindered?

Knowing who one is not

How powerful it is for a secondary leader to walk before a senior leader and yet be able to accept the fact that the senior may be preferred by the congregation or some other constituency, or have prerogatives which the forerunner himself does not! How important it is for an individual to know who he is; however, the power of John the Baptist is that he also knew first *who he was not:*

> And this is the record of John, when the Jews sent priests and Levites from Jerusalem to ask him, Who art thou? And he confessed, and denied not; but confessed, I am not the Christ. And they asked him, What then? Art thou Elias? And he saith, I am not. Art thou that prophet? And he answered, No. Then said they unto him, Who art thou? that we may give an answer to them that sent us. What sayest

thou of thyself? He said, I am the voice of one crying in the wilderness, Make straight the way of the Lord, as said the prophet Esaias. And they which were sent were of the Pharisees. And they asked him, and said unto him, Why baptizest thou then, if thou be not that Christ, nor Elias, neither that prophet? John answered them, saying, I baptize with water: but there standeth one among you, whom ye know not; He it is, who coming after me is preferred before me, whose shoe's latchet I am not worthy to unloose. These things were done in Bethabara beyond Jordan, where John was baptizing. The next day John seeth Jesus coming unto him, and saith, Behold the Lamb of God, which taketh away the sin of the world. This is he of whom I said, After me cometh a man which is preferred before me: for he was before me. And I knew him not: but that he should be made manifest to Israel, therefore am I come baptizing with water. And John bare record, saying, I saw the Spirit descending from heaven like a dove, and it abode upon him. And I knew him not: but he that sent me to baptize with water, the same said unto me, Upon whom thou shalt see the Spirit descending, and remaining on him, the same is he which baptizeth with the Holy Ghost. And I saw, and bare record that this is the Son of God.

—JOHN 1:19–34

John the Baptist knew that he was not Messiah, nor one of the Old Testament prophets, but he knew he had a role vital to the presentation of Messiah's ministry, to the nation of Israel, and ultimately to the world. He knew that he was a voice, and he had the distinct honor of facilitating God's open acknowledgement of His Son. He died in dishonor, alone in prison, at the whim of a madman and an exotic dancer. There was not a state funeral for his death. Apparently, immediately prior ot John's execution, Jesus had not expressed to him or his ministry any particular concern, and this seems to have weighed heavily either upon John, or on his followers, or both, based on the inquiry that John eventually sent to Jesus.

Defining greatness

However, Jesus commends John as having been the greatest prophet born of woman. John did no miracles, yet Jesus (God in the flesh) named him greatest. Greatness, then, does not demand the spectacular. Serving with the right heart, promoting God's agenda, even if it means personal loss and discomfort—this is great in the eyes of the Lord. John couldn't see what was behind him. He didn't know how the world would change as a result of his obedience, but he was faithful to his charge. And today, even when the forerunning secondary leader cannot understand what is going on "behind him," as long as it is scriptural (spiritual, ethical, moral, or practical), he should be willing to be the voice preparing the way of the Lord.

Flanking—Beside the Senior Leader: Aaron (and Hur)

Some secondary leaders are given the distinctive honor of walking alongside the senior leader. A key example of this is Aaron, the brother of Moses, and later Hur. The Scripture states that when Moses was called of God and he complained to God about his own lack of eloquence, God made mention of Aaron and stated that He would use Aaron to stand alongside Moses. God would speak to Moses, Moses would speak to Aaron, and Aaron would speak to Pharaoh. God ordered Aaron's steps to converge with Moses' steps and gave Aaron the grand privilege of literally being in the middle of God's deliverance of His covenant people. Aaron was Moses' elder sibling, and yet God ordained that the younger, as senior leader, would lead the elder, the secondary leader. God actually stated later that He had made Moses a god to Pharaoh and that Aaron was Moses' prophet. Aaron was ordained of God to be the mouthpiece of Moses.

Hands in hands

Later, when Moses stood upon the mountain over the battle between Israel and Amalek, it was Aaron and Hur who stood with him. Moses stood with the rod of God in his hand, but his arms grew weary; yet for him to lower his arms was certain defeat for Israel. In stepped Aaron and Hur: they put a rock beneath Moses and stood up with him and steadied his hands until the victory was won. Moses was the one with rod in his hand, but Moses' hands were in the hands of Aaron and Hur. God gave them the privilege of partnering with Moses to effect a great deliverance for His people. The potency of the ministry of the man of God was, in effect, in the hands of his secondary leaders.

Complementary gifting

So in our day, sometimes the great senior leader has an even greater lack in a certain area vital to ministry. But if God called him or her to the senior leadership position, he has called someone to compensate for that lack, be it education, eloquence, business savvy, musical skills, or administrative capabilities. Yes, one may be a fivefold minister, even a pastor, and lack any of the things listed above. It is not necessary that the set ministry gift of a church have all of the gifts; when God calls that person, He knows who has the skills, the aptitude, and the anointing to supplement and complement the vision He has given to the senior leader.

Accept God's will

Anyone who is anointed to walk beside a senior leader should not allow carnal concerns to discourage him or her, such as the fact that the senior leader may be someone that he or she led to Christ years ago. God does not choose leadership based upon chronological age or even tenure in church. Although a senior leader must be experienced to perfect his or her calling, what God calls "experienced" does not always resemble what men characterize as experienced. Moses was younger than Aaron and Miriam, and Miriam had been used of God to position Moses' mother as his nursemaid in Pharaoh's palace, yet they both were secondary in function to Moses, who was the senior leader. For the most part, it appears that they accepted God's will for their roles: when the elder siblings did murmur against Moses, the "baby" who was God's choice for senior leader, judgment fell. And God has not changed.

The sin of familiarity

One important principle for those who walk closely with their leaders is that they should avoid falling prey to the sin of familiarity, the tendency to take someone lightly because of close acquaintance. It is a classic case of "familiarity breeds contempt" or at least presumption. Just because God has granted these secondary leaders the privilege of being intimately connected with their senior leaders, they should not begin to think of that privilege as an earned right. Just as the senior leader's calling is a sovereign work of grace, so the secondary leader's association with the senior leader is an act of God's favor. It should be regarded highly and respectfully.

Counselors and advisors

> Where no counsel is, the people fall: but in the multitude of counselors there is safety.
>
> —PROVERBS 11:14

Without counsel purposes are disappointed: but in the multitude of counselors they are disappointed.

—PROVERBS 15:22

Throughout history, there have been kings, emperors, and other rulers who, though they were the senior leaders, acknowledged their need for aid in order to reign properly. And in ancient courts, as well as in modern capitals, there have been counselors who serve at the ear of the leader. A counselor can be the best or worst thing that happens to a leader or his or her jurisdiction. The Bible contains examples of senior leaders making wise or fatal decisions based upon whose advice that senior leader heeded. Many edicts issued from the throne have originated "behind" the throne.

Jethro, not Jezebel

Whether secondary leaders have official advisory positions with their leaders or unofficial "sounding board" roles, they should handle those roles with extreme care. God does not give an individual access to the heads and hearts of leaders for their manipulation. This manipulation is the true spirit of Jezebel. She is not merely spiked heels and make-up. Jezebel's spirit can manifest in a male just as readily as in a female. Whether the spirit of Jezebel is sexual or not, it includes the abuse of access and influence for control. What leaders need are Jethros, Naomis, Nathans, and Abigails who will only utilize their rapport with the senior leader in a manner that advances God's agenda.

Court jesters or encouragers?

Does a senior leader need a court jester? Not really. The Bible term "jesting" speaks of coarse, profane joking. This is sin. But leaders of old did retain on staff someone who kept the mood light. Leadership is serious, sometimes gravely so. And there are those persons who will be used of God to support their leaders by helping them to lighten up in the midst of day-to-day duty. The principle of "a merry heart doeth good like a medicine" is not to be overlooked. And as simple as it is, one may be an encourager to his or her senior leader by a smile, a friendly gesture, a card, or a commendation on a job well done. These things go a long way in preserving leaders and developing one's own leadership qualities. It was Barnabas (the son of consolation) who made Saul's (Paul's) acceptance among the disciples a smoother transition (See Acts 9:26–31). Considering his name and his prophetic anointing (See Acts 13), Barnabas was apparently an encourager.

Follow-up—Behind the Senior Leader: Apollos

There was turmoil in the church at Corinth in which schisms and factions threatened to undermine the work of God: "For every one of you saith, I am of Paul; and I of Apollos; and I of Cephas; and I of Christ" (1 Cor. 1:12). Paul writes his letter to challenge this spirit and to clarify the proper way to view ministers in association with one another instead of in comparison, contrast, or competition with one another.

Paul states that the foundation of the church is Jesus Christ. He states that he and the rest of the brethren are only ministers by whom the Corinthians believed. Then he sets up the sequence of influence with regard to his and Apollos' relationship with the Corinthian church: "I have planted, Apollos watered; but God gave the increase" (1 Cor. 3:6). The last thing is the most important thing. God is the Author and Finisher of the faith of His people. No preacher, whether he is primary or secondary in a local church, saves, heals, or transforms anyone. Only God can do this.

A founding apostle's authority

However, relative to this church, Paul evidently has an authority that no one else has. Here he may not necessarily be the local pastor, but he is the founding apostle, a father to this work who maintains apostolic oversight. In this regard, he should be seen as a senior leader here. He is the one who was used of God to establish this work, and his relationship with Corinth has continued. Apollos' role has not been foundational; instead, he has come to Corinth after Paul to refine and enhance what Paul has already set in motion. He does not come to reestablish the church; rather, he came to "water" what Paul has already "planted." It is stated in the Scripture that Apollos was eloquent (Acts 18:24). It is stated that some of the Corinthians did not think very highly of Paul's oral delivery (2 Corinthians 10:10); they thought he was a better writer than speaker. What this implies is what was stated earlier: the gifts of the secondary may complement and compensate for a lack of those same gifts in the primary leader.

Affirming and confirming the senior leader's works

To the person who is called to walk behind his leader today, he is walking there to complete and solidify that which has been initiated by the senior leader, just as Apollos did for Paul. He is not there to establish; he is there to affirm and confirm what has already been established. He is not there to lay a foundation; instead, he should in some way accentuate the ongoing construction process in the life of the local church or other ministry. Again, the same God who anoints the senior leader to lay the groundwork for the ministry anoints a secondary leader to help carry the groundwork through to fruition and maturity.

Carnality breeds division

Another note: neither Christ, Paul, Apollos, nor Cephas caused the division in Corinth. Christ and those ministers were in agreement. It was the carnal Corinthians that picked their favorite preacher and vied against one another. So today, primary and secondary leaders must decide to agree with God and with one another to bless God for each other's uniqueness, refusing to be divided because people may try to play one against another. Leaders ought to lead—not be led by—the babes and the worldly minded in the church.

Secondary leader, God trusts you with your leader's back, to protect him and the work of God from behind, not to stab him or her in the back.

Under Authority and In Authority

> The centurion answered and said, Lord, I am not worthy that thou shouldest come under my roof: but speak the word only, and my servant shall be healed. For I am a man under authority, having soldiers under me: and I say to this man, Go, and he goeth; and to another, Come, and he cometh; and to my servant, Do this, and he doeth it.
>
> —MATTHEW 8:8–9

The story from which this quote is excerpted is a powerful example of faith in Jesus Christ, beyond that of "the religious." However, the centurion's faith seems to derive from the fact that he understood and respected authority from both angles: being under authority and holding authority. He was over one hundred men ("cent-urion"), yet he would have been a part of a legion under the command of an officer called a "legate," or "legatus." (The case could readily be made that the only human beings who are conditioned to exercise authority are those who have successfully served under the authority of another.)

Somehow, this centurion inferred that the way his authority over his men worked was the same way Jesus' authority over all of nature operated. (And he was right!) He drew right conclusions about Jesus by means of having an understanding of authority.

The truth of the matter is that one cannot even be saved until one receives and declares a divine revelation of Jesus' authority: Jesus is Lord. Acknowledgement of His authority is essential to salvation.

Awareness that one may serve in an official secondary leadership capacity in one dimension of life while simultaneously carrying a primary office in another respect is empowering and liberating. It is empowering in that one may exercise the highest level of authority in one given sector of society without concern as to whether it hurts one's image to serve in a less prestigious role elsewhere. It is liberating in that the leader can have the relief of finally being a part of a system where the proverbial buck does not stop with him or her. He or she does not have to shoulder the final responsibility for success or failure.

Respect for the Secondary Leader

Leadership's effect depends on the followers' respect. People do not follow those whom they do not regard with honor. Only those who respect and reverence God follow Him. Only those who respect the senior pastor will follow him as he follows Christ. And only those who respect the secondary leader will follow him as he follows his senior pastor.

Respect is a multifaceted commodity, arising from several different bases. A measure of respect comes from the fact that one wears a respected title or holds a respected office. Another measure can come from association: if the senior leader is highly respected, the person whom he approves may automatically be regarded somewhat favorably. Another measure can arise based upon an individual's ability to fill his job description: if he is the music minister and he can minister well musically, he will tend to be respected in that realm. However, none of these measures of respect are adequate long-term and may easily dissipate if there is not another measure—the most important one: the leader's conduct on- and off-stage. This gets at the heart of this discussion.

That Which Only the Senior Leader Can Do

As stated earlier, no one can make one person respect another. As it relates to the church, the senior leader cannot force the congregation to respect a secondary leader. However, this does not absolve the senior leader of his or her responsibility to endorse the secondary leader. One of the cruelest things a pastor can do is to give a person an assignment in secret but not support him openly. Similarly, berating the secondary leader publicly over trivial matters is totally unwise and counterproductive, as these acts will tend to undermine any effectiveness that a secondary leader could hope to have and may leave him or her bitter and disillusioned. This is one of the key purposes of licensure and ordination: to say to the congregation and to the general public that the primary leader recognizes the hand of God and the character of God in the life of the designated leader. The senior leader is morally obligated to clearly point the finger of endorsement and approval toward the secondary.

> And the Lord said unto Moses, Take thee Joshua the son of Nun, a man in whom is the spirit, and lay thine hand upon him; And set him before Eleazar the priest, and before all the congregation; and give him a charge in their sight. And thou shalt put some of thine honour upon him, that all the congregation of the children of Israel may be obedient.
>
> —NUMBERS 27:18–20

Examples of the Endorsement of Secondary Leaders in the Life of Paul

Commendation of Phebe to the Roman Church

> I commend unto you Phebe our sister, which is a servant of the church which is at Cenchrea: That ye receive her in the Lord, as becometh saints, and that ye assist her in whatsoever business she hath need of you: for she hath been a succourer of many, and of myself also.
>
> —ROMANS 16:1–2

Commendation of Priscilla and
Aquila to the Roman Church

Greet Priscilla and Aquila my helpers in Christ Jesus: Who have for my
life laid down their own necks: unto whom not only I give thanks, but
also all the churches of the Gentiles.

—Romans 16:3–4

Commendation of Timothy to the Corinthian Church

Now if Timotheus come, see that he may be with you without fear: for
he worketh the work of the Lord, as I also do. Let no man therefore
despise him: but conduct him forth in peace, that he may come unto
me: for I look for him with the brethren. As touching our brother
Apollos, I greatly desired him to come unto you with the brethren: but
his will was not at all to come at this time; but he will come when he
shall have convenient time. Watch ye, stand fast in the faith, quit you
like men, be strong. Let all your things be done with charity. I beseech
you, brethren, (ye know the house of Stephanas, that it is the firstfruits
of Achaia, and that they have dedicated themselves to the ministry of
the saints,) That ye submit yourselves unto such, and to every one that
helpeth with us, and laboureth.

—1 Corinthians 16:10–16

If there is an individual who has proven to be faithful as a believer, senior
leaders should have no hesitation to speak well of him or her when others
inquire—and not only when others inquire! Speaking well of brothers and
sisters is a part of being Christlike and showing appreciation for God's work
in the lives of His people.

Moreover, on the preventative side, some ministries have had great injury
done because leaders—senior and secondary—showed up proclaiming
themselves to be great ones. Because of the typical openness of many
Christians (and non-Christians) to anyone who comes "in the name of the
Lord," individuals, marriages, ministries, businesses, and organizations
have been hurt to the point of bitterness, ruin, and disillusionment. Much of
the exploitation of the unsuspecting could be eliminated if leaders respected
the body of Christ enough to say to fellow leaders, "This brother, Sam,
would be a blessing to the youth in your ministry." Or, "I know this person
_____, is officially associated with us, but I have not observed in

him the integrity that would make me comfortable to endorse his coming to you." Or, "This sister is a tremendous speaker (administrator, intercessor, etc.) with a Christlike spirit. She will be of help wherever you assign her."

That Which Only the Secondary Leader Can Do

The senior leader has a role. However, there are things that only the secondary leader can do to garner the respect of God, the body of Christ, his or her family, the senior leader, the local church, and the world at large. Those things that the secondary leader must do are the ongoing discussion of this text.

Rewards of the Secondary Leader

In Eternity

What every believer must remember is that he or she is saved by grace through faith in the Lord Jesus Christ. The good works and faithful service of the individual are not the cause of salvation; they should be the effect of salvation. One is not more or less beloved of God based upon what he or she does. God loves all mankind because of who He is and because of mankind's value in God's sight. The Christian who does good works does them because he is on his way to heaven, not so that he may gain access to heaven.

The Lord Is Audience #1

Secondly, as the believer enters into the doing of good works, i.e., the fulfilling of what he perceives as ministry, he must have the Lord as his primary audience. No one will be successful in Christian service for long without understanding that what he is doing he is doing "unto the Lord." The prospect of a man recognizing and applauding his deeds should not be the motivating factor of his servanthood. More often than not, his service will not be acknowledged. He must keep his eyes on Jesus, understanding that although his deeds may be ignored on the earth, in the heavenlies they are being meticulously noted and recorded, and if his heart and hands are clean, he will receive rewards beyond his ability to conceive. The Bible uses the term *crowns* to signify the eternal rewards of the believer, but one may rest assured that God is not merely going to give those who are faithful a piece of fancy headgear. The crowning of the faithful speaks of their investiture with distinctions of divine glory, honor, and authority in the world to come that would challenge our human ability to comprehend.

In Time

Moreover, God has not promised to reward His faithful ones in eternity only. Peter asked Jesus:

> Behold, we have forsaken all, and have followed thee; what shall we have therefore?
>
> —MATTHEW 19:27

And Jesus responded by saying, "Verily I say unto you, that ye which have followed me in the regeneration when the Son of Man shall sit in the throne of his glory, ye also shall sit upon twelve thrones, judging the twelve tribes of Israel" (Matt. 19:28). But Jesus also stated in Mark's account of this same occasion, "Verily I say unto you, there is no man that hath left house, or brethren, or sisters, or father, or mother, or wife, or children, or lands for my sake and the gospel's, but he shall receive an hundredfold now in this time, houses, and brethren, and sisters, and mothers, and children, and lands, with persecutions; and in the world to come eternal life" (Mark 10:29–30).

Jesus promised rewards to his apostles in the age to come—"twelve thrones judging the twelve tribes of Israel"—but he also promised that they would receive a hundredfold "now in this time" with persecutions, and in the world to come, eternal life.

The Hundredfold

Some scribes would argue as to whether this "hundredfold" is literal or figurative. However, there is no debating that Jesus said that this hundredfold reaping would take place "now, in this time." Whatever this reward is, it is a reward of the here and now. As this relates to the secondary leader, it will be discussed in greater detail later, but it needs to be summarized here.

Here-and-Now Rewards of the Secondary Leader

Honor

Whoso keepeth the fig tree shall eat the fruit thereof: so he that waiteth on his master shall be honored.

—PROVERBS 27:18

- The secondary leader can expect God's honor for his faithfulness.

- The secondary leader should be able to expect the senior leader's honor for his faithfulness.

- The secondary leader may be able to expect the senior leader's congregation (or whatever his constituency) to honor him for his faithfulness.

Impartation

And Elijah took his mantle, and wrapped it together, and smote the waters, and they were divided hither and thither, so that they two went over on dry ground. And it came to pass, when they were gone over, that Elijah said unto Elisha, Ask what I shall do for thee, before I be taken away from thee. And Elisha said, I pray thee, let a double portion of thy spirit be upon me. And he said, Thou hast asked a hard thing: nevertheless, if thou see me when I am taken from thee, it shall be so unto thee; but if not, it shall not be so. And it came to pass, as they still went on, and talked, that, behold, there appeared a chariot of fire, and horses of fire, and parted them both asunder; and Elijah went up by a whirlwind into heaven. And Elisha saw it, and he cried, My father, my father, the chariot of Israel, and the horsemen thereof. And he saw him no more: and he took hold of his own clothes, and rent them in two pieces. He took up also the mantle of Elijah that fell from him, and went back, and stood by the bank of Jordan; And he took the mantle of Elijah that fell from him, and smote the waters, and said, Where is the Lord God of Elijah? and when he also had smitten the waters, they parted hither and thither: and Elisha went over. And when the sons of the prophets which were to view at Jericho saw him, they said, The spirit of Elijah doth rest on Elisha. And they came to meet him, and bowed themselves to the ground before him.

—2 KINGS 2:8–15

- The secondary leader may expect the impartation of the God-given enablement—at least some aspects of the "mantle" of the primary leader.

Experience

The secondary leader will gain priceless experience while serving with and under another, which will prepare him for greater levels of responsibility later. To have a reservoir of recollections and notations from which to pull in challenging times is valuable. Being able to ask, "What did my leader do in a moment like this?" and being able to answer it based upon having witnessed it earlier—this is a true inheritance.

Seedtime/Harvest

If the secondary leader's calling is to do what the senior leader is presently doing, he has the opportunity to sow seed into his or her own destiny. If his or her primary calling is different, that secondary leader still can expect to prosper in that assignment for having aided another in the fulfillment of God's call. The principle of sowing and reaping is going to work powerfully as the secondary goes through phases of development.

A Record of Faithfulness

The secondary leader creates for himself, by the grace of God, a record of faithfulness, a résumé (not a présumé!) that commends him to the Lord, his senior and peer leadership, the congregation, the greater body of Christ, and the world at large. (It cannot be forgotten that the world is watching.)

A Destiny of Secondary Leadership: Is This a Reward?

Some secondary leaders' destiny is secondary leadership—in fact, many will have this destiny. To have a secondary role is not to be of secondary value to God or as an individual. It is a far greater blessing to be a secondary leader in the will of God than to be a primary leader outside His will.

How unfortunate it is that some people do not consider themselves a success, particularly in ministry, unless they are the official heads of their respective institutions, at the "front of the line." Has it ever occurred to them that if everyone in the line demands to be at the front, that there will be no line? Has it ever occurred to them that being called to ministry or leadership does not demand that one be solo? No pastor of a growing ministry can pastor that church by himself or herself for long. Though there is one principal voice of God for and to that ministry, there must be plurality in the leadership if the ministry is to flourish and be healthy (and if the senior leader is going to be healthy—not burned out).

My Own *Thang*

> Better to rule in Hell than to serve in Heaven.
> —LUCIFER, IN JOHN MILTON'S PARADISE LOST

In plain terms, why is it that when an individual realizes that he has a burning passion, along with the gifts to influence, to motivate, to inspire, and to help people, he presumes that he is to run out—without being released, endorsed, or blessed by God and some father, mother, or eldership in the Lord—and "start his own thang"? Isn't this more like the American dream than the kingdom vision?

There is absolutely nothing inordinate about church planting. And every person, whether clergy or laity, should desire to do exceedingly great things for God in life. This is no improper impulse. What is inordinate is the mind-set, the paradigm, that there is no way for one person's calling in God to be fulfilled while under the auspices of another ministry established by God. It is a sense of exclusiveness, an egocentric sense of grandeur, which is poisonous.

Splits and Splinters

Consequently, many local churches never grow in quantity or quality beyond the ability of the one person to personally shepherd the flock. As soon as someone arises who could extend the ministry of the senior shepherd, he or she heads off to start his own flock—often taking some of the sheep that God entrusted to the senior leader with him or her.

And, remember that law of seedtime and harvest—it works here, too. What will the ministry look like for a person who started his or her ministry by subverting the works of another leader when reaping time comes? What kind of harvest may a leader expect who was unwilling to submit to another? What kind of members, secondary leaders, employees, or other constituents will he or she have? There are heads of ministries and organizations even now who need to repent to God and make restitution to those whom they injured "on their way up," for they know they are reaping the unsavory fruit derived from the seed of their own rebellion.

Insecure Primary Leaders

Then again, some secondary leaders have been forced out. This leads to another aspect of this issue. A lack of continuity is not just a concern on the part of the misguided aspirant; the senior leaders also may bear some guilt for secondary leaders who begin to operate beyond their calling.

Sometimes the senior leader will not acknowledge the secondary's gifts that God has literally placed at his or her disposal for fear of being displaced or replaced by that secondary leader. (See David and Saul later.) Insecurity has ripped apart precious relationships between spiritual parents and their children. Very often, the children's only goal was the fulfillment of father or mother's vision to aid in the "enlarging of their territory." For varying reasons— poor communication between the senior and the secondary; demagoguery; failures of former secondary leaders; shortcomings in the senior leaders' own spiritual parenting—these all may contribute to the demise of the connection. Many who are spiritual parents had minimal deliberate mentoring themselves, if any, and some have had mostly dysfunctional spiritual parents. Therefore, they are saddled with the challenge of being to someone else what no one ever was to them.

Fatherlessness

There is often a parallel in the spirit world to what is observed in the natural world. And in this day there is unprecedented fatherlessness. There is unprecedented abdication of responsibility by parents. There is an unheard-of measure of the tendency toward children bearing and rearing children. Even so in the spiritual dimension, there is not nearly enough "parenting"— mentoring, discipling, encouraging, and grooming—taking place in the body of Christ. There is not enough genuine, deliberate relationship, rather than superficial relationship, along denominational, organizational, or even doctrinal lines. (See "Real-ationship #1: Fathers" in chapter 2.)

Intruding Into Offices

Many people are usurping the bishopric, the apostolate, and the pastorate when they have not been weaned and groomed into spiritual adulthood. Some of them demand that others submit to their "covering" when they themselves are not properly insulated. These brothers and sisters are children attempting to rear children. And indeed, some of these truly have the callings listed above, though they may not be fully developed in those ministries; therefore, they may be bearing some fruit—sometimes dramatic, supernatural fruit—even as adolescents can impregnate, become pregnant, and deliver a full-term, healthy baby. However, the fact that an adolescent has the tools to become a parent hardly means that he or she has the skills needed for him or her to succeed as a parent.

A Faulty, Fatal Sense of Timing

Gehazi

Tangible rewards, and all good things, come with time. Outside a proper sense of timing, a leader may lose all. The story of Naaman's healing is referenced elsewhere in this text, but here we examine it in light of the issue of the timing of rewards and the principle of succession.

> Now Naaman, captain of the host of the king of Syria, was a great man with his master, and honourable, because by him the Lord had given deliverance unto Syria: he was also a mighty man in valour, but he was a leper.... So Naaman came with his horses and with his chariot, and stood at the door of the house of Elisha. And Elisha sent a messenger unto him, saying, Go and wash in Jordan seven times, and thy flesh shall come again to thee, and thou shalt be clean.... Then went he down, and dipped himself seven times in Jordan, according to the saying of the man of God: and his flesh came again like unto the flesh of a little child, and he was clean. And he returned to the man of God, he and all his company, and came, and stood before him: and he said, Behold, now I know that there is no God in all the earth, but in Israel: now therefore, I pray thee, take a blessing of thy servant. But he said, As the Lord liveth, before whom I stand, I will receive none. And he urged him to take it; but he refused.... But Gehazi, the servant of Elisha the man of God, said, Behold, my master hath spared Naaman this Syrian, in not receiving at his hands that which he brought: but, as the Lord liveth, I will run after him, and take somewhat of him. So

Gehazi followed after Naaman. And when Naaman saw him running
after him, he lighted down from the chariot to meet him, and said, Is all
well? And he said, All is well. My master hath sent me, saying, Behold,
even now there be come to me from mount Ephraim two young men
of the sons of the prophets: give them, I pray thee, a talent of silver,
and two changes of garments. And Naaman said, Be content, take two
talents. And he urged him, and bound two talents of silver in two bags,
with two changes of garments, and laid them upon two of his servants;
and they bare them before him. And when he came to the tower, he
took them from their hand, and bestowed them in the house: and he
let the men go, and they departed. But he went in, and stood before his
master. And Elisha said unto him, Whence comest thou, Gehazi? And
he said, Thy servant went no whither. And he said unto him, Went not
mine heart with thee, when the man turned again from his chariot to
meet thee? Is it a time to receive money, and to receive garments, and
oliveyards, and vineyards, and sheep, and oxen, and menservants, and
maidservants? The leprosy therefore of Naaman shall cleave unto thee,
and unto thy seed for ever. And he went out from his presence a leper
as white as snow.

—2 KINGS 5:1, 9, 14, 16, 20–27

Consider the fact that Elisha came to his prophetic ministry by the
choosing of God. However, when God chose him, God also set him under
the tutelage of Elijah. As Elisha served Elijah, he was being equipped by
God through Elijah for his own God-ordained destiny. Elijah could not call
and anoint him. What he could do was obey God's choice and mentor him.
When Elijah was to depart, God ordained that his servant Elisha would
take his place.

The next generation

Eventually, Elisha has a servant, Gehazi. He participates in the miracle
ministry of Elisha to the Shunammite woman—in the miraculous birth of
her son and in the resurrection of that same son. Upon close examination, it
is apparent that Elisha considered his anointing to be transferable, through
the obedience of Gehazi. He gave Gehazi instructions on how to use his staff,
evidently expecting the child to awaken. (Reading that text, one can only
wonder if there was something in Gehazi even then that "short-circuited"
the power.) Gehazi says, "The child is not awakened" (2 Kings 4:31).

Gehazi also is featured in the miracle of Naaman's deliverance. It is possible that Gehazi was chosen of Elisha for the same reason that Elisha was chosen of Elijah—to be equipped to fulfill his own God-ordained destiny. Even if God did not directly speak it to Elisha, the nature of such servanthood is ordained of God to prepare the next generation of leaders.

Gehazi's failure

Gehazi missed it, however, because of covetousness—because of his greed. His greed motivated him to lie to Naaman and to his master, Elisha. Sadly, the satanic malady that he had helped to get Naaman cured of was placed on him and his seed. How sad it is that the area in which one ministers deliverance to others can become the curse of the deliverer himself! And why was this?

Not the gifts, but the timing

Elisha dealt with Gehazi about the timing. He did not condemn the concept of receiving a gift. He condemned Gehazi's flesh-motivated timing. Naaman was a heathen who knew nothing of the free gift of God's mercy. He apparently expected to "pay his way," even regarding his healing. God would have used this occasion to fully demonstrate His goodness, but the demonstration was marred because of Gehazi's insolence. Let all leaders wait on God—the gifts come in His time.

Elisha's mantle

The Scripture states that Elisha died and was buried. Sometime afterward, a corpse was thrown hastily into his sepulchre in the midst of a military conflict. When the corpse touched the bones of Elisha, the man revived—resurrected by the latent, dormant power of God resident in Elisha's bones. Here is the question—did no one get Elisha's mantle? Did the failure of Gehazi break the continuity of prophetic heritage and anointing, in the "lineage of Elijah"?

Success without a successor

One thing is clear: God gets no glory from a leader dying with his or her anointing left on him or her. Notice that when Aaron died, God demanded that he remove the priestly garments before he died. These garments were passed on to his son. This seems to typify that the continuity of ministry and of anointing is not supposed to die with the passing generation. Rather, the passing generation is to transfer its unction, its faith, and its devotion to God to the succeeding generation. One prominent evangelist, who has also educated many young people for ministry, has stated, "Success without a successor is failure."

I go a step further and add this: "And the successor is not successful if he does not exceed his predecessor." This is because the predecessor has bequeathed all that he or she is and all that he or she has to the next generation. The reward of the secondary leader includes the inheritance from the senior leader. The words of the father in the parable of the prodigal son are particularly revealing as he speaks to the elder brother, his faithful, discouraged, secondary leader:

> And he said unto him, Son, thou art ever with me, and all that I have
> is thine.
> —LUKE 15:31

The inheritance of the secondary leader may not necessarily include tangible possessions. However, a legacy of wisdom, power, love, a good name, faithfulness to God, and the faithfulness of God—these are the guaranteed commodities passed on to the secondary leader as successor, and they comprise an inheritance far surpassing the value of anything tangible.

Chapter 4

THE EXAMPLE OF DAVID

And David behaved himself wisely in all his ways; and the Lord was with him. Wherefore when Saul saw that he behaved himself very wisely, he was afraid of him. But all Israel and Judah loved David, because he went out and came in before them.

—1 SAMUEL 18:14–16

Wholesome Conduct

One key to leadership's effectiveness is found in the concept of "behaving oneself wisely."

Defining "behaved himself wisely," *Strong's Concordance* (Ref. #7919) lists the following: "sakal (saw-kal') a primitive root; to be (causatively, make or act) circumspect and hence, intelligent: KJV--consider, expert, instruct, prosper, (deal) prudent(-ly), (give) skill(-ful), have good success, teach, (have, make to) understand(-ing), wisdom, (be, behave self, consider, make) wise(-ly), guide wittingly."

People look for wholesome conduct among leaders, particularly among Christian leaders. For all of one's gifts and rhetoric, if the lifestyle of a leader contradicts what he is supposed to uphold, very few people want to follow. It is interesting that even though a leader may be telling the truth (preaching, teaching, singing, administrating), if he or she is not living the truth, the sincere person does not want to hear anything—true or not—from that leader.

Sadly, one of the areas over the past several decades or so that have been fiascos for the church have been in the area of immoral conduct. Many understand can recall the public spectacle of several major Protestant ministers and ministries that were involved in moral scandals in the 1980s and '90s. Then there have been the internationally known moral scandals involving some Roman Catholic priests in the twenty-first century.

No Injury Intended

This is not an effort to exploit or aggravate what has happened in these cases. They are sad and tragic for the entire body of Christ. Those things yet pending shall be judged. Ultimately, God will judge all who are involved, because He is the One knows all the facts. Yet there are weighty lessons for leaders that can be extracted from reflecting on what happened in those cases.

Isolation—Satan's Advantage

In the sentencing of one minister, the judge allegedly said, "Mr._____ obviously began as a man who used things and loved people, but he ended up as a man who loved things and used people." Another leader involved in a scandal in which he failed morally stated that pride made him impervious to anyone who attempted to minister to him, including his own wife. He thought that he did not need to receive ministry. He thought that he should only be on the giving end of ministry. Satan, as a lion stalking wandering prey, pounces upon isolated believers. In this case, an exaggerated sense of self-importance can lead to devastation.

David as an Example

It has been said that David is an Old Testament person with a New Testament perspective. He comes closer to a New Testament relationship with God than almost anyone else in Scripture before the cross, with the possible exception of Abraham. In some ways, he is one of the greatest characters in the Old Testament narrative. What makes David so compelling is not just that he was a great man, as were others, but that, for all his flaws, he is such a comprehensive picture of the Lord Jesus Christ. He is almost the greatest Messiah type in the entire Bible, not to mention the fact that he is a celebrated ancestor of the Messiah.

Characteristics of David That Parallel Jesus Christ

- He is of the tribe of Judah.

- He is a Bethlehemite.

- A prophet is sent to announce and anoint him for God's purpose.

- The Spirit of the Lord comes upon him after the prophet ministers to him.

- The Spirit of the Lord comes upon him and anoints him initially in the presence of others.

- After the anointing, he immediately retreats into a place of solitude.

- He is a shepherd who puts himself in danger to deliver the sheep.

- He is sent by his father to his brethren.

- He is despised by his brothers.

- He defeats the enemy when no one else can or will.

- He rises from obscurity to unequalled notoriety—the masses love him.

- The "powers that be" envy him.

- He is threatened by the one(s) he came to deliver.

- He is a priest (though not a Levite), a king, and a prophet.

- He is a worshipper, a warrior, and a witness.

- He transcends the Mosaic law, not so much breaking it as lifting it.

- He vanquishes all his enemies.

- He is betrayed within his own house.

- He institutes a new mode of worship.

- He has a passion for the temple of God.

- He prepares for his son to finish and exceed his own works.

David—A Worthy Model

Jesus is the example, the model of behavior, to the church. To the degree that David is like Jesus, he is a worthy biblical example of secondary leadership as well. David "behaved himself wisely." It is obvious from the Scripture that he carried himself with virtues, such as humility, compassion for the weak (in mind or body), seriousness, loyalty and reverence for his leaders, diligence, justice, and passion for God.

David's Ethical Conduct

David did not try to step over (or on) his brethren as he waited on the word from God over his life to be established. God had chosen David to be king; David did not campaign to become king. Even if there was an aspiration for a governmental office resident in David's heart, kingship probably was not that office, because it was understood that customarily the king's son or near relatives would inherit the crown. He no doubt knew that the great prophet Samuel had been used of God to establish Saul, the son of Kish of the tribe of Benjamin, as Israel's first king. Saul was the king, and Benjamin was therefore the royal tribe—that was it.

When Samuel showed up at Jesse's house, it was a radical departure from traditional thought. It was not only radical; it was dangerous. Even Samuel knew that for him to anoint a king who was not Saul's son was to risk being charged with treason and killed. God gave him wisdom as to how to carry it out, but the elders of Bethlehem, Jesse, and his family were all still taken by surprise. An even greater surprise was when, of all Jesse's sons, God indicated that David was His choice. Samuel anointed who God had chosen.

You Don't Have to Force It

Imagine what David thought. He believed God, but he apparently believed that if God had chosen him to be king, it would come to pass without David's attempt to force it to happen. Even when Saul began to hunt him like a rabid beast, David never allowed himself to be vindictive toward Saul. David valued Saul beyond the state of their relationship at that time. Even at Saul's death, David was genuinely grief-stricken and composed an elegy in honor of Saul and Jonathan. He endeavored afterward to deal respectfully with the house of Saul.

Imitate David

What we can gain from David is to "go and do thou likewise." David conducted himself in a godly manner, and the Scripture states that God was with him. For God to be with a person in Scripture connotes that the favor of God was demonstrated toward that person. It was very evident that God was at work in David, and eventually it became evident that God was at work for David.

Too many people are busy trying to get God to work for them without giving Him the greater task of working in them. The greater work of God in the life of the believer is not the *charismata* (gifts of the Spirit, or God working for the believer) but rather character (fruit of the Spirit, or God working in the believer).

Unwholesome Conduct

On the other hand, the narrative is set up, beginning all the way back in 1 Samuel 13, to contrast the new king-designate, David, and the old king-reject, Saul.

The Attitudes/Behavior of Declining Saul versus Ascending David

Wisdom

- Samuel says to Saul, "Thou hast done foolishly." (1 Sam. 13:13)

- The Bible says, "David behaved himself wisely." (1 Sam.18:5)

Future

- Samuel says that God "would have established thy [Saul's] kingdom [reign] upon Israel forever. But now thy kingdom shall not continue." (1 Sam. 13:13–14)

- Saul later tells David, "the kingdom of Israel shall be established in thine hand." (1 Sam. 24:18–20)

Anointing

- The Spirit of the Lord came upon David.

- The Spirit of the Lord departed from Saul, and an evil spirit came upon Saul.

Courage

- Saul and all of Israel were afraid of Goliath.

- David was unafraid of Goliath and fought him in the name of God and of Israel.

Repentance

- Saul, when rebuked by the prophet of God for sin, was concerned about the people's view of him more than God's. He lost the throne and died in disgrace.

- David, when rebuked by the prophet of God for sin, was concerned about God's view of him more than the people's. He retained the throne and died with honor.

Envy

- Saul, upon hearing David praised by the women's song, grew envious of David.

- David, until Saul's death, always spoke and dealt respectfully regarding Saul. He passionately eulogized Saul and Jonathan when they died.

Loyalty

- Saul sought for those who would help him to oppose David.

- David killed the person who claimed credit for Saul's death.

Presumption/Arrogance

- Saul became presumptuous concerning his place of honor.

- David considered himself unworthy of honor without something to base that honor upon (e.g., a dowry for Saul's daughter).

Secret Thoughts

- Saul plotted to kill David.

- David plotted to keep Saul alive.

Inner Fulfillment

- The thought of impaling David to the wall with a javelin gave Saul a sense of security.

- The thought of merely cutting off a piece of Saul's robe gave David a heart of grief.

Associations I

- When Samuel encountered Saul, he was following mules (typically a symbol of stubbornness). Saul definitely became mule-spirited.

- When Samuel encountered David, he was following sheep (a symbol of humility). David said, "The Lord is my shepherd." He considered himself a sheep.

Associations II

- Many of those who held on to Saul's regime after God rejected him experienced ruin, and some even died.

- Many of those who held on to David after God anointed him (even during the times he dwelt in the wilderness and the cave) experienced promotion and enlargement.

David's Own Comments About His Attitude

I will sing of mercy and judgment: unto thee, O Lord, will I sing. I will behave myself wisely in a perfect way. O when wilt thou come unto me? I will walk within my house with a perfect heart. I will set no wicked thing before mine eyes: I hate the work of them that turn aside; it shall not cleave to me. A froward heart shall depart from me: I will not know a wicked person. Whoso privily slandereth his neighbour, him will I cut off: him that hath an high look and a proud heart will not I suffer. Mine eyes shall be upon the faithful of the land, that they may dwell with me: he that walketh in a perfect way, he shall serve me. He that worketh deceit shall not dwell within my house: he that telleth lies shall not tarry in my sight. I will early destroy all the wicked of the land; that I may cut off all wicked doers from the city of the Lord.

—Psalm 101:1–8

Lord, my heart is not haughty, nor mine eyes lofty: neither do I exercise myself in great matters, or in things too high for me. Surely I have behaved and quieted myself, as a child that is weaned of his mother; my soul is even as a weaned child. Let Israel hope in the Lord from henceforth and for ever.

—Psalm 131:1–3

These values that David writes of in Psalms 101 and 131 must be values that he had within him early, long before he became king. (How could a king not, at least sometimes, exercise himself in "great matters"?) These are attitudes that reflect God's own heart.

The Winning Combination for Leaders: Integrity and Skill

He chose David also his servant, and took him from the sheepfolds: From following the ewes great with young he brought him to feed Jacob his people, and Israel his inheritance. So he fed them according to the integrity of his heart; and guided them by the skillfulness of his hands.

—Psalm 78:70–72

David was raised up by God to lead as king. But before he led as king, he led as a servant of the king. God developed him—in his heart and in his hands. Heart development for leaders is called integrity. Hand development for leaders is called skill. God's leaders are characterized by both, but true kingdom leaders understand that the latter is driven by the former, that "faith worketh by love," and that gifts are undergirded by character.

Character is the core of our entire discussion. However, here we examine a few of the skills or practices that must be based in the integrity of the leader.

Practical Yet Valuable Skills for Leaders

Appearance

> Now he was ruddy, and withal of a beautiful countenance, and goodly to look to.
>
> —1 SAMUEL 16:12

> Behold I have seen a son of Jesse the Behtlehemite, that is…a comely person, and the Lord is with him.
>
> —1 SAMUEL 16:18

> And when the Philistine looked about, and saw David, he disdained him: for he was but a youth, and ruddy, and of a fair countenance.
>
> —1 SAMUEL 17:42

As "unspiritual" as appearance might seem, it determines, at least in part, the first and lasting impression of oneself. These details regarding David are obviously significant because they are repeated. They are significant in today's leader as well.

Groom yourself in such a way that people enjoy being near you and are not repulsed by things such as foul body odor, obtrusive dandruff, and bad breath. A leader should always be clean, physically and hygienically. A leader should dress in clean and neat attire. Personalities and tastes in clothing vary widely; however, one should observe at least the same level of discretion concerning clothing as a leader in the body of Christ as do leaders in secular positions. If you notice, the manager of a store, the supervisor of a business, the representatives of an insurance agency—all of these people tend to dress a little above average. Of course this would depend in part on the nature of the business or of the activity at hand. However, even in settings typically associated with grime and dirt, such as auto repair shops, the leader dresses above average. Also, the "higher-classed" the auto repair shop is, the more neatly everyone is dressed, regardless of rank. Generally, dressing at least a little above average, with an inclination more toward the conservative than the flashy, is a rule of thumb that will work in most settings.

Come As You Are? Not for Leaders

It is often said in church circles that God said, "Come as you are." There is no such Scripture. (Could they be thinking instead of the beloved hymn, "Just as I Am"?) Nevertheless, the principle of the seeker coming to Jesus without trying to make himself or herself acceptable (since none of us can make ourselves acceptable) is biblical.

However, once one has come to Jesus and desires to be a servant of Jesus for others, he should desire to represent Jesus—and not misrepresent Him— even in his attire. A leader should be touchable, but he or she does not have to be tacky.

Demonstrating Concern For, and Affirmation Of, Others

> And Jesse said unto David his son, Take now for thy brethren an ephah of this parched corn, and these ten loaves, and run to the camp of thy brethren…and look how thy brethren fare, and take their pledge.…And David rose up early in the morning, and left the sheep with a keeper, and took, and went, as Jesse had commanded him; and he came to the trench, as the host was going forth to the fight, and shouted for the battle.…And David left his carriage in the hand of the keeper of the carriage, and ran into the army, and came and saluted his brethren. And as he talked with them.
>
> —1 SAMUEL 17:17

Make it a habit to greet and show genuine care and concern to all, particularly those who are younger in the Lord than you are. A firm (but not too hard) handshake, accompanied by a smile, is a good start. Hugs are also effective, but one has to be careful with these, for everyone is not comfortable with close touching, particularly when it involves male/ female contact. Remember that everyone's culture and background are not always the same as yours. When hugging a person of the other gender, a looser hug—with contact around the shoulders but bodies apart—is usually comfortable for both parties and any onlookers. The key is to be courteous and caring in attitude and in actions.

Also, learn the names of the people and address them by name. This is a means of validating people as important.

Further Interpersonal Communication

Practice body language that suggests to a person, "You have my attention. You are important. You deserve to be listened to." Eye contact, not slumping or doodling when someone is speaking—all of these affirm the speaker's right to be heard, even if what he or she says is not right. Cultural norms that mean "you and what you have to say are important" should be studied and implemented.

Repeat and or rephrase to the person what he or she has said, demonstrating that you are listening to him or her and giving the opportunity for the person to state whether what you heard is what he or she meant.

Optimism: A "Can-Do/Will-Do" Attitude

> And David spake to the men that stood by him, saying, What shall be done to the man that killeth this Philistine, and taketh away the reproach from Israel? for who is this uncircumcised Philistine, that he should defy the armies of the living God? And the people answered him after this manner, saying, So shall it be done to the man that killeth him.... And he turned from him toward another, and spake after the same manner: and the people answered him again after the former manner. And when the words were heard which David spake, they rehearsed them before Saul: and he sent for him. And David said to Saul, Let no man's heart fail because of him; thy servant will go and fight with this Philistine.
>
> —1 SAMUEL 17:26, 27, 30–32

When David becomes aware that there is a challenge to his brothers, his nation, his king, and his God, he gets fired up! He sees the challenge as an opportunity to comfort the hearts of his brothers. He is mindful of the reward that has been promised by the king, but it is evident that his passion is based upon his displeasure at the insolence of Goliath and the clear distress of the armies of Israel. He says, "I can, and I will, solve this problem." He does not spend a great deal of time with his detractors—even his oldest brother. He focuses on the issue and takes the necessary steps to get in position to handle Goliath for Saul and for Israel.

The secondary leader is proactive, not reactionary. He or she is up for a challenge when it arises, even before it arises, if possible, and definitely before it takes its full toll on the group. There are no excuses and no limitations. The leader says, "By the grace of God, I can handle this—not for my glory, but to bring and restore honor to the name of the Lord." The secondary leader helps to motivate the entire group to get back on task, to see themselves as champions, and to finish their mission. David does this—and so must we.

> And David put his hand in his bag, and took thence a stone, and slang it, and smote the Philistine in his forehead, that the stone sunk into his forehead; and he fell upon his face to the earth.... Therefore David ran, and stood upon the Philistine, and took his sword, and drew it out of the sheath thereof, and slew him, and cut off his head therewith. And when the Philistines saw their champion was dead, they fled. And the men of Israel and of Judah arose, and shouted, and pursued the Philistines, until thou come to the valley, and to the gates of Ekron. And the wounded of the Philistines fell down by the way to Shaaraim, even unto Gath, and unto Ekron. And the children of Israel returned from chasing after the Philistines, and they spoiled their tents.
>
> —1 SAMUEL 17:49, 53

Chapter 5

THE TEACHINGS OF PAUL AND THE EXAMPLE OF TIMOTHY

Thou therefore, my son be strong in the grace that is in Christ Jesus. And the things that thou hast heard of me among many witness, the same commit thou to faithful men, who shall be able to teach others also.

—2 TIMOTHY 2:1–2

Faithfulness

True biblical faithfulness includes loyalty and credibility.

- Loyalty: the leader believes in the cause.

- Credibility: the leader can be believed in for the cause.

Moreover it is required in stewards, that a man be found faithful.

—1 TIMOTHY 4:2

Most men will proclaim every one his own goodness: but a faithful man who can find?

—PROVERBS 20:6

Faithfulness I: Loyalty

Why should senior leaders endorse or promote secondary leaders who are not loyal?

The secular world (all of whose righteous principles come from God) does not.

Business leaders don't do it. No business leader sanctions those who go out and badmouth the company or sell its success secrets to the highest bidder. Armies court-martial or even execute the disloyal.

God does not.

He states that He honors those who honor Him, and that those who do not will be lightly esteemed. (See 1 Samuel 2:30.) Furthermore, through the parables of the pounds and of the talents, Jesus makes it clear that the Master will only honor those who have been true and diligent in the Father's business.

The church should not.

Why should the body of Christ in general—and senior leaders in particular—ordain, license, or otherwise legitimize those who are not loyal to the Word of God and God's mandate upon a particular ministry?

Loyalty to Whom?

Loyalty to God

This is the most important loyalty of all, and it is expected of all, before anything else dealt with in this volume. Indeed, it is the overarching, underlying theme of this entire study: if one is not loyal to God, all the rest is pointless anyway. With all of the leader's heart, soul, and strength, he or she should love God, putting Him first and above all things. Loyalty to God in this study is the consummate foregone conclusion.

Loyalty to the Family

The Bible states that the key credentials of a bishop (one type of church leader) include his family relationships. Though all leaders are not bishops, the principles behind the qualifications are universally applicable to leaders.

> A bishop then must be blameless, the husband of one wife, vigilant, sober, of good behaviour, given to hospitality, apt to teach; Not given to wine, no striker, not greedy of filthy lucre; but patient, not a brawler, not covetous; One that ruleth well his own house, having his children in subjection with all gravity; (For if a man know not how to rule his own house, how shall he take care of the church of God?) Not a novice, lest being lifted up with pride he fall into the condemnation of the devil.
> —1 TIMOTHY 3:2–6

The Bible word translated *bishop* is *episkopos*, and it means "overseer." Although today the term *bishop* is applied to a minister who presides over a diocese (a district or group of churches and/or ministers), in biblical times, the term was not so strictly applied. Consequently, the term as used in 1 Timothy could apply to a presiding minister or to the heard of an auxiliary, such as the Sunday school superintendent or the usher board president.

In any case, the underlying idea is that if one is going to exercise any authority or leadership in the church, the qualifications, of necessity, include having a right relationship with his family. The husband is to rule the house and love his wife as Christ loved the church; but the wife is told to guide the house and to submit to her husband as the church should to Christ. Dependent-aged children are told to obey, and parents are told to be firm but loving, not provoking children to wrath. Elderly persons are told to model Christian maturity and purity, providing mentoring to the younger ones. Adult children are told to be prepared to repay their parents for having brought them up.

Get It Together at Home First

Anyone who does not have it together at home has to question not so much whether he or she is called but whether he or she is ready to answer the call—it will be difficult to serve outside the home with so much "inside ministry" left undone.

Now, one cannot control the attitudes of adults in one's home. Sometimes there is open hostility to the gospel in homes. As long as the Christian knows that he or she is doing all that is required of him or her by God, even when opposed or persecuted, this does not disqualify him or her from ministry. Cases have been documented in which Christian youth have been oppressed by God-hating parents. Christian husbands or wives may have family members whose only complaint with them is the fact that they love Jesus Christ. The Christian, in those instances, must be as loving, devoted, and understanding as possible—but he or she can never deny the faith.

On the other hand, one of the greatest testimonies to the authenticity of a person's Christian walk comes when someone in his or her own household is the one testifying. That family member, who may not necessarily share the Christian relative's convictions, will still admit that the Christian is serious about his or her "fanaticism" and will often vehemently defend the Christian from other unbelievers (and even from other "Christians").

Loyalty to the Senior Leader

Today, the term *armor-bearer* in church circles is used frequently (and sometimes disparagingly) to denote personal assistants to pastors and other ministry leaders. They may provide services for their leaders which free the leader to focus on their priorities in ministry. Armor-bearers may be seen driving, yet they are more than personal chauffers. They may carry the pastor's Bible or attaché case, but they are not bagboys.

It is not primarily the physical functions that they carry out that makes them armor-bearers. The believer's warfare is not primarily physical; the armor is not physical; the weapons are not natural; and therefore the essence of armor-bearing is not natural. The armor bearer's main function is to assist and protect his or her leader in the battle, and the battle is spiritual. The armor bearer must be of one heart and one soul, in sync with his leader. He is to be engaged in the spiritual conflict, protecting the protector.

> And Jonathan said to the young man that bare his armour, Come, and let us go over unto the garrison of these uncircumcised: it may be that the LORD will work for us: for there is no restraint to the LORD to save by many or by few. And his armourbearer said unto him, Do all that is in thine heart: turn thee; behold, I am with thee according to thy heart. Then said Jonathan, Behold, we will pass over unto these men, and we will discover ourselves unto them. If they say thus unto us, Tarry until we come to you; then we will stand still in our place, and will not go up unto them. But if they say thus, Come up unto us; then we will go up: for the LORD hath delivered them into our hand: and this shall be a sign unto us. And both of them discovered themselves unto the garrison of the Philistines: and the Philistines said, Behold, the Hebrews come forth out of the holes where they had hid themselves. And the men of the garrison answered Jonathan and his armourbearer, and said, Come up to us, and we will shew you a thing. And Jonathan said unto his armourbearer, Come up after me: for the LORD hath delivered them into the hand of Israel. And Jonathan climbed up upon his hands and upon his feet, and his armourbearer after him: and they fell before Jonathan; and his armourbearer slew after him. And that first slaughter, which Jonathan and his armourbearer made, was about twenty men, within as it were an half acre of land, which a yoke of oxen might plow.
>
> —1 SAMUEL 14:6–14

Jonathan, the crown prince and son of King Saul, was a courageous young leader, filled with passion and courage. Accompanying him was his armor bearer, and when he indicated that he was going on the offensive against the enemy, contingent upon God's approval, his armor-bearer came into full agreement with him. He stated to Jonathan that he was with him in carrying out all that was in his heart. Once Jonathan received the sign from God, he climbed up to the plateau where the battle would take place on his hands and feet, with his armor-bearer right behind him. When the fight began, Jonathan went forward slaying the enemies, and his armor-bearer came behind him. Based on some ancient battle depictions, there is reason to believe that they fought back to back, and God granted them victory.

What needs to be highlighted is that when Jonathan declared his zeal for God, he had someone with him who bought into the vision, not a wet-blanket spirit who spouted negativity out of fear for his own security. Moreover, while Jonathan was fighting for the nation, the armor-bearer was fighting for Jonathan. Jonathan was fighting to preserve Saul's nation; the armor-bearer was fighting to protect Saul's son. This is the true ministry of the spiritual armor-bearer: while the senior leader is ministering in his or her particular area of gifting or anointing, leading the masses to salvation and liberation, there needs to be someone on the scene to support that senior leader, to minimize distractions, and to intercede, keeping him or her covered in prayer. There needs to be someone present with him or her after the battle, a particularly vulnerable time. Every warrior needs a warrior.

> Moreover the Philistines had yet war again with Israel; and David went down, and his servants with him, and fought against the Philistines: and David waxed faint. And Ishbibenob, which was of the sons of the giant...thought to have slain David. But Abishai the son of Zeruiah succoured him, and smote the Philistine, and killed him. Then the men of David sware unto him, saying, Thou shalt go no more out with us to battle, that thou quench not the light of Israel.
>
> —2 SAMUEL 21:15–17

In this instance, David is still leading by example. However, he is now king and an aging monarch. He grows weak in battle and is almost killed by a son of the giant. (Could it have been Goliath's boy?) He is rescued by one of his men, yet another example of loyalty. Abishai and all the men of David determine that he will not go back to battle. He will still direct the warfare, but he will no longer engage in hand-to-hand combat. This is not because of his personal value—it is because of his strategic worth to the kingdom and the strategic worth of his downfall to the enemy. The team wisely decides to demand:

> Let this leader be relieved of what someone else can do,
> so that he may be fully engaged in what no one else can do,
> for the benefit of everyone.

Finally, the loyal warrior spirit of the armor-bearer is not just for that individual called to stand directly at the side of the senior leader. Every leader in the church house, the business, or the organization, regardless of the job title, should have the same conviction: that in order for the God-mandated vision to be perpetuated, the God-ordained visionary must be preserved—until God determines that the visionary (in physical presence) is no longer necessary.

To One's Local Church and Assignment

> And let us consider one another to provoke unto love and to good works: Not forsaking the assembling of ourselves together, as the manner of some is; but exhorting one another: and so much the more, as ye see the day approaching.
>
> —Hebrews 10:24–25

Even the Lord Jesus Christ made it customary to attend the synagogue, the house of worship where believers would gather on the Lord's Day. (See Luke 4:16.) He was so fiercely loyal to the preservation of reverence in the temple of God that He literally took a whip, overturned tables, and drove money changers and animal sellers out of it on more than one occasion. (See John 2:13–17 and Matthew 20:12–14.) One cannot be loyal to that of which he is not protective. A leader who believes that the community of believers is a priceless resource in the growth and maintenance of a child of God will strive to protect its atmosphere of holiness, love, power, and unity. A leader will be sensitive to remain loyal to that community, with a determination to nurture and defend it from all satanic assault.

LORD, I have loved the habitation of thy house, and the place where thine honour dwelleth.

—PSALM 26:8

One thing have I desired of the LORD, that will I seek after; that I may dwell in the house of the LORD all the days of my life, to behold the beauty of the LORD, and to enquire in his temple.

— PSALM 27:4

Pauline Examples of Faithfulness Among Secondary Leaders

All my state shall Tychicus declare unto you, who is a beloved brother, and a faithful minister and fellowservant in the Lord: whom I have sent unto you for the same purpose, that he might know your estate, and comfort your hearts; with Onesimus, a faithful and beloved brother, who is one of you. They shall make known unto you all things which are done here. Aristarchus my fellowprisoner saluteth you, and Marcus, sister's son to Barnabas, (touching whom ye received commandments: if he come unto you, receive him;) and Jesus, which is called Justus, who are of the circumcision. These only are my fellowworkers unto the kingdom of God, which have been a comfort unto me. Epaphras, who is one of you, a servant of Christ, saluteth you, always labouring fervently for you in prayers, that ye may stand perfect and complete in all the will of God.

—COLOSSIANS 4:7–12

In the Scripture cited above, Paul names several of his secondary leaders who share, along with him, concern for the work of God, including the church in Colosse. He refers to them using terms such as "faithful," "fellowprisoner," "fellowworkers," "comfort," and "always laboring fervently." This represents the spirit of New Testament loyalty to God, to senior leaders, and to one's local body of believers—a spirit so powerful that it propelled a small Jewish sect into the mainstream of the Roman Empire and transformed the whole civilized world.

A Pauline Example of Unfaithfulness in a Secondary Leader

Demas

> Luke, the beloved physician, and Demas, greet you.
> —COLOSSIANS 4:14

> Marcus, Aristarchus, Demas, Lucas, my fellowlabourers.
> —PHILEMON 1:24

Demas, whose name means "people," or "popular," was an associate of Paul mentioned in three of the epistles. Clearly, he was a young man who was dear to Paul's heart and who shared the kind of proximity to the apostle that Luke, the writer of the Gospel, had. He would have experienced many of the adventures of which Luke writes, with Paul. Could he have been with Paul on the shipwreck of Acts 27? It is very possible. Paul refers to him as a fellow laborer, which may mean that he actually ministered the Word and the Spirit of God, alongside Paul or on missions separate from the apostle as well.

What could happen to an individual who has had such opportunities to persuade him to give up on his divine destiny? Even late in Paul's life, Demas was his associate, for Paul referred to himself as "Paul the aged" in Philemon 1:9, the same epistle where Demas is called a fellow laborer. What changed Demas' heart? Whatever it was, it was so piercing that the aging apostle would have to lament as he writes in his death letter to Timothy these sad words:

> Do thy diligence to come shortly unto me: For Demas hath forsaken me, having loved this present world, and is departed unto Thessalonica.
> —2 TIMOTHY 4:9–10

Forsaken Paul?

It is vital that all leaders continually examine their hearts. In all likelihood, by the time Demas left Paul physically, he had already left God spiritually. How grievous it is to consider that there are those who are still serving in the trenches of ministry, still going through the motions of worship, but their hearts have departed from God and from their assignment. It has to have been so with the first secondary leader who defected, Lucifer, for in order for him to subvert so many of the angelic host, there had to have been a period where he was still serving as "the anointed cherub that covereth" before the throne of God, but secretly he was plotting against the throne and its Occupant. Oh, the tragedy of treachery!

Demas may not have consciously sought to overthrow or harm Paul in any way, but he did harm him. In fact, Paul took his apostasy personally, saying, "Demas hath forsaken me." A leader must know that his or her decision to give up on their God-given calling will have deathly painful effects, and most often the ones affected the most are those that the "Demases" would desire to hurt the least. It was probably not that Demas loved Paul (or God) less, but that he had come to love "this present world" more.

And, by the way, for all the Paul-figures reading this: it will probably be less painful and less detrimental if you avoid taking people's actions against or for God personally. When you are giving leadership your best and the people that you lead are walking in accordance with Scripture, you should not interpret that as your personal success. Give God the glory. And when you are giving leadership your best and people behave contrary to the things of God, you should not interpret that as your personal failure or God's. Give God the glory. They are God's people, not mine and not yours. Christ already died to save them—do not kill yourself.

Faithfulness II: Credibility

Have Faith in a Human Being?

Is it biblical to assert that people should be able to have faith in their leaders? Yes, but is not the same faith one has in God. Rather, it is respect, confidence, and honor based upon character and proven integrity.

A Problem With Trusting Humans?

> Thus saith the LORD; Cursed [be] the man that trusteth in man, and maketh flesh his arm, and whose heart departeth from the LORD.
>
> —JEREMIAH 17:5

> Some trust in chariots, and some in horses: but we will remember the name of the LORD our God.
>
> —PSALM 20:7

There are those who say, as though quoting Scripture, "Put your faith (or trust) in no man." What the Scriptures teach against is misplaced faith, meaning putting absolute faith in a human (or something else) as one's source, instead of relying upon God. This fully coheres with what is being taught in this lesson—having a human being in God's place is both idolatry and idiocy.

> Confidence in an unfaithful man in time of trouble [is like] a broken tooth, and a foot out of joint.
>
> —PROVERBS 25:19

The quote above illustrates this lesson's emphasis: the problem is the unfaithfulness of some human beings, not that no humans are trustworthy. Paul instructs Timothy in the foundational text for this chapter, 2 Timothy 2:2, to commit his message to "faithful men," people who are loyal and thus credible. Moreover, the Scripture does teach a proper kind of trust in leaders, predicated upon foundational trust in God.

> Believe in the Lord your God, so shall ye be established; believe His prophets, so shall ye prosper.
>
> —2 CHRONICLES 20:20

> It states that we should give "honor to whom honor" is due.
>
> —ROMANS 13:7

> Ye are the light of the world. A city set on an hill cannot be hid.
>
> —MATTHEW 5:14

> Let your light so shine before men, that they may see your good works, and glorify your Father which is in heaven.
>
> —MATTHEW 5:16

> Be ye followers of me, even as I also am of Christ.
>
> —1 CORINTHIANS 11:1

> And ye became followers of us, and of the Lord, having received the word in much affliction, with joy of the Holy Ghost.
>
> —1 THESSALONIANS 1:6

So it is important to have, and to be able to have, the right kind of respect for human beings, not just for God. We must give to God what belongs to God and not to man. However, there is absolutely nothing unscriptural about respecting a man or a woman in his or her place under God. There are different kinds of glory.

> There are also celestial bodies, and bodies terrestrial: but the glory of the celestial is one, and the glory of the terrestrial is another. There is one glory of the sun, and another glory of the moon, and another glory of the stars: for one star differeth from another star in glory.
> —1 CORINTHIANS 15:40–41

We are to give God His honor and give people their honor. God is a jealous God, but He is not envious. He has no problem with others receiving glory—He actually gives others glory—He just forbids them tampering with His glory. Furthermore, mature believers understand that, directly or indirectly, ultimately all glory proceeds from God and belongs to Him, because all good things come from Him.

Leaders Must Walk Worthy

As a man or woman of God, His secondary leader in the kingdom, it is crucial that a person be able to safely trust the integrity of a leader's walk with God and the character of his or her walk with men. Scripture teaches us to walk worthy of God's calling, to walk in a manner deserving of the Lord who chose us. The believer is commanded to keep himself "unspotted from the world." One of the things desperately lacking in this day is leaders that can be respected by those expected to follow them.

"Ordain Elders"—Not "Ordain Them *to Be* Elders"

The senior leader's endorsement of a secondary leader should confirm what the people already have in their hearts about him or her because of that secondary leader's proven integrity and competence. Paul instructed Titus to "ordain elders." He did not tell Titus to ordain anyone "*to be* elders."

It is unfortunate that some people equate gilded certificates and ornate vestments with proof and promotion in ministry. These things may be symbols of progress in ministerial effectiveness, but in themselves they do not prove anything about the person who receives them. In natural life and in ministry, "the certificate follows the birth"—not the other way around. No mother receives a pregnancy certificate. It is after the child has come forth that a certificate of live birth is presented. Even so, the ordination (or other) certificate "follows the birth" of mature behavior, of service, of loyalty; it doesn't produce it. If the secondary leader is not a leader before he is given a certificate, he is not a leader even after a certificate is in his hand or in a frame on his wall. The license is given to him or her because of who he or she already is, not to make him or her what he or she is not.

Interestingly, the certificate is often referred to as a "credential," a letter designed to render its holder "cred"-ible, or believeable, relative to his office. Jesus said to His contemporaries that they should believe on Him based upon His works—not a piece of paper. He taught that by the fruit of one's life and ministry, one will be authenticated or repudiated as a believer in Christ.

> If I do not the works of my Father, believe me not. But if I do, though ye believe not me, believe the works: that ye may know, and believe, that the Father is in me, and I in him.
> —JOHN 10:37–38

> Beware of false prophets, which come to you in sheep's clothing, but inwardly they are ravening wolves. Ye shall know them by their fruits. Do men gather grapes of thorns, or figs of thistles? Even so every good tree bringeth forth good fruit; but a corrupt tree bringeth forth evil fruit. A good tree cannot bring forth evil fruit, neither can a corrupt tree bring forth good fruit. Every tree that bringeth not forth good fruit is hewn down, and cast into the fire. Wherefore by their fruits ye shall know them.
> — MATTHEW 7:15–20

Leader Types Who Will Lack Credibility

The Joker (Non-Serious/Irreverent/Disrespectful)
Humor is a gift from God:

> A merry heart maketh a cheerful countenance: but by sorrow of the heart the spirit is broken.
> —PROVERBS 15:13

> A merry heart doeth good [like] a medicine: but a broken spirit drieth the bones.
>
> —PROVERBS 17:22

James says there are good gifts and perfect gifts from God. When the good gift of humor is perfected, or developed into wholesomeness, it is most appropriate and beneficial. It is a wonderful, powerful teaching tool, a healing balm, and a universal means of fellowship and getting along with others. However, the Bible teaches avoidance of corrupt communication, foolish talking, and jesting. These include the spirit of irreverence and disrespect:

> Let no corrupt communication proceed out of your mouth, but that which is good to the use of edifying, that it may minister grace unto the hearers.
>
> —EPHESIANS 4:29

> Be ye therefore followers of God, as dear children.... But fornication, and all uncleanness, or covetousness, let it not be once named among you, as becometh saints; Neither filthiness, nor foolish talking, nor jesting, which are not convenient: but rather giving of thanks.
>
> —EPHESIANS 5:1, 3, 4

The Clique Member

> Now I beseech you, brethren, by the name of our Lord Jesus Christ, that ye all speak the same thing, and that there be no divisions among you; but that ye be perfectly joined together in the same mind and in the same judgment. For it hath been declared unto me of you, my brethren, by them which are of the house of Chloe, that there are contentions among you. Now this I say, that every one of you saith, I am of Paul; and I of Apollos; and I of Cephas; and I of Christ.
>
> —1 CORINTHIANS 1:10–12

> For first of all, when ye come together in the church, I hear that there be divisions among you: and I partly believe it.
>
> —1 CORINTHIANS 11:18

The opening of the book of 1 Corinthians is based upon Paul's need to address a spirit of division in the church. The most detrimental thing in a local church is the spirit of division based upon malice and envy. One of the eight things that are detestable to the Lord, according to the writer of Proverbs is "he that soweth discord among brethren" (Prov. 6:19).

How can the secondary leader be of benefit to the whole ministry and to his or her senior leader while simultaneously pitting one part of the body against the other?

> Let nothing be done through strife or vainglory; but in lowliness of mind, let each esteem other better than themselves.
>
> —PHILIPPIANS 2:3

> For where envying and strife is, there is confusion and every evil work.
>
> —JAMES 4:12

The Liar/Covenant Breaker

The word of a leader should be dependable. And if he or she enters into an agreement or covenant, that contract—whether written or spoken, explicit or implicit in expected duties—should not be violated. The Bible has much to say about God's unfavorable view of liars:

> Wherefore putting away lying, speak every man truth with his neighbor, for we are members one of another.
>
> —EPHESIANS 4:25

> LORD, who shall abide in thy tabernacle? Who shall dwell in thy holy hill? He that walketh uprightly...and speaketh the truth in his heart. He that backbiteth not with his tongue, nor doeth evil to his neighbor, nor taketh up a reproach against his neighbor...He that sweareth to his own hurt, and changeth not. He that doeth these things shall never be moved.
>
> —PSALM 15:1–3, 4, 5

> All liars, shall have their part in the lake which burneth with fire and brimstone: which is the second death.
>
> —REVELATION 21:8

Those Who Know Not God (Irreverent/Covetous/Violent/Sexually Impure)

All of these anti-leadership traits are depicted in the lives of two scriptural secondary leaders, Hophni and Phineas, priests themselves and sons of the high priest, Eli. They and their assistants are some of the worst examples of secondary leaders with no loyalty to God, their senior leader, or the assembly of the saints. Therefore, these priests eroded their own credibility and that of the house of God:

> Now the sons of Eli were sons of Belial; they knew not the LORD. And the priest's custom with the people was, that, when any man offered sacrifice, the priest's servant came, while the flesh was in seething, with a fleshhook of three teeth in his hand; And he struck it into the pan, or kettle, or caldron, or pot; all that the fleshhook brought up the priest took for himself. So they did in Shiloh unto all the Israelites that came thither. Also before they burnt the fat, the priest's servant came, and said to the man that sacrificed, Give flesh to roast for the priest; for he will not have sodden flesh of thee, but raw. And if any man said unto him, Let them not fail to burn the fat presently, and then take as much as thy soul desireth; then he would answer him, Nay; but thou shalt give it me now: and if not, I will take it by force. Wherefore the sin of the young men was very great before the LORD: for men abhorred the offering of the LORD....Now Eli was very old, and heard all that his sons did unto all Israel; and how they lay with the women that assembled at the door of the tabernacle of the congregation. And he said unto them, Why do ye such things? for I hear of your evil dealings by all this people. Nay, my sons; for it is no good report that I hear: ye make the LORD's people to transgress. If one man sin against another, the judge shall judge him: but if a man sin against the LORD, who shall intreat for him? Notwithstanding they hearkened not unto the voice of their father, because the LORD would slay them.
>
> —1 SAMUEL 2:12–17, 22–25

The Biggest Problem of All

The first problem was the biggest one: "They knew not the Lord." No one is going to be able to successfully serve in kingdom ministry without having the heart of the King. How can godly character and conduct be expected of those who know not God?

The Irreverent, the Covetous, and the Violent

How could these priests and their servants set up a situation in which the worship of God could degenerate into a fight, at the least a tug-of-war over the meat used in sacrifice? God cannot be glorified in a context in which there is strife, and if strife is tolerated it is only because the agenda of people is considered more important than that of God. Many are the stories of arguments and battles in board meetings and even in the sanctuary, almost always initiated by people in leadership, people whose offices and titles suggest that they know God.

Moreover, the stereotype (sometimes accurate, most times not) that "all that preacher wants is my money!" is fed by attitudes like those of these Levites. Instead of waiting for the portion that was provided for their upkeep, they brashly demanded more. And as a consequence of such irreverence, "Men abhorred the offering of the Lord," meaning people associated the worship of God with the people who facilitated worship—negatively. The statement usually goes like this: "If they can do that and get to heaven, I know I'm going to heaven." Or, "If that is salvation, I don't want it." Or, "That's why I don't go to church—they're all a bunch of hypocrites." Those statements are too often made because of the misbehavior of leaders.

> Let all bitterness, and wrath, and anger, and clamor, and evil speaking, be put away from you, with all malice: and be ye kind one to another, tenderhearted, forgiving one another, even as God for Christ's sake hath forgiven you.
>
> —EPHESIANS 4:31–32

The Sexually Impure

The irreverence manifested in three ways: the first was in covetousness, then in violence, and finally in sexual permissiveness. The height of disrespect for their office as priests was the misuse of their position for sexual gratification. Any time a sexual encounter occurs between a leader and a non-authority figure, in an arrangement made possible by that leader's seniority, jurisdiction, prestige, or sense of prerogative, the leader is responsible. Even if the suggestion comes from the other party, the person with greater authority has the greater responsibility. And for the priest, the one who is to teach the flock the ways of God, not only to violate his teachings but to do it with those who look to him, this is flagrant desecration of the holy office.

> Know ye not that the unrighteous shall not inherit the kingdom of God? Be not deceived: neither fornicators, nor idolaters, nor adulterers, nor effeminate, nor abusers of themselves with mankind...shall inherit the kingdom of God.
>
> —1 CORINTHIANS 6:9, 10

Judgment

> Notwithstanding they hearkened not unto the voice of their father, because the LORD would slay them.
>
> —1 SAMUEL 2:25

The Lord did judge them. They died ignominiously, the ark of God was taken, their father Eli the high priest died, the people of God were defeated, and Phineas's wife died after having given birth to a son upon whom she refused even to look. Dying, she named the child Ichabod because of her bitter acknowledgement that the glory had departed from Israel. Death, humiliation, bitterness: this is the legacy of leaders who "know not the Lord."

A Secondary Leader Who Lost Credibility but Regained It

Mark

> And some days after Paul said unto Barnabas, Let us go again and visit our brethren in every city where we have preached the word of the LORD, and see how they do. And Barnabas determined to take with them John, whose surname was Mark. But Paul thought not good to take him with them, who departed from them from Pamphylia, and went not with them to the work. And the contention was so sharp between them, that they departed asunder one from the other: and so Barnabas took Mark, and sailed unto Cyprus; and Paul chose Silas, and departed, being recommended by the brethren unto the grace of God.
>
> —ACTS 15:36–40

Mark, having demonstrated instability in a previous mission, was considered disqualified by Paul for the next assignment. (See Acts 15:36–40.) Barnabas saw things differently—and this difference led to him and Paul actually parting company, but he held on to Mark. By the end of Paul's life, his view of Mark had changed; Paul says that Mark is "profitable to me for the ministry" (2 Tim. 4:11). Mark becomes profitable to the entire kingdom of God eventually: he writes the Gospel that bears his name. He lost his place of credibility, but by God's mercy he regained it, forever.

John Mark was the son of a woman who became a follower of Jesus Christ. She appears to have been a woman of means, for her home was large enough to house early meetings of the church at Jerusalem. Mark is depicted in church tradition as having been a very young man, even a boy, during the ministry of Jesus. It is thought by some that he was the young man who was present during the arrest of Jesus who was nearly apprehended but escaped by running out of his outer garments. (See 2 Timothy 4:11.)

Leader Types Who Will Retain and Gain Credibility

The Visible

A great contribution of a credible leader is visibility. Some leaders have referred to it as the "ministry of presence." No machine functions well with missing parts. A body does not function well when any of its organs are missing. A ministry needs its leaders visibly showing commitment to its vision.

Visible is a relative term because some roles demand that the person in that role operate behind the scenes. Nevertheless, whatever one's function, he or she should be obviously there, wherever "there" is. When the apostles are chosen, their first function is to "be with Him", Mark 3:14. When the Lord Jesus was dying on the cross, only one of His secondary leaders was present: the apostle John. Although there was nothing John could do to physically relieve Christ's suffering, because he was visible, he was able to alleviate concerns that Jesus had for the care of His mother as her firstborn Son. John's ministry of presence provided a measure of comfort for the dying Son of God.

In the last days of Paul's life, he writes to Timothy about those who have forsaken him and those who may be on various missions. He says, "only Luke is with me" (2 Tim. 4:9–10), and he asks Timothy to come to him soon—not to attempt to get him out of the prison, but to be there with him.

Visibility—presence—becomes an example for those who are up-and-coming leaders. Discipling is not only done by words. It is done by modeling proper Christian conduct to the newer disciples. It encourages the senior leader, and the entire body of believers, to be able to visually perceive the engagement of fellow believers, particularly secondary leaders.

The Rapport Builder

There are always truths that are best communicated between peers. The teacher may give eloquent discourses, but students teach other students best.

The illustration is given that, while attempting to teach "long" addition, the teacher in a country school could not get her little student to understand "carrying" certain digits in an equation. She kept insisting, to no avail, that the little boy "carry" his numbers. Finally, another little student, wise beyond his years said, "Aw, just tote it over there!" And the first little boy got it! The teacher was saying all the right things, but the second little country boy made "carry" relevant to the first little boy when he used the word "tote," which is an old Southern synonym for "carry."

Likewise, in the congregation, sometimes that which the parishioner does not grasp in a sermon or in an administrative policy or procedure can be clarified by a brother or sister in secondary leadership. Sometimes these questions do not make it to the pastor. Sometimes a new parishioner may not feel comfortable addressing the pastor, but rapport has been built with another brother or sister who has been in the congregation longer. This should not incline a brother or sister to seize prerogatives that are not his or hers. Rather, it enables the secondary leader to support what is going on "at the front" from "behind."

There have been those new disciples hurt by older (in tenure) church members who considered leaving a ministry. But because secondary leaders were watchful, they were able to intervene and encourage the new brother or sister to hold on. They have encouraged the newcomer not to judge the entire ministry by one person who behaved or spoke in a non-Christlike manner.

When Jesus spoke of going back to Judea upon the death of Lazarus, He knew that Judea was a difficult place; a death threat hung over His life there. Yet He said to His disciples that He and they should go to Judea. It was Thomas who spoke up and said that the apostles and disciples should go with Him. Thomas, a fellow secondary leader, encouraged the others, albeit pessimistically, to obey and accompany Jesus.

> Then said Thomas, which is called Didymus, unto his fellow disciples,
> Let us also go, that we may die with him.
>
> —JOHN 11:16

They all followed Jesus, even though they did not understand where following would lead them. And because He was doing what glorified God, they witnessed the greatest miracle of His ministry, the resurrection of

Lazarus, perhaps at least in part because a peer encouraged them to do what Jesus had told them to do.

Protecting the Credibility of Other Leaders

When Noah had become a husbandman and ended up intoxicated, one of his secondary leaders, his son Ham, mocked him. There are varying interpretations of what that mockery included. One thing that is certain, however, is that the other two sons, Shem and Japheth, put a garment on their backs and, walking backwards, covered the nakedness of Noah. (See Genesis 9:20–27.) As a result of Ham's improper behavior, a part of Ham's family— through Canaan—was cursed by Noah, and Shem and Japheth were blessed.

Cover Human Error, Not Rebellion

In the experience of all secondary leaders, the humanity of a senior leader, or of a fellow secondary leader, will surface. We must not deny the presence of a sinful lifestyle among leaders or attempt to rationalize it. We have already seen the damage that this can do. We must hold all human beings accountable to live righteously before God. Nevertheless, despite living right, all leaders are human and thus are capable of human error or frailty: the most anointed can seem afraid of a challenge, can seem angry about a problem, can be impatient regarding progress in an area of ministry, and may have personality flaws. These are aspects of the leader's being that everyone does not always see. God entrusts the humanity of a leader to other leaders who can see these things but who have the Christlike maturity not to be disrespectful of God's call upon that leader even when his human frailties show.

To Cover and to Confront

The Bible does not make it clear whether this was a first-time experience for Noah when he ended up drunk—was it by accident? It also does not state that the sons of Noah covered his drunkenness—they covered his nakedness, which apparently was exposed because he was drunk. They covered that which no one should see because everyone deserves to be treated with dignity, even when he or she has put himself in a compromised posture.

When Noah sobered up, somebody needed to confront him concerning his drinking. If he accidentally has gotten drunk, he needs to learn the power of fermented fruit juices. If he has developed a habit of drunkenness, he needs to acknowledge his addiction and get all the help God places at his disposal. To confront Noah is to cover him—from the potential damage to himself, his family, and his witness as a godly leader. This is a far more important "covering" than a cloth placed over his naked body! Don't let God's builder of the Ark that preserved all species of living things—including Shem, the progenitor of Messiah—die in disgrace! Don't let him bring shame to the name of his God!

The Right Kind of Covering

For the leader who becomes aware of a human frailty in another, rather than exploiting the flawed one, he or she should provide the right kind of covering: prayer and admonition or exhortation according to the leading of the Lord.

A word of caution: in dealing with one's superiors, a covenant peer or father of the leader with the flaw might need to be asked to intervene. In dealing with one's own peers, one should seek God for wisdom as to whether he or she needs to address anything himself or herself, or whether he or she should refer it to the fellow leader's superior. In any case, he or she should be sure to strictly follow the established protocol or code of ethics for that ministry or department.

However, breaking confidence, gossiping, and backbiting does nothing to resolve human issues and repair breaches. If it is not your place to speak, be silent. And when you must speak, speak to the person(s) by whom it will accomplish the most good, not the most damage. For example, why should you tell everyone in the church that Brother Strawberry, the church custodian, has a rude disposition—everyone, that is, except the pastor, who is Brother Strawberry's immediate supervisor? What does the choir director have to do with Strawberry, when Strawberry's role and that of the choir director's never converge or conflict?

When Confrontation Is Unavoidable

The best way for a secondary leader to confront a flaw in his senior leader, if it seems unavoidable, is to come humbly and with the senior leader's own principles or teachings. Notice that in the case of Naaman, his secondary leaders had to speak up to keep him from missing out on his healing:

And Elisha sent a messenger unto him, saying, Go and wash in Jordan
seven times, and thy flesh shall come again to thee, and thou shalt
be clean. But Naaman was wroth, and went away, and said, Behold,
I thought, He will surely come out to me, and stand, and call on the
name of the Lord his God, and strike his hand over the place, and
recover the leper. Are not Abana and Parpar, rivers of Damascus, better
than all the waters of Israel? May I not wash in them, and be clean? So
he turned and went away in a rage. And his servants came near and
spake unto him and said, My father, if the prophet had bid thee do
some great thing, woudest thou not have done it? How much rather
then, when he saith to thee, Wash and be clean? Then went he down,
and dipped himself seven times in Jordan, according to the saying of
the man of God: and his flesh came again like unto the flesh of a little
child, and he was clean.

—2 KINGS 5:10–14

Naaman was apparently insulted that he, a man of prestigious stature,
had been spoken to by Elisha's secondary leader—pride was at work. He
also had thought that the prophet would have been a bit more dramatic
in his healing—presumption was at work. He thought that the rivers of
Damascus were better than Israel's—comparison and competition were at
work. He nearly missed his miracle.

Enter the Secondaries—With a Two-Step Confrontation Strategy

But then Naaman's servants approached him. First, they called him "My
father." They honored him. Any leader, husband, wife, child, or any person,
for that matter, will tend to be more open to constructive admonition if he
or she is treated with high respect by the one giving the admonition. Second,
they appealed to his own sense of honor and commitment to valor. (See 2
Kings 5:1.) By these two simple steps, they were able to dismantle his rage and
help him to attain what he had gone to Israel to accomplish: the receiving of
his healing.

Naaman had come respectfully, according to protocol—he had entreated
the king. He had come sincerely, bearing great gifts of gratitude. (He did not
know the ways of the Lord.) Yet, without the respectful confrontation of his
secondary leaders, he could have died a leper. They covered his human flaw
and helped him to secure his divine deliverance. Though these people were

heathens, the principles are universal. (And incidentally, Naaman did state his intention to honor the Lord from that time forward.)

The Example of Paul and Timothy

If there be therefore any consolation in Christ, if any comfort of love, if any fellowship of the Spirit, if any bowels and mercies, Fulfill ye my joy, that ye be likeminded, having the same love, being of one accord, of one mind. Let nothing be done through strife or vainglory; but in lowliness of mind let each esteem other better than themselves. Look not every man on his own things, but every man also on the things of others. Let this mind be in you, which was also in Christ Jesus: Who, being in the form of God, thought it not robbery to be equal with God: But made himself of no reputation, and took upon him the form of a servant, and was made in the likeness of men: And being found in fashion as a man, he humbled himself, and became obedient unto death, even the death of the cross. Wherefore God also hath highly exalted him, and given him a name which is above every name: That at the name of Jesus every knee should bow, of things in heaven, and things in earth, and things under the earth; And that every tongue should confess that Jesus Christ is Lord, to the glory of God the Father. Wherefore, my beloved, as ye have always obeyed, not as in my presence only, but now much more in my absence, work out your own salvation with fear and trembling. For it is God which worketh in you both to will and to do of his good pleasure. Do all things without murmurings and disputings: That ye may be blameless and harmless, the sons of God, without rebuke, in the midst of a crooked and perverse nation, among whom ye shine as lights in the world; Holding forth the word of life; that I may rejoice in the day of Christ, that I have not run in vain, neither laboured in vain. Yea, and if I be offered upon the sacrifice and service of your faith, I joy, and rejoice with you all. For the same cause also do ye joy, and rejoice with me.

—PHILIPPIANS 2:1–18

Paul asserts some poignant truths about secondary leadership:

- First, an attitude of humility and service among believers gives the senior leader joy (vv. 1–4).

- Second, one may build credibility with God and man following the leadership attitudes of Jesus (vv. 5–18).

- Third, as we see later, Timothy embodied credible secondary leadership (vv. 19–23).

Paul's Joy Fulfilled

Paul, a senior leader in this context, taught the Philippian church about the true way in which they could fulfill his joy. They were a most generous church, and the epistle to the Philippians is Paul's "thank-you note" to this congregation for their gifts. And yet he directs them toward a means by which this church can ultimately fulfill his joy, and therein fulfill the will of Christ. Paul is not materialistic, though he is grateful for their contribution. What he is passionate about is the attitude that they should have toward one another, as listed in verses 1–4.

The Mind That Jesus Had

That attitude is the same one that Jesus had—the "mind" which was "also in Christ Jesus." Jesus allowed himself to become secondary to the Father even though He was equal with the Father. Jesus is the embodiment of all the traits of credible secondary leaders. He is also the great model of the favor and blessing of God that comes upon a faithful secondary leader.

In the latter part of the same chapter, Paul gives the Philippians a personal example of the leadership traits that not only give him joy but were also embodied in Jesus. The example is Timothy:

> But I trust in the Lord Jesus to send Timotheus shortly unto you, that I also may be of good comfort, when I know your state. For I have no man likeminded, who will naturally care for your state. For all seek their own, not the things which are Jesus Christ's. But ye know the proof of him, that, as a son with the father, he hath served with me in the gospel.
>
> —Philippians 2:19–22

Paul states that out of his own concern to know how the Philippians are faring, he will send to them Timothy. Why does Paul choose to send Timothy, out of all of his followers? Paul explains.

1) Timothy has an attitude that is rare.

Paul has churches everywhere, and yet he says that the attitude of Timothy is not common. He has "no man likeminded." Is not this the cry of senior leaders, of pastors, today? The "mind" that he refers to is the one that he prescribed and described in the early part of the chapter, the mind of Christ. And of all his protégés, none of them are as developed in Christian character as Timothy. If Paul only had one, how many are there in churches today?

Yet we believe, because of the promise of a glorious church to present to Himself at the end, there are arising men and women who will lead as Christ led: they will have the mind of humility, of servitude, and of genuine compassion.

2) Timothy is caring by nature—the divine nature, not so much human personality.

Timothy has so allowed the Spirit and Word of God to cultivate the Christ-life in him that caring is natural for him. Granted, caring might have been one of Timothy's traits from early in life, but even so, his life was affected by the godliness of his grandmother and mother. In other words, it would still have been based upon the nature of Christ.

Moreover, Paul does not deal with people "after the flesh." Timothy could have been a totally selfish person prior to salvation, but the transforming power of the Holy Spirit has conformed him to the image of Jesus. The will of God for leaders is that we do not have to consciously decide to be kind, to be thoughtful, or to be thankful. It should, and can, be "supernaturally natural" for those in tremendous authority to be gracious, courteous, outgoing, and loving. May God give us leaders who do what they do, not to impress a human audience, but out of the nature of God that is in them, even when there is not evident reward.

3) Timothy is contrasted with those who seek their own, not the things of God.

Even in Paul's day, there were those in secondary leadership who were worldly ambitious rather than spiritually zealous. Frequently, the leader desires the right thing for the wrong reason, or he is confused about the route to greatness in the body of Christ, as contrasted with greatness in the world system. How many brothers and sisters love to preach but don't like people? They desire the ministry but don't wish to serve. They actually see ministry, whether the pulpit, the choir, or the administrative office, as a means to an end, the end being self-aggrandizement. They do not understand that their anointing and talents are gifts to be given and received, not commodities to be bought and sold.

4) Timothy has proven himself by serving with Paul, as a son with a father, in the gospel.

Notice that "the proof of him" is not how well he can speak, although Timothy is clearly an able teacher and preacher of the word. In our day, Paul would probably say the proof is not that he has written a book or has been interviewed in the Christian media. The proof was that he served, and the manner in which he served. It is not even that he has a large church or outreach or that he has preached in major conferences. Those things are all legitimate accomplishments within the will of God. However, these are not the proof of Timothy's worth as a minister and his integrity before God, Paul, and the Philippians. The proof was that he served, and in the way that he served.

Serve With Me

Paul says that Timothy did not have an independent spirit. Instead he "served with [him] in the gospel." How many associate ministers who have charisma are willing to serve with a spiritual father or mother until God's time of release for replication? The widespread practice of abandoning ministries and doing one's own "thang" upon a whim flies in the face of the spirit that Paul extols in Timothy. Paul served, and Timothy joined him—emulated him—by serving.

A Son With a Father

Paul also says that the attitude of Timothy toward him was that of a son with a father. Proof of the man's integrity has to do with the fact that he honors his parent in the Lord. He does not lift up himself. Even if he is more skilled than Paul, more physically attractive than Paul, more popular than Paul—Timothy remembers who Paul is to him. And he maintains a respectful, deferential air toward him. Even when Paul is in his worst state, Timothy is faithful. We find that the very last letter of Paul is a letter addressed to whom? Timothy. And why is this? Likely, it is because Timothy was Paul's son in the faith—not just an associate minister, but one who honored and valued the divine connection that God had made between the two of them.

Attached at the Heart

In spite of the powerful doctrinal and prophetic pronouncements in the book of 2 Timothy, one can sense the deep emotion with which the book is characterized. This is not merely a sermon transcript. This is a heart-wrenching message to someone who shares Paul's heart. Paul seems to carry a great burden of responsibility for Timothy (and all those who have the Timothy spirit) at the end of his days. The fact that he tells Timothy twice to be diligent to come to him in Rome, where Paul is to be martyred, speaks of the fact that Timothy holds a unique place with Paul. It is not favoritism. It is divine favor because Timothy allowed God to develop in him the mind of Christ, a mind to "naturally care" for the state of the church, a mind to seek the things that are of God, a mind to honor his spiritual father and serve with him.

> Thou therefore, my son be strong in the grace that is in Christ Jesus. And the things that thou hast heard of me among many witness, the same commit thou to faithful men, who shall be able to teach others also.
>
> —2 TIMOTHY 2:1–2

First Faithful, Then Able

Paul tells Timothy to commit his teachings to "faithful men, who shall be able to teach others also." Paul implies that the individuals Timothy chooses should not be chosen based upon teaching talent. Paul says "they shall be able." But for the present, the critical criterion is that they are faithful. With diligence, it is possible to make a faithful person able, but it is far more difficult to make an able person faithful. This could be because the able individual is so self-centered that he has no desire to be faithful to any agenda other than one that celebrates his ability. If an individual is faithful, the gifts that lie dormant in him or her may be cultivated; techniques of leadership may be taught. However, the greatest ability in a leader is credibility, or faithfulness, to God and to man.

> Most men will proclaim every one his own goodness: but a faithful man who can find?
>
> —PROVERBS 20:6

Chapter 6

CREDIBILITY AND FAVOR

And Moses went out, and told the people the words of the Lord, and gathered the seventy men of the elders of the people, and set them round about the tabernacle. And the Lord came down in a cloud, and spake unto him, and took of the spirit that was upon him, and gave it unto the seventy elders: and it came to pass, that, when the spirit (Spirit) rested upon them, they prophesied, and did not cease. But there remained two of the men in the camp, the name of the one was Eldad, and the name of the other Medad: and the spirit rested upon them; and they were of them that were written, but went not out unto the tabernacle: and they prophesied in the camp. And there ran a young man, and told Moses, and said, Eldad and Medad do prophesy in the camp. And Joshua the son of Nun, the servant of Moses, one of his young men, answered and said, My lord Moses, forbid them. And Moses said unto him, Enviest thou for my sake? Would God that all the Lord's people were prophets, and that the Lord would put his spirit (Spirit) upon them!

—NUMBERS 11:24–29

Unofficial Officials

Eldad and Medad were not part of the seventy elders whom Moses brought forth to receive the Spirit of God. Yet God, in His wisdom and His grace, poured out upon these two whom He chose in such a way that the same thing that the "official" elders were manifesting began to manifest in these two "unofficials." This illustrates a reality that has been seen frequently in ministries and organizations: there can be a person who is a member of the rank-and-file, who does not have the spirit of an Absalom or any other insurrectionist but instead had built tremendous credibility with the congregation over time, who is used by God. As a matter of fact, this individual often has no official title or position in the church. However, the word of that individual is as weighty as that of any officer of the church—almost, if not altogether, as authoritative as the word of the senior pastor.

Official but Not Actual

And in some cases, when the senior pastor is a novice or in a system where the pastors are appointed by a congregational or Episcopal system and are not permitted to establish a long-term rapport with the people, a member of the congregation has a more authoritative word than the pastor's. Furthermore, there have been settings in which the pastor was the administrative head of the local church but not the spiritual head (under Christ, of course) of the church. Sometimes the spiritual head was "Ole' Mother Sally" or "Ole' Brother Billy"—people who had a committed walk with God, a tremendous consecration, a loving fatherly (motherly, sisterly, or brotherly) spirit, and who had established themselves as confidantes and pillars in the local house.

Understanding What Credibility Is For

In these cases when God has granted them such favor, these individuals would never strive to usurp authority or contend with the set man or woman of the local house. They understand that God has granted them this grace (they did not merit it) and that He will only use them to complement or supplement what He says and does through the senior leader. They know not to commit the sin of a "private agenda." They are mature enough to abide in their callings, and if there are concerns or insights for the church, they know how to channel those things toward their senior leader for his or her scrutiny and judgment and for the decision as to "what, when, where, why, and how" to deal with whatever matters are under consideration.

The Scarlet Letter Revisited

There have even been instances when the person who eventually became the most credible member of a congregation originally joined the church family under a dark cloud of suspicion and questionable character: "What does that low-life think he or she's doing coming into *our* church?"

But this individual comes in, is born again, becomes clothed with an attitude of true humility, and is consistent. He or she has the spirit of a disciple, a learner, a follower. Sometimes it is over the process of years, but there can come a time when that individual, at whom some of the previous members had turned up their noses, can surpass even them in the level of servanthood, compassion, diligence, and consecration. Yes, as in the classic novel by Nathaniel Hawthorne, the damaged "Hester Prynne–types" in the community can so give themselves to God that the same scarlet letter "A" that once symbolized "adulteress" can come to denote "angel." (Read the book!)

Restoring Credibility

And that leads to another area of discussion. What of the leader who has lost credibility? Is there any hope of restoration for him or her? Thank God that there is always an opportunity for redemption if an individual will follow God's instructions.

There are certain key components for the restoration of a leader that are actually components of all restoration. While this is not necessarily a perfect sequence, all of these are significant pieces involved in putting the leader's credibility back together.

Realization: Acknowledgement of One's Own Fault

The first step is to take ownership of the wrongdoing.

> For I acknowledge my trangressions: and my sin is ever before me. Against thee, thee only, have I sinned, and done this evil in thy sight: that thou mightest be justified when thou speakest, and be clear when thou judgest.
>
> —Psalm 51:3–4

A leader must understand that responsibility demands that he or she shoulder the full weight of guilt for sinful actions and the consequences of those actions. And like David, the leader must understand that the greatesr offence is against God, before his or her family, his or her kingdom, or anyone or anything else.

Repentance—Penitence

The primary thing that God always requires of an individual in order for restoration to take place is repentance.

> If my people, which are called by my name, shall humble themselves, and pray, and seek my face, and turn from their wicked ways; then will I hear from heaven, and will forgive their sin, and will heal their land.
>
> —2 CHRONICLES 7:14

> Repent ye therefore, and be converted, that your sins may be blotted out, when the times of refreshing shall come from the presence of the Lord.
>
> —ACTS 3:19

It is not enough to be sorry for wrongdoing, or even to acknowledge fault. One must then turn from the wrongdoing and the situation that precipitated the fall from the beginning.

Restitution

If there is something that needs to be repaid, replaced, or fixed, whether monetary or otherwise, the leader should accept responsibility to make it good.

> And Zacchaeus stood, and said unto the Lord: behold, Lord, the half of my goods I give to the poor; and if I have taken any thing from any man by false accusation, I restore him fourfold. And Jesus said unto him, This day is salvation come to this house, forsomuch as he is also a son of Abraham. For the Son of man is come to seek and to save that which was lost.
>
> —LUKE 19:8–10

If a crime has been committed, this will constitute answering to a charge, the paying of a fine, or perhaps incarceration, in order to make restitution. "Sorry" is not enough. Apologizing to God is not enough for a leader— indeed, merely apologizing is never enough anyway—because although God is the first One offended, He is not the only party affected by the leader's actions. Any person or group that has been affected or offended by the leader's actions should be officially addressed in proportion to the extent of the injury and their involvement. For example, the man on the street who knows of the leader's work should be given, along with the rest of the public, an official statement if the leader has fallen into some public error. However, if the public error involved infidelity with someone's spouse, that other spouse deserves more than a press release statement.

The leader must seek out that person to personally ask his or her forgiveness and to make whatever restitution is warranted. If a person or a group has not been affected or offended (actually or potentially) by the action, they do not need to be brought into an already painful situation. Not only does it serve to further embarrass the leader, it may injure other disciples who did not have to carry the wound. Do not cause babes to become disillusioned or disenchanted with God over the failure of one of God's representatives.

Repair of Rapport

The leader needs someone, who himself or herself is credible, to whom to be personally accountable and who is willing and able to support the leader through the entire process of restoration.

> And he arose, and came to his father. But when he was yet a great way off, his father saw him, and had compassion, and ran, and fell on his neck, and kissed him. And the son said unto him, Father, I have sinned against heaven, and in thy sight, and am no more worthy to be called thy son. But the father said to his servants, Bring forth the best robe, and put it on him; and put a ring on his hand, and shoes on his feet: And bring hither the fatted calf, and kill it; and let us eat, and be merry: For this my son was dead, and is alive again; he was lost, and is found. And they began to be merry. Now his elder son was in the field: and as he came and drew nigh to the house, he heard musick and dancing. And he called one of the servants, and asked what these things meant. And he said unto him, Thy brother is come; and thy father hath killed the fatted calf, because he hath received him safe and sound. And he was angry, and would not go in: therefore came his father out, and intreated him. And he answering said to his father, Lo, these many years do I serve thee, neither transgressed I at any time thy commandment: and yet thou never gavest me a kid, that I might make merry with my friends: But as soon as this thy son was come, which hath devoured thy living with harlots, thou hast killed for him the fatted calf. And he said unto him, Son, thou art ever with me, and all that I have is thine. It was meet that we should make merry, and be glad: for this thy brother was dead, and is alive again; and was lost, and is found.
>
> —LUKE 15:21-32

When the young prodigal son came home, the servants and the rest of the family received him not because of who he was (even though he was still his father's son), nor because of his performance (for he had performed miserably). He was received because his father, whose credibility was fully intact, insisted that he be received. Every leader needs accountability figures in his life who, when the leader has blown it, can speak on his or her behalf, guide and support him or her through the restoration process, and give account for the leader's completion of the restoration process.

Rest/Refreshing

Often the trauma of having to deal with failure takes a toll on all involved: spiritually, emotionally, and even physically. It is not wise for a person to jump back into high intensity activity after having just come through this process.

> Then David arose from the earth, and washed, and anointed himself, and changed his apparel, and came into the house of the Lord, and worshipped: then he came to his own house; and when he required, they set bread before him, and he did eat.
>
> —2 SAMUEL 12:20

Details will vary based on the scope of the failure, but in every case, some time for reflection and recuperation is needed for everyone involved. First, out of respect for the sacred trust of leadership, there should be a willingness in the leader to step back for a season, with that season determined by wise, loving, and unbiased counsel. Secondly, the broken leader—and all affected by his or her brokenness—need to be healed, to be ministered unto. The fact that one's gift is intact after a "fall" does not mean that one's soul and spirit are intact. There is a severe need for purging, for strengthening, repair, and renewal. This takes deliberateness, and it takes time.

Reconstruction/Renovation

The leader needs to look within, with the assistance of his accountability partners, to determine what it was that brought him or her to this place of failure.

> Who can understand his errors? Cleanse thou me from secret faults. Keep back thy servant also from presumptuous sins; let them not have dominion over me: then shall I be upright, and I shall be innocent from

the great transgression. Let the words of my mouth, and the meditation of my heart, be acceptable in thy sight, O Lord, my strength, and my redeemer.

—PSALM 19:12–14

Confess your faults one to another, and pray one for another, that ye may be healed.

—JAMES 5:16

Was it an enticement in a certain area? The leader needs to ask, "What made me vulnerable? What can I do to plug that particular leaky area in my life? What is the condition of my spirit and of my soul?"

Reorientation

Now the leader revisits the area of ministry to which he is called. He is led into a new look at the principles and practices of Christian ministry.

I will arise and go to my father, and will say unto him, Father, I have sinned against heaven, and before thee, and am no more worthy to be called thy son: make me as one of thy hired servants.

—LUKE 15:18–19

The leader needs to look at how he or she can be most beneficial to the work of God. In some settings, even legally, he or she may have totally disqualified himself or herself from functioning. He or she can be used of God, but publicly he or she may have to be used in a different capacity than before the fall happened.

The young man, the prodigal, was so glad to be restored to fellowship with the father and the father's house that he was willing to take whatever position would be afforded him. That is most definitely the attitude of the one who is being reoriented. Wherever God's Word and kingdom ethics place the restored leader—that is where he or she gladly chooses to be.

Reinstatement

The leader, under wise accountability, is formally released back into a place of service, even if it is not the original position or function, due to the nature of the failure.

And Joab sent messengers to David, and said, I have fought against
Rabbah and have taken the city of waters. Now therefore gather the
rest of the people together, and encamp against the city, and it be called
after my name. And David gathered all the people together, and went
to Rabbah, and fought against it, and took it. And he took their king's
crown from off his head…and it was set on David's head.…So David
and all the people returned unto Jerusalem.

—2 SAMUEL 12:29–31

For example, if someone has stolen church property, he or she may never be
a trustee involved with such matters again, but this does not mean that he or
she cannot serve the church in some legitimate capacity, titled or not. Though
there is always the possibility for memories of past failure to arise in the leader
or in others, he or she has proven to be humble and committed enough to
go through the process of restoration—and humility and commitment bring
with themselves a measure of credibility. The leader is well on his way to
allow God to complete the good work that He began in him or her.

There are legal considerations along with scriptural and local church or
company policy considerations that will affect placement. And whereas a
company may dismiss an individual with no hope of return, the church is
the place of hope. If an individual is willing to repent and to submit, God
has not dismissed nor forsaken that individual—somewhere in the body of
Christ, there is still a place for him or her…Selah.

The Favor Factor

One of the surest marks of the call of God to leadership upon an individual's
life is favor—favor with God, but also favor with people. Favor is a power that
attracts and elicits admiration, affection, and loyalty toward a leader.

God had said to Abraham, as He called him out of Mesopotamia:

Get thee out of thy country, and from thy kindred, and from thy
father's house, unto a land that I will shew thee: and I will make of
thee a great nation, and I will bless thee, and make thy name great;
and thou shalt be a blessing: And I will bless them that bless thee, and
curse him that curseth thee: and in thee shall all families of the earth
be blessed.

—GENESIS 12:1–3

God's Promise to Abraham

God promises Abraham much, but one of the pivotal parts of this sevenfold promise is that He will "make [his] name great," "bless them that bless [him]," and "curse him that curseth [Abraham]." This is a promise of favor.

1) The favor will be manifested as "a great name," meaning credibility and notoriety:

People will take stock in anything associated with Abram's name: "If Abram says that it's OK, then it's OK." And people, including many whom Abram does not know, will know about Abram because of God's hand upon him.

2) The favor will be manifested as a communicable (contagious) blessing:

Blessing for blessing, God says that whatever good that one does to Abram, he or she will receive a harvest of blessing, and God's harvest is always greater than man's seed.

3) The favor will be manifested as a reciprocal cursing:

Cursing for cursing—God says that whatever evil one does to Abram, he or she will receive a harvest of cursing, and a curse's harvest is always greater than its seed.

But stop! People traditionally quote or rather misquote this verse as follows: "God told Abraham 'I'll bless them that bless you and curse them that curse you.'" It is not the paraphrase from King James English to modern English that is the problem. It is the pronouns referring to the ones who bless and curse Abram. God explicitly stated, "I will bless them that bless thee." But concerning cursing, He stated that He would, "curse him that curseth thee." Notice God's choice of words, which is never haphazard—He says it exactly as He means it. He says that there is a "them" that will bless Abram and a "him" that will curse him. God is telling Abram that the "blessers" will outnumber the "cursers" in his life because of the favor of God.

For every "him" who tries to hinder you, there is a "them" that will bring you through! That is favor. Favor does not mean that there is no opposition. But in the words of Elisha, "They that be with us are more than they that be with them" (2 Kings 6:16). There will always be more people for you than are against you. That is favor!

"They Don't Like Me!" Really?

Some secondary and senior leaders become bound up and obsessed with who doesn't like them or approve of them or of their efforts. It can have a bewitching effect, a binding effect, that can hinder the move of God and the flow of the Holy Spirit's gifts in the life of a leader.

Instead, the Scripture teaches that we should walk in the awareness that, first, God is "for [in favor of] us" (Rom 8:31). Secondly, He sovereignly ordains that if we walk pleasing to Him, there will be many others that are for (in favor of) us.

A Reason Not to Like You

Caution: a leader must continually examine himself or herself to ensure that his or her walk and talk are becoming of a leader. Sometimes people dislike leaders with good reason: they may have abrasive, snobbish attitudes, a lack of tact in their speech, or an obvious lack of genuine concern for others with behavior that suggests that the people owe them deference. In those instances, people don't like them because they are frankly unlikeable.

Although there is no excuse for unkindness on anyone's part, the burden is upon the leader to be the kind of individual who makes it easy for people to relate. Also, some—maybe most—causes of dislike are unintentional; often the turnoff in a leader's demeanor or leadership style is not conscious on the leader's part. This is why one must not be afraid of assessment and evaluation of his or her leadership, and one must have people in his or her life who care about him or her so much that they are not afraid to be open with the leader about the highs and lows of his or her leadership performance and personality.

Jesus inquired of his disciples, "Whom do men say that I the Son of Man am?" (Matt. 16:13). In a real sense, Jesus was conducting a performance survey on Himself and His ministry. He wants to know how He is perceived, for He, more than anyone else knows:

> How one is perceived determines how one is received.

Assessment, Evaluation, Perception

Virtually all successful corporations and institutions know the power of assessment, evaluation, and harnessing perceptions. Again, these are kingdom principles. Scripture repeatedly exhorts believers to examine themselves. Even so, in order to maximize the favor God gives to His leader, perceptions must be assessed. Positive perceptions and realities must be optimized, and negative perceptions must be analyzed as to their accuracy and their causes.

The leader must ask himself and his confidants, "How do people see me? How do I sound to them—sincere, or smug and arrogant? What spirit subliminally exudes from me, contradicting what I say or do on a conscious level?" Even these are fair questions: "Do I stink? Do I have bad breath? Am I seen as a flirt or as a bully?" Walking with Christ's humility and compassion is obligatory for successful leadership. However, that walk must also include continued self-examination and evaluation for awareness and enhancement. To do this is to fully appropriate the promises of favor which God has bestowed on His leaders.

Self-Awareness Is Wise, Not Self-Loathing

Wise is the leader who is in touch with his or her actuality as well as with the perceptions of those around him or her. To be "in touch"—aware—is one thing, but to obsess is another: it is equally as unwise to be self-absorbed as to be totally unaware of one's own ways.

If the call of God is upon a leader, if God has given a man or woman a gift, and if that leader has totally bought in to the kingdom's agenda for the ministry, business, or other enterprise, that leader's energy should not expended on second-guessing himself or his motives. He must accept personal responsibility for his actions and supervisory responsibility for his subordinates. When he finds himself in a fault, he should be quick to repent to God, apologize to others, and take all other restorative measures as appropriate. Once he has examined himself, having rejoiced in the assets and having engaged in a strategy to minimize liabilities, he or she must go forward. Even if there have been problems, the solutions are ahead of him or her or within him or her—never behind him or her. The favor of God abides upon that leader.

Chapter 7

CHOOSING THE CHOSEN

Destined Is Not the Same as Qualified

This is a word of admonition for pastors and senior leaders. When it comes to selecting and appointing people to serve in various capacities, we should be sure to seek out "the right stuff." That is, no one is automatically qualified for leadership, primary or secondary, even though all are destined to be leaders in the general sense. We must look to the Lord, to His Word, and to His Spirit for the wisdom to select and invest in those who are to walk behind, beside, and often before the senior leader. These are people from among whom the successors in leadership are often selected. We need godly insight in order to determine the persons to whom God has given an endowment for particular tasks and the wisdom to place those people accordingly. Furthermore, we need both the godly insight to determine whom God has called for a particular assignment and the wisdom to equip them. We must choose whom God has chosen, meaning we must appoint whom He has anointed and anoint whom He has appointed.

Jesus Did Nothing of Himself But What He Saw the Father Doing

> Then answered Jesus and said unto them, Verily, verily, I say unto you, The Son can do nothing of himself, but what he seeth the Father do: for what things soever he doeth, these also doeth the Son likewise.
>
> —JOHN 5:19

If Jesus did nothing of Himself, it includes the fact that He did not put people in positions because of His own opinion. He awaited instructions from the Father and then obeyed what He saw and heard: He chose the chosen. According to Luke 6, He prayed all night and then selected the

Twelve. He selected those whom He had seen the Father selecting, including Judas.

God's Choice First, Not Ours

But there is another aspect of this that in instructive for the secondary leader, the servant, the disciple. Not only must the senior leader choose whom God has chosen to be his pupil and heir, but the secondary leader must understand how to accept God's choice for his mentor and spiritual parent. Even as it is not the prerogative of senior leaders to decide who will be God's man or woman in the next generation, it is not the absolute choice of the follower as to whom his spiritual leader will be. It is ours to accept, but God's to choose.

No One Chooses Parents—Natural or Spiritual

In the natural—the technological advances in genetic engineering and cloning notwithstanding—we do not choose our parents, and parents do not choose their children. This is left in the hands of the God of nature.

Even so, one does not have the right to choose who will be his spiritual children, and spiritual children do not have the right to "shop around" for the kind of mentor they think that they need. There is nothing in Scripture that supports this. Though it is scriptural to covet and desire the move of God that we see in others, there is a difference between merely being inspired by someone and receiving an impartation through them. God makes the impartation decision.

Joshua's Process as an Example

Then came Amalek, and fought with Israel in Rephidim. And Moses said unto Joshua, Choose us out men, and go out, fight with Amalek: to morrow I will stand on the top of the hill with the rod of God in mine hand. So Joshua did as Moses had said to him, and fought with Amalek.
—Exodus 17:8–10

And Moses rose up, and his minister Joshua: and Moses went up into the mount of God.
—Exodus 24:13

And the Lord spake unto Moses face to face, as a man speaketh unto his friend. And he turned again into the camp: but his servant Joshua, the son of Nun, a young man, departed not out of the tabernacle.

—Exodus 33:11

And Moses spake unto the Lord, saying, Let the Lord, the God of the spirits of all flesh, set a man over the congregation, Which may go out before them, and which may go in before them, and which may lead them out, and which may bring them in; that the congregation of the Lord be not as sheep which have no shepherd. And the Lord said unto Moses, Take thee Joshua the son of Nun, a man in whom is the spirit, and lay thine hand upon him; And set him before Eleazar the priest, and before all the congregation; and give him a charge in their sight. And thou shalt put some of thine honour upon him, that all the congregation of the children of Israel may be obedient. And he shall stand before Eleazar the priest, who shall ask counsel for him after the judgment of Urim before the Lord: at his word shall they go out, and at his word they shall come in, both he, and all the children of Israel with him, even all the congregation. And Moses did as the Lord commanded him: and he took Joshua, and set him before Eleazar the priest, and before all the congregation: And he laid his hands upon him, and gave him a charge, as the Lord commanded by the hand of Moses.

—Numbers 27:15–23

Who was Joshua?

Joshua, God's anointed, was appointed by Moses. The hand of God was upon Joshua seemingly from the outset, for he is seen early in the Exodus account leading the fledgling nation in war. He and Moses had a divine connection, and as Moses held up his hands, Joshua and his army were equipped to gain victory over the Amalekites. Also, when Moses went up into the mountain to receive the law of God, Aaron was left overseeing the people, but Joshua went with Moses at least part of the way up into Horeb. The first person Moses addresses, when God abruptly sends him down the mountain to confront the people's idolatry, is Joshua.

It is difficult to imagine that Joshua's spending that much time in the overflow and afterglow of the presence of God did not affect him. Furthermore, the Scripture accounts that Joshua "abode" in the tabernacle after it was built. This time spent in the presence of the Lord and of Moses was obviously critical to Joshua's development.

No guessing about succession: appoint the anointed

God later told Moses to lay hands on Joshua and to put some of his honor upon him, in order that the people might learn to obey him. Ultimately, God made it known to Moses that Joshua was to lead Israel after the death of Moses. It was not to be a natural son of Moses or Aaron the high priest or anyone of their tribe, the tribe of Levi.

Moses did not leave a situation in which the assembly would have to either seek God, campaign, or vote (all of which have legitimacy in their proper context) in order to choose the next leader after his death. He appointed Joshua, for it was clear to Moses, and probably to many others, that God had already anointed him. This example certainly extols the virtue of senior leaders having a living succession plan.

Being God's Choice: Young Samuel and Eli

The story of Samuel is such a beautiful example of the faithfulness of God from generation to generation. Samuel's birth is precipitated by the will of God and the prayers of his mother, Hannah. When he is born, she names him Samuel, which means "asked of God." He is placed under the tutelage of Eli, the high priest, whose sons should be training under their father for the holiness and purity of the priesthood. Instead, they are abominable before the Lord. (For more details, see chapter 5.)

Natural child or spiritual offspring?

Sadly, it is possible for a person to be the natural son or daughter of a spiritual father but not the spiritual offspring. Also, it is possible for God to use a person who has dysfunction in his life to impact and groom another for His service. As stated earlier, a spiritual father or mother may have gross personality flaws, but that does not preclude their having a measure of unction to bless the next generation. In fact, the succeeding generation is responsible to bring their forebears' work to perfection.

Sight despite dim eyes

Even though Eli had lost his sight naturally, and somewhat spiritually, he retained enough discernment to know that God was dealing with the child Samuel. And God used Eli to equip Samuel to respond to His call. It was only after Samuel responded to the call, with an awareness of who it was that called him, that revelation was birthed in his life and the unfolding of his prophetic destiny began.

"Teach me how to respond"

What a powerful truth, that someone must teach us how to respond to the call of God. Even though God calls and anoints, He will use some man or woman to prompt us and to train us how to respond to what God is doing in our lives.

Interestingly, when Samuel heard God, he thought he was hearing Eli. Eli had been the voice of God to Samuel, and to others, for some time. If one has a true spiritual mentor, God sounds like that mentor to the neophyte. What the young one learns later is that, at his or her best, the mentor sounds like God.

Eli perceived that even though Samuel was not his biological son, he was God's choice. There is nothing stated about Eli's feelings concerning the fact that this calling of Samuel was something that his sons could never hope for again, given their state of apostasy. He knew his sons were wicked, and he did not have the fortitude to fully execute discipline against them. However, God in His mercy used him to appoint Samuel, the one whom He would anoint to be prophet, priest, and judge over Israel.

Side Note

Though Samuel was the natural son of Elkanah, he lived in the tabernacle community for all of his life: in that sense, Eli may have seemed like his father more than Elhanan ever did. (Interestingly, Samuel's sons failed also; they did not emulate the integrity of their father. Did Samuel get any of his fathering skills, or lack thereof, from Eli?)

Almost Missing God's Choice: The Old-Man Samuel and David

> And the Lord said unto Samuel, How long wilt thou mourn for Saul, seeing I have rejected him from reigning over Israel? fill thine horn with oil, and go, I will send thee to Jesse the Bethlehemite: for I have provided me a king among his sons. And Samuel said, How can I go? if Saul hear it, he will kill me....And Samuel said unto Jesse, Are here all thy children? And he said, There remaineth yet the youngest, and, behold, he keepeth the sheep. And Samuel said unto Jesse, Send and fetch him: for we will not sit down till he come hither. And he sent,

and brought him in. Now he was ruddy, and withal of a beautiful countenance, and goodly to look to. And the Lord said, Arise, anoint him: for this is he. Then Samuel took the horn of oil, and anointed him in the midst of his brethren: and the Spirit of the Lord came upon David from that day forward."

—1 SAMUEL 16:1-2, 11-13

After Saul's failure, God spoke to Samuel and told him that He had selected a king among Jesse's sons, not Samuel's sons, and that Samuel should go to Bethlehem and confirm this. Having followed God's strategy for getting to Bethlehem without losing his life, Samuel went to Jesse's house, and there Jesse had all of his sons to pass before the prophet. Samuel saw the eldest, an apparently impressive-looking young man named Eliab, and presumed to anoint him. God had to stop him.

And it came to pass, when they were come, that he looked on Eliab, and said, Surely the Lord's anointed is before him. But the LORD said unto Samuel, Look not on his countenance, or on the height of his stature; because I have refused him: for the Lord seeth not as man seeth; for man looketh on the outward appearance, but the Lord looketh on the heart.

—1 SAMUEL 16:6-7

Samuel's trauma

Samuel had experienced the life-shattering trauma of seeing someone he had raised up in leadership go afoul of God's plan for his life. He had watched Saul, the son of Kish, go from being an unassuming, even bashful young man, whose only aim had been to obey his father and secure his runaway mules, to becoming the first monarch in Israel. He had seen Saul's brilliant beginning, when the anointing of God had moved him to stand up for his people against their enemies, the Ammonites. He had watched, and grieved, as Saul's 1) disobedience (or partial obedience), 2) unwillingness to accept responsibility for his actions, 3) greater concern for public image than heartfelt penitence, and 4) loss of relationship with God (calling God "the Lord your [Samuel's] God" in 1 Sam. 15:30), cost Saul the kingdom. And then he, the same prophet and father-figure who had inaugurated Saul's administration, had to pronounce judgment against Saul's reign.

Samuel's affection for Saul

Samuel is an aging man whose own sons had been a disappointment. He had no doubt seen his dreams rekindled somewhat in Saul, though he and God were not in favor of a monarchy. Yet there must have been some special affection in Samuel's heart toward Saul: when he prepared to anoint him, he kissed him—something that was, in all likelihood, not in the script. (Note, for example, that he did not kiss David when he anointed him to be king.)

The Bible deliberately states that Saul looked the part of a leader: he was a fine-looking specimen, and he stood "head and shoulders" taller than any of his countrymen. In other words, he was, literally, outstanding. And Saul was, most importantly, God's choice for king. Some people allege that God never really wanted Saul as king anyway, presuming that God could not have chosen Saul when the Messiah was to be born through David. But God does not play with people's lives. Saul eventually adopted David, even in his demonized state. With the love that Jonathan had for David, if Saul had continued to obey God, why could not David still have become king, with Jonathan as co-regent or vice-regent? According to Jonathan, this is what he (Jonathan) expected anyway! No, Saul had been God's choice for his particular season, and Saul had had "the look."

Another Saul: Eliab had "the look"

How Samuel had cried and prayed over this former spiritual son of his! What did he pray? Perhaps he had asked God for a second chance for Saul to finish his term as king. The Bible does not say. What it does say is that God interrupted Samuel's dirge. God was ready to move on and had sent Samuel after a new king.

And now, after all his disillusionment, God appeared to be giving the aged prophet one more chance to anoint a young man who appeared eligible to be going places in the kingdom. Yes, Eliab may well have reminded Samuel of Saul in his earlier years. The Bible says that Samuel "looked on Eliab, and said, Surely the Lord's anointed is before him" (1 Sam. 16:6). It does not say that he prayed about it, got any references on Eliab's behavior, or checked his record of obedient service; it simply says that Samuel "looked." God mentioned "countenance" and "height of stature"—apparently Eliab had both. Like Saul before him, Eliab had "the look."

But God had already looked

Samuel informed God that His anointed had to be standing in front of him, right then, in the person of Eliab. This must be the one! Unfortunately, Samuel had not considered that God had already checked Eliab out. God did not merely say, "I did not choose him." That would have been simple enough. No, God said, "I have refused him." Does that mean that as Samuel spoke, God refused Eliab, or does it mean that in some other realm of life Eliab had aspired to leadership? We find out later that he was a military man. Had someone, perhaps Jesse, tried to have him promoted to a place of prominence and influence and God had said no because He saw something toxic in Eliab that wasn't visible to others?

God says to Samuel, "Look not on his countenance, or on the height of his stature; because I have refused him: for the Lord seeth not as man seeth; for man looketh on the outward appearance" (v. 7). This may not be connected to Samuel's relationship to Saul, but the parallel cannot be overlooked.

They have "the look"

How many senior leaders, old in age, or in experience, or in feelings— or in some combination of all three—have yearned for someone who would serve with them, and perhaps succeed them? And then, in came or up rose somebody with "the look"? Perhaps, like Samuel, their offspring have disappointed them, but God has used them to groom another son or daughter who has their spirit. Or, perhaps these spiritual sons or daughters are also flesh of their senior leader's flesh.

At any rate, they are polished and professional in their bearing. They know how to dress, how to groom themselves, how to use the King's English, and how to flash that winning smile. Their qualities could garner attention in any sector of life: business, finance, and so on. And they are so well-mannered, always deferring to the senior leader as "the man (or woman) of God" or "my mother (or father) in the Lord." Above all, they appear to be gifted, charismatic in their abilities, and capable of inspiring the people.

Insecurity can result in faulty choosing

The insecurities of spiritual parents are sometimes manifested in their attempts at vicarious success or success by association. Insincere spiritual children, hypocrites who know how to flatter and cajole, can exploit these insecurities. The leader, after having been persecuted or rejected, may earnestly desire to be accepted, to be affirmed, to look good and to have good-looking people about him. Finally it looks like there is someone who will give the ministry an image of validity, professionalism, and breadth. At last, here is an asset instead of a liability.

If a leader is desperate for the image or whatever good looks that his spiritual child seems to provide, he or she may compromise previously established standards. The guidelines that the other children have been held to may be blatantly violated by the golden child, with no repercussions.

But…

Must there always be a "but"? Not always. However, in this case, God said "but." And if God says "but," we must take note.

Before we look at God's "but," let us protest, using the senior leader's "but":

- "But God, I'm old (overextended, sick, tired, ready to retire). I need somebody who can take over this aspect of ministry."

- "But God, he (she) can preach up a storm."

- "But God, if you don't give people positions, they will leave you."

- "But God, that's my son (daughter). I can't promote someone else and not him (her)."

- "But God, he (she) has been here from the beginning."

- "But God, he is the most talented (most anointed, most liberally giving, most popular with the power brokers) person in this ministry."

- "But God, I promised him (her) this position."

- "But God, she (he) is a professional. She (he) adds validity to our ministry."

- "But God, I love him (her). I have poured myself into him (her)."

- "But God, You said…"

God's use of "but"

God says, "But the Lord looketh on the heart." Despite all of the supremely painful protests above, have you checked out this candidate's spirit? Though he or she is anointed, have you noticed that the attitude is one of apathy toward the things of God? Do you notice that she or he is not a team player and only gets excited about an event in which he or she will shine? Does he or she appear during the behind-the-scenes moments of ministry (prayer meetings, Bible studies, rehearsals) or only during the big events? Though magnificently gifted, what does the character look like? This person seems humble now, but if authority were granted to him or her, would he or she switch and become domineering?

Only God knows what is in an individual's heart. Our striving must be to remain tuned in to God's heart, even if we don't know specifically what is in the prospective secondary leader's heart.

We do not know exactly what, but God saw something in Eliab that Samuel had missed. "The Lord seeth not as man seeth" means that God's perception and perspective is different from that of man. God does not see as man does. However, thank God, man can be equipped to see as God does, at least in part. This equipping is essential for Samuel, and all "Samuel figures," if they are going to act on behalf of the Lord's choices.

Principle: *"Every plant, which my heavenly Father hath not planted, shall be rooted up" (Matt. 15:13).*

- We do not have the right, in the body of Christ, to appoint the unanointed; neither do we have the right to anoint the unappointed. In fact it is most dangerous to presume to establish someone in a ministerial office or capacity for which God has not sanctioned him or her (Rom. 12:3; 1 Cor. 12:1–12; Eph. 4:11–16; Col. 2:19; Heb. 5:4).

- The Old Testament is filled with examples of the judgment that befell individuals who intruded into holy offices. (The principle is no less valid in the New Testament: remember the seven sons of Sceva.) Others are disqualified because although

they legitimately entered those offices, they became lifted up
in themselves and changed their disposition toward God.

Anoint the Appointed

It turns out that God had been thinking about and talking about David
in chapters 14 and 15 of 1 Samuel. There is no definite indication that He had
yet revealed Himself to David, but He had already purposed him to be king
over Israel in the stead of Saul. God had already appointed him, referring to
him as "a man after His own heart" and a "neighbor of thine, that is better
than thou [Saul]" (1 Samuel 13:14; 15:28).

When David comes into the presence of the prophet, the Lord instructs
him to anoint David because "this is he." God has already appointed him
king. The prophet Samuel's job is to anoint him for the appointment and for
the tedious process of becoming what God has declared. (Being anointed and
"becoming" are not the same.) Yet the alignment of anointing and appointing
is critical. Leaders must view upcoming leaders through eyes of God.

Picking the Wrong One

It occurred more than once in Scripture that an otherwise godly person
chose someone whom God had not chosen. Abraham, though he knew that
Ishmael was not the will of God for his life, petitioned God that Ishmael
might be the chosen one. Isaac became almost blind in his later years, and he
seemed to have a measure of spiritual blindness as well: he was determined
to bless Esau, although Jacob was God's choice from the beginning. And
when Jacob had the divine insight and foresight to cross his hands and bless
Ephraim, the younger of Joseph's sons, above Manasseh the elder, Joseph
was offended.

Abraham, Isaac, and Joseph were inclined to pick the wrong one. And
this poor choosing, though perhaps well-intended, was based upon human
preference, rather than upon divine appointment. In each case, God intervened
to reveal His choice: Isaac, not Ishmael; Jacob, not Esau; and Ephraim, not
Manasseh.

There are cases even now of demagoguery, political systems, and the
like in which the choice of man seems to prevail over the decree of God.
This does not negate the authority of God's set man or woman, but it does
set in motion a series of events by which God will prove His will. It may

also create tension between the individual "candidates" that perhaps could have been avoided had the spiritual authority figure been led by the Lord from the beginning, choosing His chosen, before following his or her own prejudices. It is our privilege and solemn responsibility to seek, sense, and accept the Lord's choices—and to choose them.

Appoint the Anointed

> Now there were in the church that was at Antioch certain prophets and teachers; as Barnabas, and Simeon that was called Niger, and Lucius of Cyrene, and Manaen, which had been brought up with Herod the tetrarch, and Saul. As they ministered to the Lord, and fasted, the Holy Ghost said, Separate me Barnabas and Saul for the work whereunto I have called them. And when they had fasted and prayed, and laid their hands on them, they sent them away.
>
> —ACTS 13:1–3

The church at Antioch ministered unto the Lord and fasted, and God spoke to them concerning His plan regarding Barnabas and Saul. This account shows that Barnabas and Saul were already in proven ministry as teachers and/or prophets. God commands the church to set these two apart unto Him. He further states that He has called them. He is not calling them at the moment of the separation. The separation follows the call of God—a call that Paul said was from his mother's womb (Gal. 1:15–16) and even from before the foundation of the world.

In other words, God now instructs the church to appoint (ordain) Barnabas and Saul to do that for which He has already anointed them. And in another sense, He instructs the church to anoint (pray over and bless) those whom He has already appointed.

Matthias: The Thirteenth Member of the Twelve
This briefly mentioned Bible character has been the cause for some debate over the years, but the principle again applies: choose the chosen.

> These all continued with one accord in prayer and supplication, with the women, and Mary the mother of Jesus, and with his brethren. And in those days Peter stood up in the midst of the disciples, and said, (the number of names together were about an hundred and twenty,) Men and brethren, this scripture must needs have been fulfilled, which

the Holy Ghost by the mouth of David spake before concerning Judas, which was guide to them that took Jesus. For he was numbered with us, and had obtained part of this ministry.... For it is written in the book of Psalms, Let his habitation be desolate, and let no man dwell therein: and his bishoprick let another take. Wherefore of these men which have companied with us all the time that the Lord Jesus went in and out among us, Beginning from the baptism of John, unto that same day that he was taken up from us, must one be ordained to be a witness with us of his resurrection. And they appointed two, Joseph called Barsabas, who was surnamed Justus, and Matthias. And they prayed, and said, Thou, Lord, which knowest the hearts of all men, shew whether of these two thou hast chosen, That he may take part of this ministry and apostleship, from which Judas by transgression fell, that he might go to his own place. And they gave forth their lots; and the lot fell upon Matthias; and he was numbered with the eleven apostles.

—ACTS 1:15–17, 20–26

Matthias: man's choice or God's choice?

Various scholars have stated that Matthias was the choice of the apostles because of a vote. They teach that Matthias was not God's choice but that he was man's choice; and furthermore, Paul was God's choice for the "twelfth apostle." The following observations seem to contradict their ideas:

1.   Unless Peter was mistaken, the criteria for the twelfth apostle included the fact that the replacement had to have known Jesus on earth and have witnessed His earthly ministry, from the baptism of John to the resurrection. Paul never followed Jesus (many think he never once met Him) in His earthly ministry.

2.   Unless Peter was mistaken, he expected God to honor their prayer to guide them concerning the replacement for Judas.

3.   The baptism of the Holy Ghost had not yet taken place: therefore, casting lots, an Old Testament practice, was proper as they sought God's will. After Pentecost, we have no record of the apostles casting lots.

4.   Furthermore, it has been said that the proof of Matthias not being a legitimate apostle is that nothing is written of him

after he is selected in Acts 1. However, if documented activity in the Scripture is the test of apostolic legitimacy, then seven or eight of the others were illegitimate as well.

a. Peter is featured prominently in Acts up until chapter 11; then he fades as Paul takes center stage. He writes two books of the New Testament.

b. John is featured briefly in Acts and writes five books of the New Testament.

c. James, the brother of John and son of Zebedee, is killed in Acts 12 by Herod.

d. Matthew writes the gospel of Matthew.

e. Phillip, in the book of Acts, chapters 8 and 21, is generally thought of as the deacon from Acts 6, not one of the Twelve.

f. James, who wrote the book of James, is held to have been the Lord's half-brother, not "James the Less," one of the Twelve.

g. Jude, who wrote the book of Jude, is thought to have been another of the Lord's half-brothers, not the apostle by that name.

h. Luke, writing under the inspiration of the Holy Spirit, refers to the apostles as "Peter standing up with the eleven," not "the ten legitimate plus one illegitimate" (Acts 2:14).

i. He later in Acts 6:2 refers to all the apostles as "the Twelve," and together they speak the mind of the Lord.

j. The conclusion that Paul is the "twelfth apostle" lends itself to the cessationist view that there never were but twelve apostles of Jesus Christ. Granted, there were only twelve "apostles of the Lamb," but there are other people in Scripture, not just the Twelve, who are directly or indirectly referred to as apostles.

k. Jesus is also called the Apostle and High Priest of our profession. No one is an Apostle as He is.

l. The Twelve were selected to be eyewitnesses who would walk intimately with Him on the earth and attest to His life and ministry. No one else is an apostle as they were.

m. There are other persons who are not qualified to be apostles in the sense that Christ or the Twelve were, and yet they are called apostles also. Examples include Paul, Barnabas, and James, the Lord's brother.

n. The other seven or eight members of the Twelve, including Matthias, are not mentioned in the book of Acts by name again. Are they all illegitimate?

Surely these points are worth consideration. In the final assessment, Matthias was identified through the casting of lots, but he was actually chosen by God. The apostles chose whom God had chosen. And in the next chapter, Acts 2, God anointed all of those whom He had appointed.

Always supernatural—not always spectacular

Why is it that believers tend to think that the proof of God's supernatural choosing of an individual must be a spectacular display? Granted, Matthias was not knocked down to the ground and blinded by a light, but neither were the other members of the Twelve. God deals with each individual as He wills. Our responsibility as leaders is to be sensitive to His choices, whether God makes it known by thunder or by whisper. Then we have the grand privilege of confirming on the earth what He has already decreed in heaven by choosing His chosen.

Chosen to Be Second

Then Saul's anger was kindled against Jonathan, and he said unto him, Thou son of the perverse rebellious woman, do not I know that thou hast chosen the son of Jesse to thine own confusion, and unto the confusion of thy mother's nakedness? For as long as the son of Jesse liveth upon the ground, thou shalt not be established, nor thy kingdom.

Wherefore now send and fetch him unto me, for he shall surely die. And Saul cast a javelin at him to smite him: whereby Jonathan knew that it was determined of his father to slay David.

—1 SAMUEL 20:30–33

And Jonathan Saul's son arose, and went to David in to the wood, and strengthened his hand in God. And he said unto him, Fear not: for the hand of Saul my father shall not find thee; and thou shalt be king over Israel, and I shall be next unto thee; and that also Saul my father knoweth. And the two made a covenant before the Lord: and David abode in the wood, and Jonathan went to his house.

—1 SAMUEL 23:16–18

And the Philistines followed hard upon Saul and upon his sons; and the Philistines slew Jonathan.

—1 SAMUEL 31:2

And David lamented this lamentation over Saul and over Jonathan his son.... Saul and Jonathan were lovely and pleasant in their lives, and in their death they were not divided.... How are the mighty fallen in the midst of the battle! O Jonathan, thou wast slain in thine high places. I am distressed for thee, my brother Jonathan: very pleasant hast thou been unto me: thy love to me was wonderful, passing the love of women. How art the mighty fallen, and the weapons of war perished!

—2 SAMUEL 1:17, 23, 25–27

The First Crown Prince of Israel

Jonathan somehow came to the awareness that God had chosen him to be second to David, even though traditionally he was to have been first, heir to his father's throne: he was the first crown prince of Israel. Therefore, he was caught in the tension between God's will (his secondary position in David's reign) and his father's will (his inheritance of the primary leadership position as king).

Today's Jonathan

This is a difficult place in which many leaders and aspirants in this hour find themselves. They have a sense of the will of God: to follow God's chosen into a cave and through hostile environments. But at the same time, the other route is so accessible, so convenient, so comfortable, and seemingly so right. Add to this the complexity of having family relationships involved in the conflict. Not only must he or she choose between what *seems* right and what *is* right, but the choice is between the wishes of natural relatives (who may also be spiritual family) and God's will (a spiritual family which may or may not include natural relatives).

And finally, there is ambition, that trait that makes a person desire to do more, be more, and have more. Ambition is not necessarily good or evil, but it must be tempered with a commitment to achieve God's way and for God's purpose, not the worldly way for self-aggrandizement. There is what is referred to as "blind ambition," which means that the ambitious person becomes insensitive to anything or anyone in his way as he scales the heights of success. He will resort to anything, from flattery to treachery, to get his way. Even a pure desire to be more in God can be perverted by the flesh and the devil: one can want the right thing for the wrong reason, or want what is wrong for a right reason. It is harder to identify the latter than the former. The wrong reason is typically an impure motive. However when there is the right reason—such as a pure motive to help, to bless, or to be a blessing—it may harder to determine what a wrong thing might be.

Jonathan's End

Tragically, Jonathan died because he did not actively embrace God's choice for him to be second to David. Apparently, his loyalty to his natural father (good reason) overrode his loyalty to the heavenly Father (bad thing). Doing a bad thing for a good reason cost him his life and his potential place in God's plan and in the Holy Writ.

To Avoid Jonathan's Fate

A leader therefore must invest much time and energy in examining his heart and cleansing his heart in the presence of God. He must continually remind himself that he is a servant, and that as a submitted servant, God has chosen him, and others around him, to do His will. He should remain alert, preparing himself, sharpening his gifts, and helping others to do likewise. In this process, God will begin to reveal his anointing more fully, and God will ensure that the appointment that accompanies that anointing will be made. Whatever the position God has ordained, it will ultimately match and satisfy the longing to serve that resides in that leader. Leaders may be reassured that God did not give them abilities without the intention of releasing them into an arena He has prepared. Whatever "product" God manufactures through you has a "market" awaiting it. You must know that there is a God-given something in you: administration, the arts, political savvy, healing—and God didn't give you something for nothing.

Chapter 8

THE PRINCIPLE OF REPLACEMENT

Transition for Leaders Is Real

As people grow, as they age, and as the breadth of ministry, business, or their organization changes, it requires transition, movement, and the changing of posts among leaders. Transition is real. There are two basic dynamics of position change in the kingdom: succession and replacement. Chapter 7 dealt with succession under the topic "Choose the Chosen." This chapter deals with the other side.

With or Without Us

God loves His people. He loves leaders. He loves secondary leaders. And for each, He has as a unique role. Patiently, He awaits each of us to get in, or back into, our place. He is most longsuffering with those who draw back from His plan. Nevertheless, there comes a sad point when God and His kingdom have to move on. With us or without us, the program of God will survive and thrive. It is our privilege, but also our prerogative, to say yes to the Lord in regard to His calling us to serve or not serve.

Elijah's First Servant

The ancient prophet Elijah has a servant, someone who ministers to his needs as he ministers to those of the nation of Israel. This servant is left unnamed, but he participates in the miracle ministry of Elijah in 1 Kings 18.

This young man apparently witnesses the fire when Elijah calls it down from heaven. He is a participant (albeit a blundering one) when Elijah prays the rain down from heaven. He witnesses the power of God come upon the prophet so intensely that he is able to outrun some of the best horses in the country, the king's own, on foot.

These are the documented miracles that this person witnesses, but given Elijah's reputation, the servant likely observes many other supernatural acts. He sees God use his mentor to usher in national revival. One can imagine the surge of pride that this up-and-coming young man feels when he sees all of Israel stand in awe of Elijah and Elijah's God.

A Defining Moment

> Then comes the servant's defining moment: Elijah is put under a death threat, and the servant has to decide what his position will be. "And Ahab told Jezebel all that Elijah had done, and withal how he had slain all the prophets with the sword. Then Jezebel sent a messenger unto Elijah, saying, So let the gods do to me, and more also, if I make not thy life as the life of one of them by to morrow about this time. And when he saw that, he arose, and went for his life, and came to Beersheba, which belongeth to Judah, and left his servant there. But he himself went a day's journey into the wilderness, and came and sat down under a juniper tree: and he requested for himself that he might die; and said, it is enough; now, O Lord, take away my life; for I am not better than my fathers. And as he lay and slept under a juniper tree, behold, then an angel touched him, and said unto him, Arise and eat.
> —1 KINGS 19:1–5

Notice that what happens is that Elijah is stricken with fear—which is quite uncharacteristic of this prophet—when he receives the message of Jezebel's intentions. Elijah leaves Jezreel and goes to Beersheba in desperation, and there he leaves his servant.

The first question is, "Why does the prophet leave his servant?" Why does Elijah determine this to be the best course of action? Perhaps it was that Elijah did not wish to endanger the servant. Perhaps it was because the servant would have been an encumbrance because he would not have been able to survive and maneuver under the harsh conditions that would accompany being a fugitive from the law.

How Was Elijah Able to Leave Him?

The second, more important question for our purposes is, "How was the prophet able to leave his servant?" If the servant had truly been loyal to the man and his mandate, would he not have refused to part company with Elijah? Would he not have protested until the end? Why did he agree to what appears to have been Elijah's decision to leave him? Was he a "fair-weather friend" who was willing to be associated with Elijah the celebrity but not Elijah the fugitive? Why didn't love force him to disobey this time? Why didn't he cling to Elijah?

"The Cling"

One of the first determiners that an individual is the chosen of God to be a protégé in ministry, a spiritual offspring, is the fact that he or she will exhibit a quality to which we refer as "the cling." "The cling" speaks of loyalty, consistency, and tenacity based in divine love and purpose. It is a determination to remain in a posture of humility and service so that the plan of God may be realized in one's life.

Illustrating "The Cling": Remember Ruth?

And Naomi said unto her two daughters in law, Go, return each to her mother's house: the LORD deal kindly with you, as ye have dealt with the dead, and with me. The LORD grant you that ye may find rest, each of you in the house of her husband. Then she kissed them; and they lifted up their voice, and wept. And they said unto her, Surely we will return with thee unto thy people. And Naomi said, Turn again, my daughters: why will ye go with me? are there yet any more sons in my womb, that they may be your husbands? Turn again, my daughters, go your way; for I am too old to have an husband. If I should say, I have hope, if I should have an husband also to night, and should also bear sons; Would ye tarry for them till they were grown? would ye stay for them from having husbands? nay, my daughters; for it grieveth me much for your sakes that the hand of the LORD is gone out against me. And they lifted up their voice, and wept again: and Orpah kissed her mother in law; but Ruth clave unto her. And she said, Behold, thy sister in law is gone back unto her people, and unto her gods: return thou after thy sister in law. And Ruth said, Intreat me not to leave thee, or to return from following after thee: for whither thou goest, I will go; and where thou lodgest, I will lodge: thy people shall be my people, and thy God my God: Where thou diest, will I die, and there will I be buried: the LORD do so to me, and more also, if ought but death part thee and me. When she saw that she was steadfastly minded to go with her, then she left speaking unto her.

—RUTH 1:8–18

Before going on with Elijah's story, "the cling" is beautifully illustrated in the story of Ruth. It is portrayed in the attitude of Ruth toward Naomi after the two of them, and Orpah, had been left widows and Naomi prepared to return to her homeland. Naomi advised them to return to their own homeland with the hope of their finding husbands, a true necessity for the survival of women in those days. They kissed and wept. Naomi attempted to convince them of the futility of staying with her, stating that even if she gave birth that night, it would be totally unrealistic for them to wait on her new offspring to grow to marrying age. They broke down and wept again, realizing that what she said was true. Orpah left, but Ruth stayed. She had "the cling."

> But Ruth clave unto her. And she said, Behold, thy sister in law is gone back unto her people, and unto her gods: return thou after thy sister in law. And Ruth said, Intreat me not to leave thee, or to return from following after thee: for whither thou goest, I will go; and where thou lodgest, I will lodge: thy people shall be my people, and thy God my God: Where thou diest, will I die, and there will I be buried: the LORD do so to me, and more also, if ought but death part thee and me. When she saw that she was steadfastly minded to go with her, then she left speaking unto her.
>
> —RUTH 1:14–18

"The Cling" Made the Difference

Ruth went with Naomi, even against what Naomi considered her better judgment. Somehow Ruth's commitment to what she saw and had received in Naomi, a knowledge of the God of Israel, overrode Naomi's genuine concern for Ruth's own long-term well-being. Somehow Ruth sensed that her destiny was tied to this old, embittered, now barren woman, her people, and her God.

The same inner battle between going back and remaining was fought by Ruth and by Orpah. They both cried; they both resisted; they both held on to Naomi. But ultimately one released her and the other clung to her. Ruth had "the cling," and if you know the rest of the story, you know that "the cling" made all the difference in Ruth's life, in Naomi's, in the people of Israel's, and even in ours today. She became the ancestor of David and of David's Son and Lord, Jesus Christ. All of this was made possible because Ruth had "the cling."

Back to Elijah (and "The Cling")

While in the wilderness, Elijah had a fresh encounter with God. He received reassurance, rejuvenation, and redirection, a part of which was that the prophet would appoint his successor.

> And the Lord said unto him, Go, return on thy way to the wilderness of Damascus: and when thou comest, anoint Hazael to be king over Syria: and Jehu the son of Nimshi shalt thou anoint to be king over Israel: and Elisha the son of Shaphat of Abelmeholah shalt thou anoint to be prophet in thy room. And it shall come to pass, that him that escapeth the sword of Hazael shall Jehu slay: and him that escapeth the sword of Jehu shall Elisha slay.
>
> —1 KINGS 19:15–16

Elisha: God's Choice, Not Elijah's

Elisha was not Elijah's choice; there is no proof in the text that he even knew Elisha prior to this event. Elisha, however, was God's choice. When Elijah placed the mantle of adoption upon Elisha, Elisha recognized the symbolic gesture and may well have recognized Elijah himself from his reputation, if not from having seen him before. Notice that when he ran behind Elijah to express his willingness to follow the prophet, Elijah did not say anything about the word that God had given him concerning Elisha. He rather coldly responded, "Go back again: for what have I done to thee?"

Harsh Till the End

It seemed that from the start, Elijah did not intend to be gentle with Elisha, and to the end he maintained that intention. When it was time for Elijah to be taken away, he stated that this servant, Elisha, that he should stay put in Gilgal, while he journeyed on alone. This decision was similar to the one he had made regarding the previous servant, but the reaction of Elisha was much different from that of his predecessor. Whereas the previous servant had allowed Elijah to deposit him safely inside Beersheba and outside the annals of history forever, Elisha essentially says, "Not so!"

> And Elijah said unto Elisha, tarry here, I pray thee; for the Lord hath sent me to Bethel. And Elisha said unto him, As the Lord liveth, and as thy soul liveth, I will not leave thee.
>
> —2 KINGS 2:2

When Elijah leaves Bethel, he gives Elisha another opportunity to resign, but Elisha refuses to accept. Finally, leaving Jericho for Jordan, Elijah commands Elisha to remain there, and again Elisha refuses to stand anywhere other than by his man of God.

This story is well known, and one element that we have omitted thus far is the "sons of the prophets." According to some scholars, these were Bible-college-like students who were being groomed for ministry by the prophetic fathers of their day, with Elijah as the preeminent voice. It is thought that this academic structure was originally built under the auspices of Samuel the prophet and continued through the succeeding prophets' administrations. At each of the cities where Elijah attempted to leave Elisha, the sons of the prophets came forward with a revelation for Elisha.

> And the sons of the prophets that were at Bethel came forth to Elisha, and said unto him, Knowest thou that the Lord will take away thy master from thy head today? And he said, Yea, I know it; hold ye your peace.
>
> —2 KINGS 2:3

They came flexing their spiritual muscles and showing forth their savvy in the spiritual gifts.

Parking-Lot and Kitchen-Table Prophets

Many believers today consider themselves special because the manifestations of the Spirit operate in their lives. They set themselves apart as spiritual giants because certain of the giftings of their fathers begin to manifest in their lives. And these gifted believers attempt to use God by their anointing, instead of allowing God, by His anointing, to use them. They have a show-off spirit.

Often people in the secondary role are so busy trying to prove to someone how anointed that they are that they miss the big picture. These are of the sort who corner people in the church parking lot or in their homes and proceed to prophesy. (Some do prophesy, while some prophe-"lie.") Even if the gift is legitimate, the context is illegitimate if this ministering is not done under some biblical authority, for the Scripture teaches that personal prophecy, for example, should be subjected to judgment: Who is going to judge the parking-lot and kitchen-table prophecies? (See 1 Corinthians 14:29–33.)

Uncommitted/Unsubmitted

Often this is the sort of believer who will not commit and submit to a local ministry, at least not after God begins to manifest Himself in his or her life. (Interestingly, the name Jezebel literally means "unmarried." Unmarried carries the connotation of being uncommitted and unsubmitted. Have we discovered the true spirit of Jezebel? More about this spirit later.) There are actually those who believe that once the Lord's power shows itself in their lives, they can never again serve as ushers, parking attendants, choir members, or children's Sunday school teachers. They would not be caught at a simple prayer meeting or Bible study session; they are now too deep for these kinds of activities. It gets worse: some are even too deep to have a job or go to school! They are full-time, big-time.

Tragically, once something of God's grace begins to show itself in these believers' lives, they presume that they have arrived. It is now beneath them to serve. They are offended if they are not given the highest seats in the sanctuary. They are offended if they are not referred to according to their ecclesiastical rank.

Elisha Is Anointed, Too

Elisha is anointed also. Let it never be thought that the only people in the church who are anointed are those who have official leadership capacities. The entire body of Christ is anointed; Christ means "the Anointed One." We are the body of the Anointed One.

And in addition to this, there are those who are in the trenches of obscure servitude who are greatly anointed. There are some church janitors who are more anointed than some clergy. This is not intended to deprecate the clergy. It just means that the favor of God does not necessarily follow titles and hierarchy, but it does follow sincerity, humility, and tenacity.

When the sons of the prophets came "struttin' their stuff" to Elisha, he let them know that he was seeing in the Spirit as well. He knew, apparently by divine revelation, that Elijah was to be taken away. However, he was willing to put his gifts on the back burner in order to serve. He knew that this was not the time to exhibit his charismata; rather, it was time to demonstrate character. And because he had the spirit of a servant, he had "the cling."

Elisha was not sitting back, waiting on somebody to roll out a carpet and invite him to Bethel, to Jericho, or to Jordan. Elisha's attitude was, "If God has sent my master there, even if He didn't call my name, He has sent me there as well. Whatever the assignment of my leader is from God, it is my assignment as well. I will not stop until my Elijah stops, and he will not stop until God says to stop." Elisha was committed and determined to finish his term of service, regardless of the task, even if Elijah did not seem to appreciate it.

Mentors, Meanness, and Other Issues

This brings us to another concept implicit in this story. There is a psychological element with which secondary leaders must come to terms in order to establish a record of longevity in service to God's men and women: their leaders' human personalities do not always render them the easiest persons with whom to work. Some mentors are mean and tough.

Defining Meanness

Urgency

Most senior leaders are extremely passionate people. They are usually very compassionate as well, and in some areas of life they may even be too giving and forbearing. But when it comes to those areas that they consider their calling or their mandate, they tend to be extreme. They are often characterized as rigid workaholics, people who don't know when or how to stop. They may be perfectionists, micromanagers, or nags because they are driven to fulfill their ministries.

Many of them love God and His people with such intensity that they may overemphasize some areas and underestimate other worthy causes, concerns to which they do not feel called. Sometimes these senior leaders need others who love them to remind them of these concerns, which may include their own health, their family relationships, and other aspects of life.

The secondary leader must be aware that often the senior will strive to portray indomitable physical, emotional, and spiritual strength before the masses to keep up the morale. Meanwhile, privately, the same leader may be struggling with physical illness, financial insufficiency, insecurities, relationship difficulties, and any of the challenges that are common to man.

Special satanic warfare

In addition, there is a special warfare that the enemy wages against shepherds, because the smiting of the shepherd will cause the sheep to be scattered and ravaged. He takes special aim at the prayer life, the physical and mental health, the marital relationships, the parental relationships, and the finances of all believers, but especially of shepherds. Jezebel put out a death threat against Elijah, and most scholars believe that she was a priestess of Baal, or a witch. Consequently, she may well have unleashed demonic opposition against the prophet.

There are Jezebel personalities among us in this day. Thus, these are all reasons why spiritual armor-bearers—intercessors—are integral to the success of a leader and of ministry. Someone must love the man and woman of God enough to hold them up in fervent prayer on a consistent basis.

The leader's vulnerability

Also, pastors who have people in their hearts are very vulnerable toward them. If a member or staffer says or does something that negatively affects the ministry or the minister directly, it tends to cause that leader indescribable pain. He or she may not only take the fallout personally, but often feels personally responsible for anything that goes wrong in ministry or among the membership.

For example, if someone leaves another church, a member who remains may think, "Good riddance—he was a problem anyway." This is similar to the view Joab had of Absalom. Absalom had been a problem, and in

Joab's mind, David should have been glad to be rid of him. However, David mourned greatly. He felt responsible (and in that case, he was partly responsible). And so the senior leader may feel, "What did I do or not do? Did I counsel enough? Did I spend enough time with this individual? Was his complaint about me or the ministry legitimate?"

The temptation of the secondary leader may be to think, "Why is Pastor so concerned about him? Pastor acts as if he is more important to him or her than I am. I'm always in place, and Pastor acts as if he or she doesn't even notice!" (See the elder brother in the prodigal son story.)

Feeling the Burden, Bearing the Brunt

Those who serve closest to the senior leader may feel the burden of ministry to a greater degree than those who are more distant. When that man or woman is wrestling with some challenge, he or she may seem to attack or tread over anything or anybody who appears not to be as passionate as he or she is. Furthermore, the senior leader may seem too demanding, behaving as if the secondary leader is supposed to read the senior leader's mind. He or she may behave with impatience toward anyone who is not as driven as he or she is concerning the mandate of ministry.

Therefore a secondary leader must be armed with discernment to differentiate between the leader's emotions and his motives. The weak and the insecure are not ready to walk closely with a passionate leader.

On the other hand, senior leaders must know how to temper their urgency with practicality and sensitivity. They must appreciate those who submit to serve and ask God to help them to be kind—never abusive and rarely abrasive. If a senior leader does "miss it" in the way that he or she speaks or reacts, he or she should demonstrate true humility and repent to God and earnestly apologize to the one he has mistreated, making any necessary restitution as well. To be serious about God's business is one thing, but there is never a godly reason to behave in an ungodly manner.

Unction

Another situation, similar to the others, in which a senior leader may seem uncharacteristically sharp is when he or she senses the anointing of God and is attempting to minister in that anointing. Those secondaries who are supposed to facilitate that anointing's flow may find themselves being dealt with bluntly and directly during those times. They may find the leader pushing them to hurry and get in place, to focus on the spiritual, to be more fervent in prayer, and to minimize distractions. When there is an intense anointing, the preaching and teaching are stronger. When an anointing for personal ministry, such as the altar call or prayer for individuals in need, is present, the senior leader may become irritated with ushers who can't seem to get those who are coming for prayer in the proper order so that this season of ministry can begin.

Often, the senior person has a wonderful rapport with the secondary leader in everyday situations, but in this context he or she is not operating as a fishing partner or shopping buddy: he or she is attempting to minister the grace of God to the needy, and any impediment is viewed with disdain. This is the moment that the senior leader has been preparing for and praying for—a moment when God will move powerfully on those who come. Therefore, it is supremely frustrating to him or her to be hindered or slowed down due to a secondary leader who is out of tune with the atmosphere, did not anticipate the number of respondents to the altar call, or did not come prepared to assist in ministering.

Sometimes secondary leaders are so caught up in their own issues that they are not sensitive to minister to others in need. If one is going to be a leader in the house of God, then one must realize that in the assembly, his or her needs have to be put last. One of the surest ways to be reprimanded is to be out of place when the anointing is flowing.

Blatant unkindness

Those of us who have either observed or come through "old-school" leaders know about the harsh, ungracious manner in which some of them handled (or rather mishandled) even their most loyal followers.

There is no excuse for a lack of kindness; nevertheless, these personality problems do not necessarily disqualify a person as a spiritual parent. There are, as in the natural, spiritually dysfunctional parents. And very often it is because they themselves had poor, if any, spiritual parenting in their formative stages. And again: no one chooses his own parents.

Caution!

"Personality problems" do not include willful sin, a lifestyle of immorality, abuse and manipulation of followers, or the demand for blind obedience. These things are unacceptable in God's sight and disqualify any person from active leadership, even though they may be highly gifted, except through repentance and restoration. Don't love or commit to a human being more than you fear God.

However, there are some people whose communication, management, and discipline styles are distasteful to the secondary leader, not as a matter of sin but as a matter of lack of tact. Elijah was very harsh with Elisha. It may have been because of his own personality or his past. Then again, it could have been a deliberate test.

Test?

Elijah dealt with Elisha this way, perhaps, because he had to know if Elisha had "the right stuff." Perhaps he had to know that Elisha would not quit under a little pressure. The mantle and the mandate were too precious to be entrusted to a spiritual wimp. The times in Israel were too critical for a leader with a limp wrist. Elijah had to be sure that the banner would be held high. Elisha may not have known that he was being processed and proven. Many times senior leaders, and God Himself, are testing future leaders to see them function under pressure. And one thing that helped Elisha was "the cling." Everyone who aspires to the fulfillment of God's will must have "the cling."

In conclusion, the first servant may have been as talented, gifted, handsome, and eloquent as Elisha, or even more so. However, he missed his opportunity to take Elijah's mantle because of his inability to discern what was most important. Therefore the former was replaced by the latter.

Let all be warned—God needs somebody. He will use somebody, but it does not to have to be you. No individual is indispensable to the plan of God. One has a choice to be used, or not. And if he or she cannot hold on, cannot endure hardness, cannot "cling," he or she is disqualified. There is someone waiting to take his or her place.

How sad it is to think that I could be replaced! It is tragic, and it is mournful…but it is also biblical.

Biblical Examples of Replacement

- Because of Adam's sin, he was replaced with the Last Man Adam.

- Because Ishmael was a work of the flesh, he was replaced by Isaac.

- Because of Esau's despising of his birthright, he was replaced by Jacob.

- Because Reuben was unstable, he was replaced by Joseph.

- Because Moses disobeyed God, he was replaced by Joshua.

- Because Eli refused to chasten his sons, his judgeship was replaced with that of Samuel.

- Because Saul, son of Kish, disobeyed God, he was replaced by David.

- Solomon replaced Absalom and Adonijah.

- Because Judas fell through sin, he was replaced by Matthias (not Paul—he doesn't qualify to be one of the Twelve).

- Because Barnabas allowed his contention with Paul to separate him from Paul, he was replaced by Silas.

- Because, officially, the Jews rejected the gospel, though personally thousands embraced it, the major Jewish leadership and movement of the church were temporarily replaced by the Gentiles.

Note

We *do not* subscribe to so-called *replacement theology*. God made an unconditional covenant with Abraham, which included his natural descendants, regardless of their spiritual condition. The Jews have not been replaced; they are still God's chosen, and their "blindness" as to the identity of Messiah shall be removed. All of the promises of God to natural

Israel shall continue to be fulfilled. However, it is a fact that they missed their opportunity to accept the King the first time. Consequently, the disproportionate quantity of those who accepted and proclaimed Jesus of Nazareth as the Christ has been the Gentiles.

> He came unto his own, and His own received Him not. But as many as received Him, to them gave he power to become the sons of God, even to them that believe on His Name.
>
> —JOHN 1:11–12

Incidentally, as of this writing, many natural Jews are coming to faith in Jesus Christ in record numbers, becoming, along with natural Gentiles, "one new man"—a sign, we believe, of the prophetic times.

Reinstatement

In the case of Jews, they are the example of a displacement that is not destined to be permanent. They shall fully occupy their position once again, as Paul prophesies that "all Israel shall be saved" (Rom. 11:26), and God Himself foretells in Zechariah that His beloved Jewish nation "shall look upon me whom they have pierced and mourn for Him as one mourneth for his only son" (Zech. 12:10). The revelation of who Jesus is shall restore them to the fullness of their divine destiny.

Does God Have Duplicates?

The principle of replacement is so powerful that sometimes the person who replaces another even resembles the one whom he or she replaces, either naturally in some way or in spirit. It seems that God intends for a certain "spirit type" or personality type to fulfill a certain role in the house of God. And when one won't comply, God will raise up another, and sometimes, though not in every case, the replacement will have some of the same traits and even a similar demeanor as his or her predecessor.

More About "the Cling"

On the other hand, many of those mentioned above, as well as others, were not supposed to make it, but they did anyhow because of "the cling":

Jacob, noted above, was a supplanter, but he knew how to "cling" to a divine birthright. When he could no longer wrestle with the angel, he just continued to "cling" until he received the blessing.

Joshua was a man of war, but he knew how to "cling" in servitude to Moses as well as to the vision of Moses—he and Caleb asserted that if the Lord delighted in the Israelites, they were well able to take Canaan. He became the leader of the next generation.

David sinned against God, but he knew how to "cling" in repentance, and he was restored.

The Shunammite woman, when her son had died, determined to "cling" to the feet of Elisha until he came back to her house and raised her son from the dead.

Mary of Bethany knew how to "cling" at Jesus' feet, even when Martha disapproved—and she got the good part. When Lazarus died, Martha's approach provoked a sermon from Jesus; however, Mary's coming elicited a groaning in His spirit, and Jesus moved toward the tomb.

"The cling" is an attitude and an act that demonstrates faith in God. (Ask the woman with the issue of blood and the Canaanite woman with the demonized daughter.)

Clinging While Maintaining Deference

Someone has said that familiarity breeds contempt. It is equally as important to the one who clings that he maintain a high level of regard for his man or woman of God. When he is serving, he should not presume upon access to leadership as an opportunity for him to edit his ideas onto the agenda or to have impromptu counseling sessions. If he has concerns, he should plan to address them in the same orderly manner as others, granting that the working relationship between him and the leader may well make it possible for him to be heart-to-heart more frequently than others.

However, if the one who clings does not understand that access is a privilege and not a guaranteed right, he may come to demand that to which he has no right. It is actually difficult for some people to live and work up close to anyone and remain respectful. Those people are not prepared to walk in the Joshua, David, and Elisha roles. They will always have to be fed from a distance; if not, they may tend to bite the feeder's hand.

Privacy and Confidentiality

When the senior leader is conversing with someone in a private matter, be it a counseling session or receiving a guest minister, it is not the prerogative of the secondary leader to intrude upon the conversation. If he or she is not invited into the exchange, he or she should have nothing to say. Furthermore, it should be understood practice that when there is an exchange taking place, that unless one has been asked to do otherwise, he or she should leave the immediate area. This may seem rigid, but there is great freedom when one can say, "I heard nothing, and I know nothing."

In the event that a secondary leader is made privy to confidential information or private conversation, the rule of confidence should govern his or her conduct. Therefore nosy, garrulous, gossiping, lying individuals are disqualified from secondary leadership. They may be ever so gifted and goodhearted, but if they are talkative, if they are "news-carriers," and if they are those who tend to take the facts and distort them to "make the story sound better," it is wise not to allow those people into any leadership role in which they might encounter anyone's qualified information.

What would happen if, while the pastor is counseling someone who is experiencing marital strife, a secondary leader were to go out and spread it throughout the congregation? The pastor's effort is to so handle the matter that no other congregant knows that it even occurred, so as not to damage the credibility of either spouse—but now everyone would know. (This is not with regard to abuse or other endangerment to a spouse; the pastor himself would be legally obligated to report some things to the legal authorities, though not to the "gossip committee." Rather, the issues referred to here are the kind that any married couple could confront.) Now, and even when things are resolved between the spouses, people will have taken sides. They will have decided who the offender is, who is the victim is, what the "crime" was, and the "penalty" should be. They will have decided whether either or both of the spouses are qualified for service in the house of the Lord ever again. And all of this happened because a secondary leader could not keep his or her mouth closed.

"The Cling" Includes Practical Accountability

Sometimes the idea of accountability is not associated with the concept of "the cling" because the cling seems so spiritual and accountability seems so practical. Even when it is practiced, sometimes it is not practiced in a pure spirit. For example, in the case of a leader needing to be absent, accountability means more than a call a few minutes before service begins, saying, "I won't be there." The call a few minutes before should be an emergency call based upon unforeseen circumstances.

When circumstances are foreseeable, there should be planning done to prepare for those circumstances. Suppose an individual serves as an usher and is assigned to work on a given Sunday. Let's say the fourth Sunday is his day to serve. If he decides that he is going out of town this weekend to see his cousin and he will not be back in time to serve, he should inform his usher president as early as he knows. If he knew in July that he would be absent in September, he is not truly accountable if he waits until Sunday morning at 10:30 a.m. to call the church and leave a message for his president. Even Saturday night would probably be difficult because the substitute usher should have a uniform ready, but he may not.

Almost everyone who holds a job of any kind knows that if he or she is to miss work, it is far more preferable and professional to inform the supervisor as far in advance as possible, the exception being a totally unforeseen crisis. And even then, there is supposed to be a standing emergency or contingency plan for whoever has to fill in for the missing professional. How is it that the same person who is so professional in the execution of his secular duties can be so unconcerned about his function in the house of the Lord?

Within One's Authority

"The cling" of accountability also includes staying within one's measure of authority and privilege. If one is not authorized to make purchases on behalf of the ministry, he should not be amazed when he is not reimbursed for his purchase: his purchase becomes a gift. If the decision about the menu is not left in the hands of the servers, then they should not attempt to change what has already been established by the dieticians. If the decision about what song is to be sung has already been made by the minister of music, the associate director should not modify the day's repertoire without first conferring with the minister of music.

Replacement versus Succession

Simply put, transition is a natural part of natural and spiritual existence. All things present must give way to things to come. However, replacement is a judgment upon an individual because of a lack of obedience and submission to God. Succession is promotion; replacement is often demotion, or at least disqualification for the "next level." Succession is progress—one may have one function in the body of Christ for a season, and then, after proven faithfulness in that function, be moved to another. In Acts 6–8, Stephen and Philip go from serving tables to preaching the gospel with signs and wonders. In Acts 13, Paul and Barnabas go from being local prophets and teachers to the apostleship and the greatest missionary work in the New Testament. All leaders should be preparing themselves and those around them for their inevitable transitions, that succession may be expected and welcomed. And all leaders, senior and secondary, should strive to live and walk in such a way as not to be replaced.

Chapter 9

ZEAL: AN ESSENTIAL INGREDIENT IN LEADERSHIP

All Successful Leaders Have Zeal

The people who become leaders and do great things for God are those with great zeal for Him. Some great kingdom leaders are orators; some are not. Some are talented singers; many are not. Some are shrewd administrators; some are not. But all successful kingdom leaders have zeal. In fact, all successful leaders, in every aspect of human society, have zeal.

Zeal is an ingredient that stands out above most others in the life of a kingdom leader. In the Hebrew it is *qaena,* a word that means "to make zealous, jealous, or envious." Elijah refers to his having been jealous for God, meaning he was possessive (jealous) over God's people and envious of the worship being given to other gods that should have been given to God. Paul claims a similar jealousy over the church at Corinth: "For I am jealous over you with godly jealousy: for I have espoused you to one husband, that I may present you as a chaste virgin to Christ" (2 Cor. 11:2).

Heat

The Greek term for *zeal* is *zelos,* and it literally means "heat" and figuratively speaks of "ardor...jealousy as of a husband." It is derived from *zeo* which means "to be hot (boil, of liquids, or glow, of solids)." So it is semantically accurate to describe the zealous as "on fire" for a thing, such as "on fire for God."

Taken together, zeal is a fiery passion and possessiveness (or protectiveness) toward someone or something. The object of zeal may be God or man, place or thing, concrete or abstract.

Characteristics of Zeal

To be zealous toward a certain cause is to be turned on or driven concerning that cause. It is often difficult to harness zeal or the individual who has it. And unbridled zeal, like fire, can burn out—or burn up—the zealous one and his or her surroundings. Yet, also like fire, it is indispensable to the advancement of civilization (or spiritually, the kingdom of God). The greatest accomplishments in society have been birthed through zeal.

Zeal brings with it a resilience, a relentlessness. Regardless of opposition or hardship, zeal refuses to be denied. The spirit of the patriarch, the prophet, the pioneer, the trailblazer, the explorer, the philanthropist, the revolutionary, the reformer, the civil rights leader, and the entrepreneur— all of these include the essential component of zeal. The zealous are often characterized as the Type-A personalities who are loud and adamant about their beliefs. But then one may be zealous with an inner combustion, not as readily obvious, but just as fervent.

Some Tendencies of the Zealous

- A person with zeal will joyfully volunteer service, not out of guilt or obligation.

- A person with zeal will come early and stay late to advance the cause.

- A person with zeal will dream of ways to enhance procedures creatively.

- A person with zeal will brave the elements and laugh in the face of calamity.

- A person with zeal will probably be branded as a fanatic.

- A person with zeal will have an infectious affect upon most others.

- A person with zeal will tend to make his or her non-zealous (or just plain "worn out") senior leader tired from trying to keep up with him or her.

- A person with zeal will consider excellence and achievement their own reward.

- A person with zeal has the best questions in the company meetings.

- A person with zeal has questions and ideas even when there is no meeting, because he or she thinks about the cause constantly.

- A person with zeal tends to be more optimistic than not.

- A person with zeal will be quick to repent and regroup if he falls.

- A person with zeal will strive to protect the integrity of God and of the ministry or other organization.

Natural Zeal

There is natural zeal, and there is divine zeal. Natural zeal, as all natural and supernatural gifts, comes from God. Natural zeal covers a broad spectrum of expressions, from an avid sports fan debating the fan of another team to a medical researcher tirelessly pursuing a cure for cancer.

Misguided Zeal

Nevertheless, natural zeal can be misguided. One may energetically oppose that which he should actually promote, due to misinformation or plain ignorance. The apostle Paul is a classic example of that fact. In his life as Saul the Jewish rabbi, he was "exceeding zealous" of the traditions of the fathers, Galatians 1:14. He was sincere but sincerely wrong. His misguided zeal manifested in the horrific persecution of the church, Philippians 3:6. Saul and his contemporaries in Judaism were zealous, Romans 10:1, but "not according to knowledge." It took a dazzling visitation of the Lord Jesus Christ Himself to redirect Paul's zeal, sanctify it, and superimpose upon it His supernatural zeal. As a result, it is widely held that, second only to the Lord Jesus Himself, Paul is the greatest proponent of Christianity in all of history.

The Example of Paul's Zeal: First Natural, Then Divine

The zeal of Saul the Rabbi was redirected and intensified into the fuel that propelled Paul the apostle to the Gentiles through most of the known world of his day.

- His zeal caused him to be misunderstood. (Acts 9:20–24)

    - Early on, even the church did not trust him. (Acts 9:26)
    - His former associates sought to kill him, implying that they anticipated the power of his zeal. (Acts 9:23–24)

- His zeal caused him to accept suffering.

    - He said that he gloried in infirmities (sufferings) that the power of Christ might rest upon him. (2 Cor. 12:9–10)

- His zeal made him protective of the flock of God.

    - Read Galatians and all of the Pauline epistles.

- His zeal caused him to come down very strongly on those who threatened to harm those whom he sought to develop and protect for Christ.

    - He stated that those who preached another gospel should be accursed. (Gal. 1:8–9)
    - He stated that he could wish for the Judaizers who troubled the Galatians to be "cut off." (Gal. 5:12)

- His zeal caused him to be extreme in his passion toward the church, particularly in addressing issues that needed correction.

    - He referred to the Galatians as "foolish Galatians" because they had departed from the teachings of Christ, which he had imparted to them. (Gal. 3:1)

- His zeal made him intolerant of hypocrisy.

    - He withstood Peter when it seemed that he withdrew from the

Gentiles after having fellowshipped with them earlier. (Gal. 2:11–14)

- His zeal made him "less than patient" with the indecisive.

  – Paul refused to take John Mark on another missionary journey because of Mark's earlier desertion. (Acts 15:36–41)
  – He later changed his perception of Mark and called him "profitable to [him] for the ministry." (2 Tim. 4:11)

- His zeal for the development of people was greater, for a time, than his zeal to go to be with the Lord.

  – He said he had a dilemma: to remain in the flesh or to go to be with Christ, but that for the sake of the people in Philippi he would remain in the flesh. (Phil. 1:21–26)

- His zeal preserved him from a sense of having "arrived," in spite of his tremendous accomplishments. Rather, he continually "pressed" for more of God. (Phil. 3:12–14)

  – He said to the Philippians that if he died for their development in the faith that he would glorify God. (Phil. 1:16–17)
  – He said that he could wish himself accursed from Christ for the enlightenment of his Jewish brethren. (Rom. 9:2–3)
  – He called himself the least of the apostles and less than the least of all the saints. (1 Cor. 15:9; Eph. 3:8)

- Finally, his zeal helped to sustain him to the very end.

  – Read 2 Timothy 1:7–14.

Jesus and Divine Zeal

Zeal is one of God's attributes. Jesus is God; therefore, we would expect zeal to manifest in His earthly life and ministry.

- Even before He came to adulthood, at age twelve Jesus demonstrated zeal for the Father's house. (Luke 2:41–50)

- It was predicted in the prophets that the Messiah would be zealous. (Isa. 42:4; 59:15–20)

- Jesus demonstrated divine zeal in the cleansing of the temple. (John 2:13–17)

- He demonstrated divine zeal in His ministry to the woman at the well. (John 4:27–34)

- He demonstrated divine zeal in His determination to go through with His Passion, surrendering to the Father's will over His own. (Luke 12:50; Matthew 26:41)

Zeal and the Fruit of the Spirit: A Fruit Cocktail

Which fruit of the Spirit is synonymous with divine zeal?

1. Love produces zeal. Love is passionate, possessive, and protective.

2. Joy produces zeal, and zeal can produce joy.

3. Zeal brings the steadiness of peace.

4. Zeal empowers a person for longsuffering.

5. Zeal can make the harshest person sensitive (or gentle).

6. Certainly a person can be zealous toward that which is good.

7. Faith and faithfulness are characterized by zeal.

8. A teachable spirit (meekness) is found in the person who is zealous for knowledge.

9. Zeal constrains a person unto self-control.

Zeal is related to virtually all of the fruit. It is a spiritual "fruit cocktail" because it involves and overlaps many of the Spirit's virtues.

Zeal and Leadership

God wears zeal as a cloak (Isa. 59:15–20). It is a coat of many colors. Our God is a zealous God, and inasmuch as we are sons of God, we have His nature. Our aim should be to mature in His attributes—in this case, in zeal. The people who do great things for God are those with great zeal for Him and for His house. Even without great gifts, those with great zeal can do great things. God can do more with the "zany zealous" than with the "learnedly lazy" or lethargic. Nevertheless, zeal must come to maturity in order for it to fulfill its purpose—to drive the zealous, and those whom he or she influences, toward destiny.

Awareness of the Zealous: It Takes One to Know One

Senior leaders must be on the lookout for the zealous. He or she should recognize zeal when it manifests, because undoubtedly it is a trait of his or her own. If one is a God-ordained leader, he or she has been processed for the job. And the only way to survive and thrive in the making process is to have a zeal that is hotter than the fiery trials that arise. A truly zealous person often passes tests without realizing that testing was taking place because of the intensity of his or her focus. Senior leaders must identify the zealous and help to protect and develop them. The zealous must be protected from themselves and from some others.

Protecting the Zealous From Themselves

The danger that zealots face from themselves is the risk of overshooting God's timing for fulfillment of divine calling. They may tend to be frustrated with slow progress and impatient with the less- or non-zealous. Their seeming impulsiveness and spontaneity may lack proper sanctioning, planning, and tact. Many "preemies," as discussed in chapter 3, are over-zealous babies that could not wait for the gestation period to be completed. They enthusiastically lunge out of the womb into a harsh environment for which they are not properly prepared. The fatherly counsel that zealous people hear often, and hate most, is *wait*. Nevertheless, if this word is given through a spiritual parent who has the mind of God and the best interest of the zealous at heart, it can save the zealot from many unnecessary blunders and woundings.

Protection from the Non-Zealous

Secondly, the zealous must be protected from those who have no zeal. Either they have had it and lost it, or they never had it. Supernatural zeal is an anointing, and remember that the greatest opposition to the anointed comes from those who used be anointed or ought to be anointed.

Only one example is necessary. Lucifer used to be anointed, and he was and is the greatest opponent to Christ, the Anointed One, and His followers, Christians, the anointed ones. He is the adversary who seeks to stifle Christians' zeal for God by any means possible.

Moreover, a zealous person may cause the complacent to become uncomfortable because he or she reminds them of what they should be about. In days past, when some of the saints became complacent, they referred to this complacency as being "settled" or "seasoned" in God. When a young person (in age, experience, or spirit) arose with the glowing fire of God's presence, it scorched the "frozen chosen" and they tended to react negatively to the zealous.

Wounded in the Father's House

The most painful type of rejection and persecution is that which comes from among brethren from within the Father's house. Divine zeal will eventually culminate in success, but it is so disheartening for someone to experience success and have no one who really knows the story to celebrate the success. There are those who, instead of joining in the celebration—because they know what the zealot came through to get where he or she is—prefer to sit back and scowl. Some even pray that success won't last so the zealot can become more humble. This is a witchcraft spirit, and God does not answer such "prayers," but Satan may oblige, coming through the open doorway of envy to attack the unsuspecting zealot. One knows to expect arrows from enemies, but it is always difficult to anticipate the dagger of Brutus or the kiss of Judas.

Zeal: The Mark of the Next Generation's Leaders

Senior leaders, therefore, must be conscious of the zealous, because it is from among the zealous that the next generation of leaders arises. Whether or not he or she has special training, education, gifts, looks, or other gifts, if a person has zeal, zeal has a way of propelling him or her a long way past many obstacles. A man or woman with zeal will not be denied. Zealous people are extreme, and therefore they will act when they see a need. Because they are willing to take risks, they will make mistakes. However, because of their zeal toward the things of God, a wise shepherd will correct their errors without killing their essence.

Peter's Example

For example, zealous disciples will be defensive concerning the ministry; therefore, they may, like Peter in the garden of Gethsemane, "draw the sword" of protection at the wrong time, leaving Jesus (or the senior leader) to clean up the mess. Like Peter, they may be reactionary, but like Jesus, their leaders must see the greatness of their hearts and develop them. Zealous people will lay down their lives for the cause, just as Peter was risking his life at that point. He did get into fear later, and he did deny the Lord; however, he was operating in natural zeal at that time, and natural things can run out. Nevertheless, once he began to operate in supernatural zeal, he never denied Jesus again, and tradition says that he died by martyrdom, still zealous for Christ. It is said that at the point of his own crucifixion, he requested to die upside down because of his zeal to keep Jesus uplifted, even regarding the manner of His death "in a class by Himself."

Divine Zeal and Natural Ambition:
The Similarities and the Contrasts

There are numerous similarities between zeal and ambition. The most fundamental difference, however, between zeal and ambition is simple—the motive. A person with zeal is driven for the sake of the Savior, the saints, the sinner, and society. A person with ambition is usually driven for the sake of self, self, self, and self.

If Christ is the center, it is zeal. If self is the center, it is the worst kind of ambition. Is ambition inherently wrong? No, it is not necessarily wrong, especially if it is a means to an end, but the end must always be the glory of God in Christ. Zeal, divine zeal, always looks to the object, the goal, and the prize, which is God and His kingdom's advancement.

Other Aspects of Zeal

To the Zealous

Here are some principles that will sustain and develop the zealous.

Be careful in choosing those with whom you share your dream.

Your heavenly Father and spiritual father will rejoice, but half-brothers may grow envious. "Whole brothers" esteem and promote each other.

Embrace discipline.

Fire is a powerful tool or a destructive agent, based upon whether it is controlled or allowed to run wild.

Honor your father, mother, and spiritual family.

You may have discovered a precious aspect of the kingdom for which you burn and others do not, at least not as intently. Nevertheless, you cannot advance the cause of Christ by not being Christlike toward your family in God. If God has enlightened you, He can kindle them. Besides, if He does not, you cannot. You will have to show love unconditionally, even if others do not understand your zeal. The proof of your discipleship is not intense activity or chasing devils; it is love. Respect your leaders and your peers.

Refuse to compete with your family.

If you are one of the overt, outspoken zealous, do not compare yourself with your quieter siblings who may be equally as passionate, just not as articulate. Gifts come from God, so no one has the right to boast of one over another. Avoid preaching competitions, singing battles, and prophesying contests. Do not vie over finances, popularity, or prestige. (This does not prohibit basketball, spelling bees, trivia contests, etc. These are at the discretion of individuals and leadership. The competition spoken of here is the spirit of emulation, schism, envying, and contention. That spirit has no place in a kingdom leader's life.) You never have to destroy another's work to build your own.

Trust God with your life's itinerary.

Your job is to prepare yourself for the journey. His job is to order and direct your steps on the journey. If you are obedient to Him, you will arrive on time. You will not miss your moment.

Know zeal's limitations.

Zeal is essential, but so is training. So is humility. So is organization. Make the quality decision to garner the other necessary elements that complement zeal. Zeal is of God—ruthlessness is not. Zeal may get you "there," but only character will keep you there.

Absolutely avoid pride.

Regardless of how God blesses you, do not think of yourself more highly than you ought. Pride has been the undoing of many powerful zealots. God resists the proud (1 Pet. 5:5).

Keep your zeal.

The greatest deterrent to success can be success. Once a person sees progress in life, he can become complacent and "park," making a destination out of a rest stop. No, keep the zeal. Also, persecution and misunderstanding will come. As long as your life is in order with God and all others to whom you are accountable, just keep glowing and growing, trusting God to handle the adversity. Keep your fire. It is not nearly common enough. Remain intense for God until it becomes contagious. God values passion, and He makes dreams come true. He will place within your grasp the resources necessary to bring them to pass.

The Satanic Weapon of Discouragement

People who are driven tend to crash very hard when discouragement takes root. People who feel intensely feel *everything* intensely, the good and the bad. In discouraging times, the opposition they face will take on an exaggerated significance. It will seem that everybody is against the zealous one, when in most cases it may be one or a few individuals with a misunderstanding or, unfortunately, with malicious intent. The inclination to think "I'm the only one" is typical for the zealous. We mentioned Elijah earlier, the prophet of fire, who became discouraged and told God that he was the only prophet left and that he was living under a death warrant.

Elijah began to operate under a death wish. He asked God to let him die. God mercifully dispatched a special angelic messenger to nourish him. Zealous people can plummet to the depths of discouragement, particularly when this is accompanied by other variables like Elijah's: fatigue, a sense of futility, and loneliness. The angel's advice to Elijah is the word for other discouraged zealots:

> Arise and eat; because the journey is too great for thee.
>
> —1 KINGS 19:7

- "Arise"—Get up; look up; lift up; cheer up. Nothing Godward is accomplished without an "up" attitude.

- "Eat"—Take something in for your own nourishment. Zealots are always pouring out—now be poured into.

- "The journey is too great for thee"—You are not finished. Destiny is ahead of you. A new day is ahead of you. A fresh God encounter is ahead of you. Instructions for the next level are ahead of you. You are called to usher in the next generation of zeal.

And If You Lose Your Zeal...

Go back to prayer.

Prayer reignites the fires and the passions. Prayer intensifies the anointing upon a life. And if you just can't seem to pray, still get in position and persevere.

Go back to fasting.

Fasting has a way of helping one to break through barriers—walls that are impeding your flow and intensity. Fasting complements the prayer effort.

Go back to the Word.

Remembering what God said can, and will, rekindle the flame of zeal. Get in an anointed atmosphere of preaching and teaching. Meditate and saturate in the Bible and in Bible-based writings and recordings in public and in private.

Go back to praise and worship.

Praise can help one to regain focus, clearing out the "cobwebs" of distraction. Worship has a way of clearing our minds and resensitizing our spirits. Worship can help us to lose our sense of offense for a suffered wrong. Praise and worship provide an atmosphere for the anointing to manifest and lift us above circumstances.

Associate with zealots.

Find somebody who is as extreme as, or more extreme than, yourself. Let it be someone whose fire makes you a little uncomfortable because they provoke you to a higher plane. Hang around people who prompt you to repentance, to action, to worship, and to praise. Find someone who believes in you as much as, or more than, you believe in yourself.

Preview your inheritance.

Visit places or circumstances that represent where you are going in God. Walk in places that you are called to conquer and possess. Revisit your visions, and re-dream your dreams.

Get back in your element.

I was fishing some time ago, and someone had caught a fish and left it in the grass. By the time we decided to throw it in the water, it appeared dead. Still, I threw it in, and sure enough, it lay still on the surface—for a second. Suddenly the fish righted itself, flicked its tail, and sped away under the water. What had happened was that although the fish was nearly dead, as soon as it reconnected with its realm, its domain, it was reinvigorated. Even so, if you are anointed to preach, or teach, or give, or show mercy, or intercede, or sing, or administrate—whatever your area is, that is your "element." As water is to a fish, so is a believer's area of anointing and service. Get back to doing what you are really called to do, and you will be rejuvenated, perhaps before you even realize it.

Chapter 10

ABOUT THE PREACHER'S SPOUSE

Secondary #1!

Perhaps the most significant secondary leader in a local church, at least potentially, is the spouse of the senior pastor. This is true on the conditions that the senior leader is married, the spouse is genuinely a part of the body of Christ (is saved and growing in God), and the spouse is a devoted part of the local ministry. If the senior leader is married, he or she is obligated to love, honor, and protect his or her spouse, even if the spouse is unsaved. However, if the spouse is not a believer, that spouse cannot lead in the house of God, though he or she may certainly attend and support natural community-enhancing activities.

The Most Complex Secondary Leadership Position

Being the spouse of the preacher is also potentially the most difficult secondary leadership position to hold in a ministry, or at least the most complex. Partly it is because there exists such a high volume of role-casting ideas relative to the pastor's wife—or husband, if the senior leader is a female. The range of concepts extends from one in which the spouse has co-equal, or shared, leadership of the flock to another in which the spouse is "just another member" with absolutely no authority and no say in the life of the church.

This is complicated further by the nomenclature applied to the spouse's role. In the far more prevalent case, the preacher's spouse is female, and in some settings she is the co-pastor; in others she is the first lady; in others she is the elect-lady; in others, she is automatically Mother _____ (insert the preacher's last name) or Evangelist _____; and in others, she is simply Sister or Mrs. _____ (insert the preacher's last name). In some cases, these titles bring with them tremendous significance, but in others, the same title has little or no meaning.

What should the preacher's wife do? Some expect her to pray, play an instrument (usually piano), teach the children or the women, dress well (but not too well), always be in a pleasant mood, expect unexpected guests, be gracious answering the phone (even at 11:35 p.m.), cook expertly (but not better than all the sisters in the church), raise perfect children, accompany the preacher on all engagements, always understand when the preacher is late coming home due to the needs of the parishioners, always understand when the preacher leaves suddenly due to the needs of parishioners, and never expect to have a holiday without her husband being on call for the flock. In some settings, she is to sit with her husband on the platform; in others, she is to sit alone (or with the children) in the second seat from the front, often with a large hat with a brim wide enough to cover most-to-all of her lovely (but not too lovely—lest she be labeled a "Jezebel") face.

In the meanwhile, in the eyes of many, she should never have a viewpoint, or if she has it, she should keep it to herself. The preacher's spouse—and the children—are really secondary, or tertiary, or even at the back of the line.

The problem is that a leader often places his or her household second to the wrong people: the family of the preacher is to be second, in the preacher's life, to God only. It must be so. Is it not taught in 1 Timothy 3:2–5 and Titus 1:6, alongside Ephesians 5:22–33 and Ephesians 6:4 that the preacher's wholesome relationship with his spouse and family are a major criteria for his fitness for ministry? As with all the other secondary leaders, and even more than all the other secondary leaders, the preacher's spouse (and family, in many cases) can make or break the success or failure of the preacher's ministry. On the other hand, the making or breaking may be either a response to wholesome treatment by the preacher or a reaction to abuse and mishandling by that same leader.

Herein are some helpful principles for the senior leader's family, often called the "first family."

The First Lady

> Moreover the Lord said unto me, Take thee a great roll, and write in it with a man's pen concerning Mahershalalhashbaz. And I took unto me faithful witnesses to record, Uriah the priest, and Zechariah the son of Jeberechiah. And I went unto the prophetess; and she conceived and bare a son. Then said the Lord to me, Call his name

Mahershalalhashbaz..." Behold, I and the children whom the Lord
hath given me are for signs and for wonders in Israel from the Lord of
hosts, which dwelled in mount Zion.

—Isaiah 8:1–3, 18

In the life of Isaiah, the senior leader's wife's role is depicted in a measure.

A. The senior leader, a prophet, is married to a prophetess. All
    first ladies may not have the same gift set as her husband,
    but her walk with God will complement his calling in the
    Spirit.

B. She is unnamed in the Scripture, though Isaiah's name is
    all over: often the first lady will not have the limelight and
    will not be acknowledged, though she is vital to Isaiah's
    ministry and success.

    1. However, Isaiah (and any senior leader) must honor his
        wife in public and in private.

    2. This may illustrate the fact that Isaiah—who is the
        writer—attempts to protect her from the glaring, merci-
        less light of public scrutiny as much as possible, an
        honorable attitude.

C. Isaiah's associates are named, although they do not invest
    nearly as much as his wife does. Sometimes others in
    ministry will be celebrated for contributing less than the
    spouse does as an individual.

D. Though Isaiah has ministry partners, God wills it that the
    prophetess gives birth to the incarnation of his prophecy.
    The godly spouse of a godly minister will be specially,
    divinely used to help bring to pass the word of the Lord
    upon his or her life.

Some Imperatives for the First Lady (and for the Preacher Man Who Belongs to Her Secondly)

The First Lady...

...Must walk in the Spirit, not in the flesh.

...Must seek God for strength not to be insecure: a) in regard to her husband's role and b) in relation to their parishioners, male or female.

...Must accept the fact that her spouse, and therefore her marriage, is not "normal" because of the call of God. Their mode of existence will not be that of the average family down the street.

...Must accept the fact that she is sharing her spouse with God and with the outside world in ways that most people do not have to. Consequently, she may never have the quantity of attention and time with/from her spouse that others who are not called to this role may have. But God is God of recompenses: what is lacking in quantity will be compensated for in quality.

...Must accept her responsibility to intercede for her man of God. She is his first and most intimate armor-bearer.

...Must accept her responsibility to seek to know the heart and God-given vision of her man of God. There is an automatic tendency toward disconnect that comes if he perceives her as oblivious to his passion.

...Must live by the rule of confidentiality and discreetness.

...Should be kept in the inner circle, in the know of the ministry, by the senior leader.

...Must be provided for, materially, by her husband.

...Should understand that her mannerism should convey respect to and for her man of God: often friction will come—not because of any difficult subject matter she raises, but because of the way she presents and deals with the subject. God's Word teaches that men need a sense of being respected.

...Must be understood as often bearing the brunt of spiritual attack meant for the husband because of her intercessory posture. Therefore, she must have intercession on her behalf.

...Must be understood as sometimes bearing the brunt of emotional and psychological attack because someone considers her unworthy of her husband or desires her position.

...Should be honored by the congregation as being of equal value, even if not the same function, as the husband.

...Should be respectfully protected by the congregation in the absence of the husband: when the husband is on the battlefield on behalf of the ministry, if he were to fall sick, fall into sin, or die.

...The pastor must not show favoritism to anyone, but he must bestow honor and affection to his wife above all others in the congregation; furthermore, if she is with him in the ministry, she must be shown to be distinct from every other member in her relationship to him and in sharing and supporting his pastoral position.

...Must not be publicly reprimanded (except in an official case of "public" sin, i.e., sin that is known in the church community or the community at large). And in this case, and all cases of ministerial reprimand, it must be done with dignity and love.

...Must be extremely cautious in word and action because she can undermine his influence with the congregation by contrary behavior to his teachings or she can underscore them by conforming behavior to his teachings.

...Must be assured that her husband does not counsel the other gender without her unless:

> Someone else is present to hold him and the female accountable.
> The subject matter is appropriate.

...Should strive to emulate the spirit of the senior leader.

...Should not be unjustly compared to the spouse; should not be made to feel obligated to fit a stereotype.

...Should not yield to the temptation to compete with her husband.

...Must not be overlooked because of her compliance.

...Must have her exclusive communication, time, and space with her husband (and their family) protected.

...*Should be a woman.*

...Should prioritize ministering to her husband as a man. This includes deference and romance: she must know that in ministering to him in this dimension, particularly after a season of warfare (whether a win or a lose) is protection for him.

The First Lady must know that she is divinely destined to give birth to her husband's prophecy (his destiny's fulfillment); thus, it is *their* prophecy.

The First Gentleman

> But while he thought on these things, behold the angel of the Lord appeared unto him in a dream, saying, Joseph, thou son of David, fear not to take unto thee Mary thy wife: for that which is conceived in her is of the Holy Ghost. And she shall bring forth a Son, and thou shalt call His Name Jesus: for he shall save His people from their sins.... Then Joseph being raised from sleep did as the angel of the Lord had bidden him, and took unto him his wife: and knew her not till she had brought forth her firstborn Son: and he called his name Jesus.
>
> —MATTHEW 1:20–21, 24–25

When a woman is a carrier of the Word, beginning with Mary having carried the Incarnate Word, her man must be specially prepared. Neither the world nor the church is completely comfortable with women in leadership generally, or in leadership in the church particularly.

There are "first gentleman" principles seen in Joseph, the husband of Mary, the mother of Jesus, that are universal.

A. Matthew refers to Joseph as a "just" man. He was a man of God first, irrespective of his relationship with Mary. He knew God for himself. The "First Gentleman" must be God's man before he can be her man.

B. Joseph evidently cared deeply for Mary, and this, along with his love for God, disposed him to deal as delicately with Mary's situation as the law provided for, tempering justice with mercy and love. The "First Gentleman," then, must love God and his wife completely. That way, all his dealings with her will be righteous and loving.

C. Joseph apparently was told the truth that Mary was "with child of the Holy Ghost," but information and revelation are not the same. God gave Joseph a revelation through a dream of what He was doing in Mary, and Joseph's issue was resolved. The husband of a woman of God needs

a personal revelation of what God is doing in her, that
his commitment to her work may be based on divine
conviction.

D. God gave Joseph a series of supernatural revelations,
directing him in protecting and caring for his wife and
God's Son born through her. The "First Gentleman" must
therefore be continually Holy Spirit–led in providing for his
wife and God's work through her.

Though Joseph was a just man, it took God dealing with him directly
in order for him to grasp what was actually happening in the life of his
betrothed wife.

The temptation exists, then and now, to feel as if the husband has been
betrayed when the wife is carrying something that he does not understand.
However, Joseph was given the greatest honor that could be bestowed
upon a husband and father: the opportunity to be the covering for God's
Incarnation, to be co-caregiver with Mary and the adoptive father of Jesus.
Granted, Joseph is an obscure character, not seen again after Luke 2 (some
believe he died early in the life of Jesus). Nevertheless, Jesus comes to be
known as "the carpenter's Son" and "the Carpenter." It is clear that Joseph
helped to shape Jesus for His divine destiny. He housed and protected that
Holy Thing which Mary carried and brought forth. Even as the original
New Testament First Gentleman, today's First Gentleman is called to help
secure the "holy thing"—ministry, leadership, purpose—that God has
wrought in his wife.

Imperatives for the First Gentleman (and for the Preacher Woman Who Belongs to Him Secondly)

The First Gentleman...
...Must walk in the Spirit, not in the flesh.
...Must come to grips with a biblical apologetic regarding women in
ministry.
...Must come to terms with a personal conviction regarding women in
ministry.

...Must come be aware of the various views that exist regarding women in general and women in ministry and leadership in particular, and must have a response for those views.

...Must seek God for strength not to be insecure a) in relation to his wife nor b) in regard to their parishioners, whether male or female.

...Must accept the fact that his spouse is not "normal."

...Must accept the fact that he is sharing his spouse with God and with the outside world in ways that most people do not have to. Consequently, he may never have the quantity of attention and time with or from his spouse that others who are not called to this role may have. But God is a God of recompenses: what is lacking in quantity will be compensated for in quality.

...Must accept his responsibility to intercede for his woman of God. He is her first and most intimate armor-bearer.

...Must accept his responsibility to seek to know the heart and God-given vision of his woman of God. There is an automatic tendency toward disconnect that will come if she perceives him as oblivious to her passion.

...Must retain his responsibility to ensure material provision for his wife and children, regardless of what her role or her income may or may not afford.

...Must live by the rule of confidentiality and discreetness.

...Should be kept in the inner circle, in the know of the ministry, by the senior leader.

...Must be understood as bearing the brunt of spiritual attack meant for the wife because of his intercessory posture.

...Must be understood as sometimes bearing the brunt of emotional and psychological attack because of the unique position of being head to his wife as spouse and yet submitted to her as pastor.

...Must be understood as sometimes bearing the brunt of emotional and psychological attack because someone considers him unworthy of his wife or desires his position.

...Should understand that his mannerism should convey honor, affection, and commitment to his woman of God. Often friction will come not because of any difficult subject matter, but because of the way the subject is presented or dealt with. His wife needs his love and honor.

...Should be honored by the congregation as being of equal value, even if not the same function as the wife.

...Must not be publicly reprimanded (except in an official case of "public" sin, i.e., sin that is known in the church community or the community at large).

...The pastor must not show favoritism to anyone, but she must bestow honor and affection to her husband above all others, particularly men, in the congregation; furthermore, if he is with her in the ministry, he must be shown to be distinct from every other member in his relationship to her and in sharing and supporting her pastoral position.

...Must be treated as a man by his wife, even though the wife is senior leader.

...Must be given his position as head of the marriage and of the household despite her headship of the church (under Christ).

...Should be respectfully dealt with by the congregation in the absence of the wife: when the wife is on the battlefield on behalf of the ministry, if she were to fall sick, fall into sin, or die.

...Should strive to emulate the spirit of the senior leader.

...Must be assured that his wife does not counsel the other gender without him unless:

Someone else is present to hold her and the male accountable.

The subject matter is appropriate.

...Should not be unjustly compared to the spouse and should not be made to feel obligated to fit a stereotype.

...Should not yield to the temptation to compete with his wife.

...Must not be overlooked because of his compliance.

...Must have his communications, time, and space with his wife (and their family) protected.

...*Should be a man.*

...Should prioritize ministering to his wife as a woman

This includes serving, listening, and romance. He must know that in ministering to her in this dimension, particularly after a season of warfare (whether a win or a lose) is protection for her.

He is destined to protect, nurture, and nourish her prophecy (the fulfillment of her destiny). Therefore, it is *their* destiny.

The Senior Leader's Family: Asset or Liability

The family of the leader, the household, or the extended family can be the greatest human asset or the greatest human liability.

The family will be an asset...

...If the family loves God

...If they respect the senior leader as God's man and do not sin the sin of familiarity or insubordination

...If the senior leader is not so ignorantly zealous about his or her ministry that he or she abuses or neglects them for the ministry or in an effort to prove to or convince the people that he or she does not wrongfully exalt his family.

...If they respect the church as distinct from the family's personal property.

...If the church respects the senior leader's and family's personal property and life as distinct from, yet complementary to, the church.

...If they sincerely strive to live according to the pastor's Bible-centered teachings.

...If the pastor and church do not hold them to an unrealistic, manmade set of demands because they are the pastor's family.

...If they consider the house of God as worthy of reverence.

...If the church considers the senior leader's house as worthy of respect.

...If they do not presume special status above that which God has given them and do not use their honor as a means of attaining offices or mistreating non-family members.

...If the church respects the senior leader's family as due honor because of the family's sacrifice and support of the leader in order for him or her to serve.

It becomes the senior leader's responsibility to guide the establishment and maintenance of these attitudes and behaviors on both sides—that of his or her family and that of the church. God is a God of families. There are blessings and anointing that reside in families. The senior leader's family can become a living testament of the will of God, to the church, and to the world.

Chapter 11

THE GREATEST DEFENSE: PRAYING FOR LEADERS

The Most Important Things

The most important things that a secondary leader can do for a pastor or senior leader are to live out the teachings of that senior leader, support the senior leader as he or she lives out and carries the message to others, and pray for that senior leader. The first two are explored in other places—let's take a closer look at prayer for leaders, and particularly for senior leaders.

The Apostle Peter

Peter's deliverance from death row in Herod's prison was precipitated by the prayers of the saints.

> Peter therefore was kept in prison: but prayer was made without ceasing of the church unto God for him....He came to the house of Mary the mother of John, whose surname was Mark; where many were gathered together praying. And as Peter knocked at the door of the gate, a damsel came to hearken, named Rhoda. And when she knew Peter's voice, she opened not the gate for gladness, but ran in, and told how Peter stood before the gate. And they said unto her, Thou art mad. But she constantly affirmed that it was even so. Then said they, It is his angel. But Peter continued knocking: and when they had opened the door, and saw him, they were astonished.
>
> —ACTS 12:5, 12–16

When he got out of prison, he went to the place where they were praying. The power of their prayer transcended their own understanding—some couldn't believe it was Peter already released and knocking on the door until they saw him! This prayer meeting took place at the home of Mark's mother. Mark became one of Peter's greatest protégés, one of his secondary

.id later the writer of the gospel that bears his name. Scholars .hat Peter was one of Mark's great sources for his gospel's content, .e gospel of Mark is in some respects Peter's telling of the story. Would gospel have been possible without somebody praying for Peter?

The Apostle Paul

Paul repeatedly asked the believers that were under his leadership to pray for him. There is no implication that he felt that since he was the great apostle to the Gentiles, no one less than an apostle could pray for him. No. He asked for prayer all the time from the churches.

> Now I beseech you, brethren, for the Lord Jesus Christ's sake, and for the love of the Spirit, that ye strive together with me in your prayers to God for me.
>
> —ROMANS 15:30

> Ye also helping together by prayer for us, that for the gift bestowed upon us by the means of many persons thanks may be given by many on our behalf.
>
> —2 CORINTHIANS 1:11

> Praying always with all prayer and supplication in the Spirit, and watching thereunto with all perseverance and supplication for all saints; And for me, that utterance may be given unto me, that I may open my mouth boldly, to make known the mystery of the gospel.
>
> —EPHESIANS 6:18

> For I know that this shall turn to my salvation through your prayer, and the supply of the Spirit of Jesus Christ.
>
> —PHILIPPIANS 1:19

> Withal praying also for us, that God would open unto us a door of utterance, to speak the mystery of Christ, for which I am also in bonds.
>
> —COLOSSIANS 4:3

> Brethren, pray for us.
>
> —1 THESSALONIANS 5:25

Finally, brethren, pray for us, that the word of the Lord may have free course, and be glorified, even as it is with you.

—2 Thessalonians 3:1

But withal prepare me also a lodging: for I trust that through your prayers I shall be given unto you.

—Philemon 1:22

Pray for us: for we trust we have a good conscience, in all things willing to live honestly.

—Hebrews 13:18

Some people question whether Paul wrote Hebrews. Whoever it was, it was a leader who requested prayer.

The Lord Jesus Christ

Our ultimate example is the Lord Jesus Christ, and though He was God in the flesh, He relied upon the supply of the Holy Spirit. He prayed continually, throughout the course of His life, during the highs and the lows.

And in the morning, rising up a great while before day, he went out, and departed into a solitary place, and there prayed.

—Mark 1:35

Now when all the people were baptized, it came to pass, that Jesus also being baptized, and praying, the heaven was opened, And the Holy Ghost descended in a bodily shape like a dove upon him, and a voice came from heaven, which said, Thou art my beloved Son; in thee I am well pleased.

—Luke 3:21–22

But so much the more went there a fame abroad of him: and great multitudes came together to hear, and to be healed by him of their infirmities. And he withdrew himself into the wilderness, and prayed.

—Luke 5:15–16

And it came to pass in those days, that he went out into a mountain to pray, and continued all night in prayer to God.

—Luke 6:12

And it came to pass, as he was alone praying, his disciples were with
him: and he asked them, saying, Whom say the people that I am?

—Luke 9:18

And it came to pass, that, as he was praying in a certain place, when
he ceased, one of his disciples said unto him, Lord, teach us to pray, as
John also taught his disciples.

—Luke 11:1

And he was withdrawn from them about a stone's cast, and kneeled
down, and prayed.... And being in an agony he prayed more earnestly.

—Luke 22:41–44

Jesus even prayed throughout His suffering on the cross. In fact, His last
words were a prayer. There is much to be learned from the prayer life of the
Man Christ Jesus. Amazingly, when He was at His most intense moment
before being arrested, He asked His disciples to join Him in prayer (Matt.
26:38–44). Some may argue that He did not ask them to pray for Him.
However, there is no doubt that He expected them to pray while He prayed.
The crushing emotional state that Jesus was in was such that He could draw
strength from knowing there were those about Him who loved Him and—
to the best of their ability—were in emotional and spiritual support of Him.

And therein lies the pattern. Jesus taught that there is power unleashed
when there is agreement in prayer (Matt. 18:19). Great grace and much
encouragement come to a senior leader who is surrounded by secondary
leaders who are sensitive enough to pray while their senior leader prays,
calling upon God with—and for—that leader.

Praying for Secondary Leaders

Not only is Jesus our example in calling on secondary leaders to pray,
but, as discussed earlier, He prayed for the secondaries. In John 17, there is
an example of Christ praying for the secondary leaders as a whole group.
He prayed for the apostles, the other disciples He had then, and all the rest
of the Christians that would come to Him through those He left behind.
In Luke 22:31–34, there is an example of Christ praying for one particular
secondary leader who was actually already under satanic assault without
his knowledge. The Lord told Peter that although the devil had petitioned

to have him, He had already prayed for him. He was so confident that His prayer was effective that He told Peter that when—not if—he was converted, that he should strengthen the brethren.

Therefore, there is precedent for a senior leader to pray for those who share with him or her in leadership. And there is a pattern set for intercession on behalf of individual secondary leaders and their struggles. If there are any individuals in the ministry who will come under satanic attack, second to the senior leader, it will be those who stand to do the most good or the most harm: the secondary leaders.

The scriptures teach that the work of the Lord Jesus Christ in heaven is intercession on behalf of His secondaries, the church. The ministry of the Holy Spirit includes intercession on behalf of believers, all of whom are His individual secondary leaders. Therefore, senior leaders and the church as a whole are well advised to pray unceasingly for secondary leaders: collectively and individually.

> Wherefore he [Christ Jesus] is able also to save them to the uttermost that come unto God by him, seeing he ever liveth to make intercession for them.
>
> —HEBREWS 7:25

> Likewise the Spirit also helpeth our infirmities: for we know not what we should pray for as we ought: but the Spirit itself maketh intercession for us with groanings which cannot be uttered. And he that searcheth the hearts knoweth what is the mind of the Spirit, because he maketh intercession for the saints according to the will of God.
>
> —ROMANS 8:26–27

What Does One Pray About for Leaders?

- That God will turn their hearts as He will (Prov. 21:1).

- That God will give them the spirit of wisdom and revelation (Eph. 1:15–23).

- That God will cause them to increasingly walk in love and unity (Eph. 3:14–21).

218   *Building Credibility in Leadership*

- That God will give them boldness to declare His Word and that signs and wonders will follow (Acts 4:28; Eph. 6:19).

- That God will cause them to walk in love, discernment, discretion, and excellence (Phil. 1:9–11).

- That God will cause them to walk in righteousness (Phil. 1:11).

- That God will cause them to know His will and to have a lifestyle worthy of association with His name (Col. 1:9–10).

- That God will cause them to be strengthened with supernatural power and that this will enable them to endure with joyfulness (Col. 1:11).

- That God will let His Word have free flow and access (2 Thess. 3:1).

- That God will deliver them from wicked and unreasonable men (2 Thess. 3:2).

- That God will give them opportunities to declare His truth and protection from the enemy when those opportunities arise (Col. 4:3).

- That God will deliver them out of persecution (such as imprisonment) for the cause of Christ (Acts 12:5; Phil. 1:19).

- …and everything else that the Word declares to be God's will for His leaders.

Inclusive, Not Exclusive Prayer

Let us remember to pray not only for leaders in the "sacred" context, but also in the "secular" arena (1 Tim. 2:1). Presidents, kings, senators, judges, governors, mayors, entertainers all need to be covered in prayer continually. Their influence affects billions of people, from the macrocosmic to the most intimate details of their lives. Their hearts are in God's hands (Prov. 21:1), and He can turn them as He will.

Chapter 12

CONCLUSION OF THE WHOLE MATTER

Ending at the Beginning

What is the "conclusion of the whole matter"? If we follow God's example, and He always ends at the beginning, we will have come full circle. At the beginning, we talked about having a clearer vision of the church. Then we examined the critical role of primary and secondary leadership in the church, which is Christ's body and God's great means of taking man through Plan B back to Plan A—and again, God's purpose shall not fail.

For the Perfecting of the Saints

The church is a living organism that shall never end. God gave the five-fold ministry to the earth for the perfecting and equipping of its members, the saints, which will prepare all of us for the work of serving. This, in turn, will build up the body of Christ, quantitatively and qualitatively. God says that this will continue "until ..."

Until

Until means "up to the moment in time when," but it also means "with the outcome being" or "to the extent that." *Until* suggests that a time will come, but it also suggests that preceding events will prepare us for that time. It is the time when we will all arrive in the vehicle of the unity of the faith and of the knowledge of the Son of God unto a perfect man. The development of individual believers will culminate in the maturity of the collective body of Jesus Christ.

Unto a Perfect Man

Unity is not the object of Ephesians 4:11–12. Rather, it is the means by which the church will move toward the objective. Unity is the garment that will adorn the body of Christ when the object is finally realized: a perfect Man in the measure of the stature of the fullness of Christ—the composite Christ—will perfectly reflect God's likeness throughout the whole earth. It will be God's dream come true.

Jesus prayed that His church would become one. Sometimes that statement is lifted out of its context to emphasize unity, but Jesus did not promote unity for unity's sake. (Unity apart from God's agenda can result in a Tower of Babel.) Christian unity is to be the medium through which the world will receive and believe the message that God sent Jesus. The oneness of believers will provide for powerful witness to the manifold wisdom of God—oneness for witness.

A Corporate Perspective

The Individual—A Temple

Much teaching has been done about the individual believer and who he or she is in Christ. We have been well-advised to search and re-search the epistles for all of the "in Him," "in whom," and "in Christ" statements, for they provide the map of our divine genome, our spiritual DNA—they tell us who we are in Christ. They tell us what we have within us, now, which is the Holy Ghost's presence in our regenerated spirits.

As individuals, we are affirmed and taught that each of us has unlimited possibilities within: the fruit of the Spirit, virtues, gifts, wisdom, knowledge, understanding, and unction. Each of us is a temple of the Holy Ghost, replete with His wealth.

The Temple on Other Levels

And yet, suppose we looked at the other dimensions of the temple ("Measure the temple"—this prophetic instruction is given in Ezekiel and in Revelation.) The temple has two other New Testament applications, in addition to the individual believer as the temple. The local church assemblage is the temple, and the universal body of Christ is the temple of God. Most of the energy has been spent on learning what God says is in Christ regarding each individual member of the body. What would happen if we assessed what we have in Christ from a corporate perspective?

Collective Blessing

In other words, suppose we left the Scriptures as they are written? When the scriptures refer to "our" blessings and provisions, let us not trivially replace the words *we* and *us* with *I* and *me*. Instead, we should rejoice that "'I' am in the 'we'" and "'me' is in the 'us.'"

For example, Christ is made wisdom "unto us" (1 Cor. 1:30)—this goes infinitely beyond the capacity of an individual possessed of wisdom. We must see it as the collective wisdom within the body of Christ. What could we not do if we tapped into an awareness of the collective potency of our "in Christ" qualities in the local church?

For example, as musically proficient as individuals are, suppose there was more merging of musical gifts within a local church, or a region of the church, rather than the "Battle of the 'Baddest' Choirs"? What songs and symphonies could be written if the formal, systematic training of one musical group could be integrated into the spontaneous, prophetic orientation of another?

Save the Chicken and the Fish

And what evangelism could be accomplished if those who do it well would avail themselves to share their secrets with other congregations who are willing but unsure of how to undertake a campaign? If there were more of a "Christ's body" perspective rather than a "my thing versus your thing" perspective, resources would make it into the hands that need them and could properly utilize them.

One part of the Body has the personnel; another has the plans; yet another has (or has access to) the capital to make ministry happen on an unprecedented scale. Worship centers, daycares, clinics, auditoriums, coliseums, feeding centers, shelters, schools—all these things, which are needed to fully propagate the gospel, could be strategically attained, and readily so, if the body saw itself as one.

Fundraisers and such have their place, but there will never be enough fish-fries to support twenty-first-century ministry—that is, unless God gives a multifaceted fish franchise or marketing strategy to a part of the body, to use its profits for the kingdom! Thank God for chicken sandwiches and spaghetti suppers, but if the individual members of the body and the larger subunits of the body embraced oneness and gave themselves mutually for the kingdom's agenda, not so many chickens and fish would have to lay down their lives to save mankind. (And all the chickens and the fish said..."Amen!")

New Wineskins

We must seek God for new wineskins for this new wine. Some efforts have been made along these lines in various settings, sometimes resulting in success, at other times resulting in disillusionment and exploitation. But surely God must have somebody in the church who is "saved enough" to handle His resources (including His people) properly. As a matter of fact, I am convinced that the greatest ingathering and outpouring of resources for the kingdom is ahead for the church. God is trying the hearts of leaders, primary and secondary, to show whom He can trust. If He cannot trust us with mammon, He most definitely cannot trust us with the true riches of Himself and souls. And interestingly, He tries us with the true riches first:

> But seek ye first the kingdom of God, and His righteousness: and all
> these things shall be added unto you.
>
> —MATTHEW 6:33

But He will not commit the true riches unto us until we have proven faithful, even in the lesser valuables.

Christ said that He would have a glorious church upon His return. And all the things aforementioned, and many others, accompany the glory. There must be, and there is ongoing, a changing of mind-sets and attitudes among the leaders of Christ's body. With an abandonment of selfishness in and among Christians, we can galvanize our God-given gifts, anointings, and insights, along with our tangible commodities, to become what He has called us to be.

Now Unto Him

> Now unto Him that is able to do exceeding abundantly above all that
> we ask or think, according to the power that worketh in us, unto Him

be glory in the church by Christ Jesus throughout all ages, world
without end. Amen.

—EPHESIANS 3:20–21

Often the Scripture quoted above has been applied as a promise to an
individual. In fact, it is a declaration concerning God's relationship with
a group of believers, the church at Ephesus, and ultimately the church
everywhere. Many of the promises that believers have attempted to appropriate
will only partly be realized as they seek to grasp them as individuals, for
individuals. Yes, the individual is integral to God's plan, but God has greater
intentions for us: local "us," networked "us," and universal "us," His body.

The Starting Point for Leaders: Humility

Humility Toward God
And where does it start? It starts with us—leaders—humbling ourselves.
First, we are to humble ourselves to God. He is the Head of all things, our
Father, our Creator. We owe the Lord Jesus Christ allegiance because He is
our Savior, our Redeemer, and the Head of the church. By the Holy Ghost,
He guides, grooms, grows, and empowers us.

Humility Toward the Family
Second, we are to be humble toward our families. If one does not submit
to giving quality time and attention, along with every available resource,
to the building of the family as a house of God we may be public successes
and private failures who bring dishonor to the essence of our calling. If we
are in the business of "giving out God" and God is love, then why don't our
spouses and children get any? God is love; therefore, the man of God is the
"man of Love" and the woman of God is the "woman of Love," aren't they?
Or, are they?

Humility Toward Other Believers
Third, we must submit to our brethren in Christ: spiritual parents, peers,
and protégés. If we as leaders demonstrate to our followers that we don't
merely tolerate other leaders, but that we earnestly desire and need our
brethren, it would help to make it more natural for the followers to submit
to each other.

Let's face it: many of us who are now in senior ministry served rigorously during our spiritual upbringing as faithful followers, but most of our parishioners were not there to witness it. As it is sometimes said, "They see the glory, but they don't know your story!" And consequently, with the leader as the role model, the people tend to emulate what they think they see. If they perceive the leader as lofty, untouchable, superior, always the answer-giver and problem-solver, never needing or receiving from anyone, never collaborating with anyone on an equal, or even subservient, basis—that leader can teach mutual submission all day, but the followers may never get it. Our students tend to become what we are, not what we teach—what a scary thought! "Like people, like priest."

Senior Leaders Need to Be Seen Serving

So they need to see us—their leaders—needing other brothers and sisters in ministry, meaning cleaving in covenant relationship to each other. They need to see us cooperating, collaborating, submitting to, and obeying each other—willingly and joyfully. They need to see us celebrating someone else's accomplishments. They need to hear us quote from other living servants of Christ whose words and works have blessed us.

This is true for all senior leaders. Our people—actually, the Lord's people—need to see us striving to be united with the greater body and within the local body. They need to see us "endeavoring to keep the unity of the Spirit in the bond of peace" (Eph. 4:3).

> But Jesus called them unto him and said, Ye know that the princes of the Gentiles exercise dominion over them, and they that are great exercise authority upon them. But it shall not be so among you: but whosoever will be great among your, let him be your minister; And whosoever will be chief among you, let him be your servant: even as the Son of man came not to be ministered unto, but to minister, and to give his life a ransom for many.
> —MATTHEW 28:26–28

Grab Something

We should grab a broom, a rag, a crying child, a needy elder—whatever—whenever we have opportunity. The apostles said that it was not meet to leave the Word of God and serve tables; nevertheless, they were not endorsing a snobbish and lofty detachment that prohibits leaders from being actively involved in meeting the felt needs of those around us. As we have opportunity, it should be the norm for us, not merely a Kodak moment.

> Whatsoever thy hand findeth to do, do it with thy might; for there is no work, nor device, nor knowledge, nor wisdom, in the grave, whither thou goest.
>
> —ECCLESIASTES 9:10

Secondary Leaders Need to Be Seen Serving

And so it is true for secondary leaders as well. We must practice submission and cooperation with those whom God has placed over us and beside us. Those whom we assist in leading should see us as premier servants, out-served only by senior leader-servants themselves.

And it is not so much the fulfilling of menial tasks that proves that we have a servant's heart, though that may demonstrate that we can take a servant's posture. But duties vary. Some will be servile, but others will carry great prestige. Rather, it is the joyfulness, the willingness with which we accept whatever God sends our way. We see it as an opportunity to please Him, our ultimate Lord and Master. Wherever He sends us, to whomever, and under whomever He calls us to serve—we are willing and obedient. Our "little" brothers and sisters in Christ will tend to take their cues from us and will emulate what they see in us—resulting in a unified house, a unified network, and a unified body of Christ.

> Not with eyeservice, as menpleasers; but as the servants of Christ, doing the will of God from the heart; With good will doing service, as to the Lord, and not to men: Knowing that whatsoever good thing any man doeth, the same shall he receive of the Lord, whether he be bond or free.
>
> —EPHESIANS 6:6–8

> But if ye be willing and obedient, ye shall eat the good of the land: But ye refuse and rebel, ye shall be devoured with the sword: for the mouth of the Lord hath spoken it.
>
> —ISAIAH 1:18–19

We Are Willing

> The Lord said unto my Lord, Sit thou at my right hand, until I make thine enemies thy footstool. The LORD shall send the rod of thy strength out of Zion: rule thou in the midst of thine enemies. Thy people shall be willing in the day of thy power.
>
> — PSALM 110:1–3

We are willing because we have a grasp of God's vision. We may not know all, but we believe in what God is doing. We know that He is up to something, and it's not business-as-usual or church-as-usual. We believe in the hour of His glory revealed in His body, the church. Therefore, we commit our lives. We dedicate every iota of our being to His coming. We believe that He is coming for the church, but we believe that He is coming again *in* the church!

This world is about to have another encounter with the Man from Nazareth, the Lord Jesus Christ. They will see Him Hispanic, black, and white. They will see Him male and female. They will see Him young and old. And yet He will look the same—the same purity, the same power, the same holiness, the same hope that radiated two thousand years ago on the shores of the Galilee. The last Adam will have accomplished fully what the first accomplished only partially and tragically. He will have been fruitful; He will have multiplied. He will have replenished the earth and subdued it. Yes, and He will have dominion—He will be declared to be Lord.

This will be fully fulfilled in the Millennium, Christ's literal one-thousand-year reign on the earth, after the Second Coming. But *now, now, now*, He is ready to invisibly but supernaturally and dynamically rule "in the midst of His enemies"—through His body, the church.

> For he must reign, till he hath put all enemies under his feet.
>
> —1 CORINTHIANS 15:25

The Lord Jesus has been instructed to sit at the right hand of the Father until He (the Father) makes His (Christ Jesus') enemies His footstool, a place for His feet to tread. And His feet are in the body, the church! The church will stand in victory above all the enemies of Jesus, awaiting His promised return. Only then will He leave His seat to return for his own, the *glorious church!*

But as it is written, Eye hath not seen, nor ear heard, neither have entered into the heart of man, the things which God hath prepared for them that love him. But God hath revealed them unto us by his Spirit: for the Spirit searcheth all things, yea, the deep things of God.

—1 CORINTHIANS 2:9–10

Even as Christ also loved the church, and gave himself for it; that he might sanctify and cleanse it with the washing of water by the word, that he might present it to himself a glorious church, not having spot or wrinkle, or any such thing; but that it should be holy and without blemish.

— EPHESIANS 5:25–27

Arise, shine, for thy light is come, and the glory of the Lord is risen upon thee. For behold the darkness shall cover the earth, and gross darkness the people: but the Lord shall arise upon thee, and his glory shall be seen upon thee.

— ISAIAH 60:1–2

NOTES

Introduction

1. Maxwell, John. "Leadership Quotes." ThinkExist.com. 199-2010. http://thinkexist.com/quotation/leadership_is_influence/329074.html. Accessed April 4, 2011.

ABOUT THE AUTHOR

MICHAEL A. BLUE was born in North Carolina and was reared from infancy in Sellers, South Carolina. He was educated in Marion County and at the Francis Marion University in Florence, South Carolina. He is a veteran educator of twenty-five years. Blue preached his first official sermon in July 1980. He and his wife, Malinda, are the founding pastors of The Door of Hope Christian Church in Marion, South Carolina. Bishop Blue also serves as presiding prelate of The Christian Covenant Fellowship of Ministries.

CONTACT THE AUTHOR

Michael A. Blue

401 Martin Luther King Jr. Blvd.

Marion, SC 29571

843.423.0340

www.dohcc.com

www.buildingcredibilityinleadership.com

ADDITIONAL RESOURCES AVAILABLE FROM MICHAEL BLUE

God Shall Supply

Bishop Blue and the Voices of Hope offer up electrifying praise and worship through this live musical event produced live at The Door of Hope Church by Steven Ford, featuring legendary musicians Jeff Davis, Jonathan Dubose, and others!
Available in CD format only

The Rewarder

This three CD compilation features Bishop Blue, The Voices of Hope, and a congregation of prayer warriors ministering unto the Lord in a live, intense season of intercession, adoration, and travail, interspersed with songs of worship and praise. WARNING: this is "raw, old-school" prayer. The first two CDs present the prayer service, and on the third CD, Bishop Blue reads Scripture passages pertaining to prayer. All are designed to be a tool for the believer who desires to pray more fervently.
Available in CD format only

The Anointing of Jesus

This teaching/preaching series highlights Jesus' declaration of His God-appointed mission in the synagogue at Nazareth—the world has never been the same since that day! Bishop Blue delves into the historic and prophetic significance of what was implied when Jesus read, "The Spirit of the Lord is upon Me..."
Available in CD and DVD format

Kingdom of God Seminar 2011: "Total Buy-In"

This series of teaching guides the student of the Word deeply into an awareness of an aspect of Kingdom empowerment: God's gifts and calling, invested in each human being. Whether spiritual gifts or natural, they all are from God, for His glory. The key to fully manifesting and accomplishing destiny is that the believer would submit the gift to the Giver and, in the words of Paul to Timothy, "give (himself or herself) wholly..." to his or her development in whatever gift or calling God has bestowed.

Paul predicted that Timothy's profiting would become apparent to everyone if he would "totally buy in" to the mandate entrusted to him by God. The same is true for believers today! God calls us to "Total Buy-In."
Available in CD and DVD format

Other teaching DVDs and CDs by Bishop Blue are availab[

Contact: DHCC Media Ministry • The Door of Hope Christian Ch[
401 Martin L. King Jr. Blvd• Marion, SC 29571 • 843.423.034[
www.dohcc.com • www.buildingcredibilityinleadership.c[
thedoorofhope@gmail.com

Elder Adena H Russell